Winters of Discontent

Winters of Discontent

The Winter Olympics and a Half Century of Protest and Resistance

Edited by

RUSSELL FIELD

UNIVERSITY OF ILLINOIS PRESS
Urbana, Chicago, and Springfield

Library of Congress Cataloging-in-Publication Data

Names: Field, Russell, editor.
Title: Winters of discontent : the Winter Olympics and
    a half century of protest and resistance / edited by
    Russell Field.
Description: Urbana : University of Illinois Press,
    [2025] | Series: Sport and society | Includes
    bibliographical references and index.
Identifiers: LCCN 2024023878 (print) | LCCN
    2024023879 (ebook) | ISBN 9780252046377
    (hardcover; acid-free paper) | ISBN 9780252088445
    (paperback; acid-free paper) | ISBN 9780252047664
    (ebook)
Subjects: LCSH: Winter Olympics. | Winter Olympics—
    History.
Classification: LCC GV841.5 .W56 2025 (print) |
    LCC GV841.5 (ebook) | DDC 796.9809—dc23/
    eng/20240827
LC record available at https://lccn.loc.gov/2024023878
LC ebook record available at https://lccn.loc.gov/2024023879

Contents

Winters of Discontent

Introduction

The Winter Olympics as a Site of Protest and Resistance

RUSSELL FIELD

As the Olympic movement put the pandemic-delayed Tokyo Summer Games (originally scheduled for 2020) behind it, the international sporting world turned its attention to the 2022 Olympic Winter Games. Held in Beijing—with bobsleigh, luge, and Alpine events taking place on artificial snow in the Xiaohaituo Mountain region near Yanqing (90 kilometers from the center of Beijing) and Nordic events located in Zhangjiakou (220 km from Beijing)—the event should have been eagerly anticipated. The Chinese capital became the first city to host both a summer and winter Olympics. However, the circumstances surrounding the Games being awarded to Beijing by the International Olympic Committee (IOC) did not pass without controversy as activists sought to draw attention to the Chinese government's human rights record.

At the time of the announcement in July 2015, an official with Human Rights Watch (HRW) warned that, "in choosing China to host another Games, the IOC has tripped on a major human rights hurdle." Pointing to the 2008 Summer Olympics and concerns over "massive forced evictions, a surge in the arrest, detention, and harassment of critics of the government, repeated violations of media freedom, and increased political repression," HRW's China director, Sophie Richardson noted, "the Olympic motto of 'higher, faster, and stronger' [sic] is a perfect description of the Chinese government's assault on civil society."[1] Minky Worden, HRW's Director of Global Initiatives, warned that "major sporting events are also accompanied by human rights violations when games are awarded to serial human rights abusers."[2] Referring to both the Beijing bid and a competing one from Kazakhstan for the 2022 Winter Olympics—neither put forward from a nation renowned for its human rights record—Worden urged the IOC to enforce its own reforms, which included requiring host cities to sign a contract ensuring human rights protections. Among the grave concerns was the treatment of the Uyghur people in northwest China, which hearkened back to the protests over China's treatment of Tibet that accompanied the 2008 Olympic torch relay. As the 2022 Games approached, officials in Canada, the UK, and elsewhere called for a boycott—partly in response to China's imposition of a national security law in Hong Kong—while activists continued to highlight a range of human rights abuses.[3]

In addition to human rights issues, athletes had concerns about the selection of Beijing as a *winter* Olympic host. Following the 2014 Winter Olympics, which was hosted in the summer resort town of Sochi, the decision to return to another city not known for snowfall accumulation was troubling for many. "Hosting the Winter Olympics in a place with no natural snow is crazy," noted US Olympic biathlete Tim Burke. "I don't know any other way to put it." The influence of nondemocratic governments (e.g., Russia and China) was not lost on athletes, as were other elements of the selection process. "I know it seems quite obvious that to host a successful Winter Olympics you need venues that have snow," noted former Canadian Olympian and onetime IOC and athlete commission member, Beckie Scott, "but when committee members hear very persuasive, well-funded proposals that address this point with manmade snowmaking and other technical solutions, the subtleties of things like the reliability and durability of the snowpack and the impact on racing can quickly get lost." Beyond concerns for competitor safety and the athletic experience, others expressed disappointment that such hosting choices did not contribute to the growth—in participation and infrastructure—of winter sports. Most significantly perhaps, scholars and activists noted that hosting the event provided China with an opportunity to "sportswash" its global reputation, drowning out the criticism brought to bear on human rights abuses with the feel-good stories of medal-winning performances.[4] Similar critiques were levied at FIFA for its decision to host the 2022 men's World Cup in Qatar.[5]

When criticism of China's human rights record (in addition to concerns over environmental protection) was expressed in advance of Beijing hosting the 2008 Summer Games, then-IOC President Jacques Rogge, reiterated the longstanding position that such "politics" have no place in the Olympics. He asserted that "the Olympic Games are not the place for demonstrations."[6] Nearly fifteen years later, the position that sport and politics need to be kept separate is increasingly untenable (it always was a fanciful notion), as the impact of the #MeToo and Black Lives Matter movements on how sports conducts itself as an institution has made clear. Athletes, activists, and broader social movements have responded to these cultural shifts and used the tools of social media to make their politics more vocal and more visible. As sporting events increasingly become the focus of activism and protest—both efforts aimed at reforming sport as well as initiatives that capitalize on the visibility of "sport mega-events" (SMEs) to advance a wider social agenda—the institution of the Olympic Games has been no stranger to such resistance.

What was perhaps most striking about Beijing's winning 2022 bid was not the vote tally, which the Chinese capital won 44–40, but that the Beijing bid won out over only one other contender: Almaty, Kazakhstan. A number of potential candidate cities, headlined by the Norwegian capital, Oslo, had withdrawn their bids—most often in response to a lack of public support. A Krakow bid failed in a local referendum, while in October 2014, the Norwegian government withdrew its support of a potential Oslo bid, citing both the costs of hosting the Games and a lack of public support for the bid (see chapter 7). Even before this, cities such as Lviv, Munich, St. Moritz, and Stockholm had removed themselves from consideration. But it was the withdrawal of a city such as Oslo—northern and wealthy, possessing both existing facilities and a well-developed winter sport culture—that would appear to be an ideal Winter Olympic host that was particularly telling. This scenario was not unique to the Winter Olympics, as evidenced by the well-organized and ultimately successful opposition ("No Boston Olympics") to Boston's bid for the 2024 Summer Olympics. However, the continued participation of high-profile metropolises like Los Angeles, Paris, Madrid, and Istanbul in bidding for and (in the cases of Paris and L.A.) winning the rights to host Summer Games suggests that the recent trend of wavering interest in the Olympics bidding process may be a more significant issue for the Winter Games.

These patterns have continued despite the December 2014 introduction by the IOC of "Agenda 2020," a series of reforms that were, among other things, intended to streamline and reduce the cost of bidding, while emphasizing sustainability and the use of existing facilities (rather than insisting that potential Olympic hosts invest in new sporting infrastructure). As former Nordic combined gold medalist Bill Demong observed, the selection of Beijing for 2022 was "another example of the IOC deviating from their own 2020 agenda toward more sustainable sport."[7] The situation did not improve for the subsequent 2026 Winter Olympic bidding cycle. Again, potential candidate cities chose not to pursue bids without public and/or state support. In October 2018, the civic government in Stockholm (which had briefly declared an interest in bidding for the 2022

Games) decided not to support the Swedish Olympic Committee's choice of their city as the country's 2026 bid candidate, citing a desire not to use taxpayer funds in this way. (Despite this, the Swedish Olympic Committee continued to support a joint Stockholm-Åre bid, which ultimately finished second in the selection process to a joint bid from Milan–Cortina d'Ampezzo, Italy.) Three other potential candidates from the developed global North had already withdrawn from the 2026 bidding–Graz, Sion, and Sapporo–as did a Turkish bid from the city of Erzurum. (Officials from Sapporo have shifted their attention to the 2030 Games; see chapter 8.) In North America, a potential Calgary bid for 2026–which already had support from multiple levels of government and was proposing to reduce expenses by reusing facilities built for the 1988 Games (consistent with Agenda 2020 and framed by local organizers as an opportunity to revitalize existing facilities)–faltered when a public plebiscite in November 2018 returned 56 percent in favor of not proceeding with the bid.

The year 2018 was a challenging one for the Winter Olympics–and not only because Calgary and Stockholm continued the pattern of prominent cities opting out of the bidding process. Four years after the Sochi Games had attracted the attention of protesters over the Russian government's stance on LGBTQ rights among other issues and raised eyebrows among anti-Olympic advocates with its $51 billion (US) price tag (see chapter 5)–making it the costliest Olympics ever–the IOC hoped for more positive narratives surrounding the 2018 PyeongChang Games. The two Koreas marching into the Opening Ceremony behind the "unification flag" and the creation of a united Korean team competing in women's ice hockey hinted at the sport-contributing-to-the-greater-good rhetoric that is at the heart of the Olympic movement's mandate. Yet these Games were also the subject of public outcry as protest groups sought to raise awareness over the damage that Olympic construction and development caused to the natural environment, and in some instances, traditional spiritual sites (see chapter 6). In addition, civic leaders in PyeongChang objected to proceeding with costly facilities without greater support from the central government.

The dearth of potential bids for 2022–to say nothing of the antidemocratic governments supporting them–was notable because for decades the Olympic Games have been an attractive SME for many cities that boasted of their winter sport culture and sought a share of the prestige and the economic benefits and boost in tourism that it was thought accompanied hosting such events. This book, though, is not just about failed Winter Olympic bids. It examines the issues that have led to the resistance that has scuppered recent bids, but also chronicles the ways in which the issues raised by anti-Olympic advocates have increasingly become part of a mainstream discourse—from concerns over the use of public funds in a neoliberal economy to the varied impacts of development on Indigenous rights, the living circumstances of local residents, and the natural environment, all of which occur in the context of a rapidly deteriorating climate.[8] While these issues have been at the forefront of resistance to the Summer Olympic Games and other events (primarily the FIFA men's World Cups in South Africa [2010], Brazil [2014], and Qatar [2022]), they intersect in unique ways in the preparations for and operation of the Winter Olympic Games. The latter draw from a smaller set of countries—primarily northern and developed ones—than their summer counterparts. And the IOC's insistence that what for many nations are indoor winter sports (e.g., basketball and volleyball) remain on the Summer Olympic program means that the Winter Games are focused outdoors in nonurban locales, resulting in frequent clashes between the development deemed necessary for venues and environmental stewardship, while at the same time ensuring that this development occurs most often far removed from urban eyes.

While protests have occurred at both the Summer and Winter Olympics and also impacted potential bids for both events, the Winter Games, featuring events that are most popular among northern, developed countries, offers a coherent set of cases around which to consider the meanings and impacts of anti-Olympic protest movements. The Winter Games have a distinctly different origin story to the Summer Games. Culminating in 1896, the efforts of a minor French aristocrat, Baron Pierre de Coubertin, were the driving force behind the modern Olympics. Inspired by the example of sport at elite British "public" schools, Coubertin married to the exclusive amateur ideal promoted by these institutions the vitality of healthy youth and notions of the health of the nation—all cloaked in nineteenth-century neo-Classicism—to "revive" ancient Greek traditions as the modern Olympic Games.

The Winter Olympics are a different kettle of fish entirely. They reflect an at-times uneasy compromise rather than a set of invented traditions. The prominence of debates over environmental conservation versus commercial (sporting) development—and the rights and resources of governments to privilege one over the other—are embedded in the historical origins of the Winter Olympics and the source of some of the continued resistance to the event. To grasp the unique circumstances of the Winter Olympics, and the evolving nature of resistance to them, it is best to start with the event's origins.

A Brief History of the Winter Olympics

While the modern Olympic Games were invested with what Eric Hobsbawm and Terence Ranger famously label "invented traditions," their neoclassically inspired rites and symbols do little to suggest winter sport competitions.[9] The Olympic Winter Games (the official title) were instituted more than three decades after Coubertin formed the IOC, which held the first modern Olympic Games in Athens in 1896. Coubertin and others in the Olympic leadership were initially resistant to the idea of adding a separate event of winter sports to the Olympic calendar.[10] The notion was contentious enough that it was only after the fact that the Winter Sports Week, held in late January and early February of 1924 in Chamonix, France, was retroactively labelled the first Olympic Winter Games. Emerging as a compromise of sorts between Scandinavian proponents of Nordic sport traditions and the operators of affluent Alpine resort towns, the Winter Olympics have been characterized—without any recall to ancient Greek traditions—by commercialization, facility development, and consequent environmental destruction, all of which have inflected numerous anti-Olympic protests.

Winter sports first appeared on the Olympic program at the Games in London in 1908, when four figure skating events were held in late October on the artificial ice at the Prince's Skating Club. Significantly, winter events were not repeated four years later in Stockholm. Col. Viktor Balck was head of the 1912 organizing committee, and while he "sought to promote his country through sport," he opposed the inclusion of winter sports in the Olympic program.[11] An official in Swedish gymnastics, rowing, and skiing organizations, as well as an original member of the IOC, Balck was also a founder of the *Nordiska Spelen* (variously translated as the Nordic Games or the Northern Games). First conceived in 1899, the Nordiska Spelen were held every four years from 1901–1917 and again in 1922 and 1926 (with the fact that these Games ended as the Winter Olympics were becoming established not a coincidence). The multisport event included competitions in Nordic skiing, bandy, cross-country running, and skijoring (where competitors on skis were pulled by horses).

But the significance of the Nordiska Spelen extended beyond the specific events. They were conceived as a manifestation of the Scandinavian pursuit of *Ski-Idræt* (in Norwegian; *Ski-Idrott* in Swedish): "an attachment to old folk tradition, to active life in the outdoors, to wholesome all-around qualities blending body and soul of the individual into a good citizen; and by extension the whole community, even the nation would benefit."[12] Within such a configuration, Balck was supportive of a broader geopolitical mandate for the Nordiska Spelen, which were created under the auspices of the Swedish Central Association for the Promotion of Sports. In conceiving of the event, Balck asserted "above all we placed the national goal of rendering a service to the fatherland and bringing a higher honor to our country."[13] In this way, the Nordiska Spelen were more than a celebration of what were constructed as pan-Scandinavian cultural practices—and athletes from Sweden, Norway, Finland, Denmark, and Iceland competed—they also reflected Swedish political and cultural dominance of the region as well as resistance to rule from Stockholm. All but the 1903 Nordiska Spelen were held in the Swedish capital, with the 1903 event held in Kristiania (now Oslo), Norway.

Winter sport practices, skiing in particular, were especially central to Norwegian cultural identity, and as E. John B. Allen notes, the Nordiska Spelen "were originally intended to keep Norway within the Swedish-dominated pan-Scandinavian bloc."[14] Norway achieved its independence in 1905, but its skiers remained active participants in the Nordiska Spelen, as well as in the annual Holmenkollen event, which had started in 1879, before moving to the hill of the same name in Oslo in 1892. Efforts to incorporate skiing within the Olympics met a cool reception in Norway—the cultural home of Ski-Idræt—as Arne Martin Klausen details: "Norwegian skiing was associated with a romantic communion with nature, and was strongly influenced by the sharp criticisms of competitive sports by Norway's national hero, the Arctic explorer Fridtjof Nansen."[15] While Swedish organizers had opted not to include winter sports during the 1912 Games in Stockholm, the plans for the 1916 Berlin Olympics (subsequently canceled by the First World War) had included skiing events in the Black Forest. Postwar efforts by "the Scandinavian bloc" to maintain the "pure" nature of Ski-Idræt and keep Nordic skiing out of the Olympics were met with opposition, including "a wish on the part of their own skiers to show their prowess in the international arena."[16]

In 1921, following the inclusion of ice hockey at the previous summer's Olympics in Antwerp, the idea of a winter Olympic Games emerged. At the IOC Session in Lausanne, representatives from Canada, France, and Switzerland proposed a resolution to establish Olympic competitions that featured winter sports. While the resolution passed, it was opposed by the Finnish, Norwegian, and Swedish delegates. In trying to appease its Scandinavian members, and in deference to the apparent tensions between Nordic and Alpine winter traditions, the IOC opted to offer its patronage to a Winter Sports Week to be held in January-February 1924 in Chamonix, where French officials could act as host before the country held the Olympics in Paris later that year.

Sigfrid Edström of Sweden, IOC member and president of the then-International Amateur Athletics Federation (and future IOC president) "assured the IOC that the Scandinavians would have no objection to a Winter Sports Week."[17] He did suggest that Scandinavian participation was partly contingent on the event not being labelled "Olympic" but "international," writing to Coubertin that as the Nordiska Spelen were waning in significance, "I much more believe in the upcoming international Games at Chamonix and I am doing my best to persuade the northern countries to take part there."[18] Nonetheless, as Allen observes, "if there was a degree of care within the IOC not to offend the Norwegians and Swedes, elsewhere the Chamonix 'Week' was openly called the Winter Olympics."[19]

Athletes from sixteen nations—including Finland, Norway, and Sweden—gathered in Chamonix to compete in bobsleigh, curling, figure skating, ice hockey, speed skating, and Nordic skiing (which included competitions in cross-country skiing, ski jumping, Nordic combined, and military patrol). The absence, in an Alpine setting, of the events (downhill and slalom) that comprised the emerging discipline of Alpine skiing was noteworthy because of the tensions between skiing traditions. By contrast, the inclusion of Nordic events engendered consternation in some quarters. As Roland Renson notes, "because the Chamonix competition was an admitted success, representatives from the Norwegian, Swedish, and Finnish ski associations met in Stockholm on June 5, 1924 to send a strong message to the IOC president, asserting that 'skiing and other winter sports must not be part of the Olympic Games.'"[20]

The president, however, was unmoved. Coubertin noted that Chamonix was a "snowy prelude" to the 1924 Paris Games and had been "a great success from every point of view, helping to calm the ill-feeling and weaken the prejudices of the Scandinavians, whose champions naturally distinguished themselves."[21] (Norway won all but one of the ski races and led the way with seventeen medals overall; Finnish athletes were second with eleven.) Whether this was an accurate rendering of Scandinavian sentiment proved irrelevant when a year later, at its 1925 Congress, by a vote of 45–15, the IOC established "a separate cycle of Winter Olympic Games."[22] Another year later, at the 1926 IOC Session, the Chamonix event was formally recognized as the first Olympic Winter Games.[23] The establishment of the Winter Olympics played a role in effectively minimizing the significance of the Nordiska Spelen. The death of Viktor Balck in 1928 also contributed to the event's demise as no one stepped into this void to champion the event, and the final Nordiska Spelen were held in 1926. Nevertheless, the tensions between Alpine and Nordic approaches to skiing persisted, as did the sentiment in some quarters that winter sports had no place in the Olympic program.

The dominant narrative of the Olympic Winter Games' origins focuses on the tensions between Nordic (Scandinavian) and Alpine (primarily, but not exclusively, French and Swiss) pursuits. Andrew Denning, however, argues that although "the international skiing community came to be defined by a certain geographical determinism," the emergence of Alpine skiing is best read as a representation of modernity.[24] He contends that the fast, aggressive nature of downhill skiing combined with the technical expertise of the slalom meant that Alpine skiing reflected the modern athletic tastes "that were also embraced by the Olympic movement."[25] While "Alpine skiers claimed to represent the future of sport," Denning asserts, "much of the Alpine-Nordic friction in the 1920s and 1930s arose from attempts by Scandinavian skiers to check the ambitions of 'faddish' Alpine skiers over what they regarded as their patrimony."[26]

Such portrayals of Alpine enthusiasts as social dilettantes—or less-than-serious sportspeople—points to a second, related tension in the origins of the Winter Olympics. While Alpine sport offered alternatives to traditional Nordic practices, the former had not historically or exclusively been framed around skiing. Indeed, many Alpinists (i.e., mountaineers) resented the impact that sportification was having on Alpine settings. As Allen notes of these interrelated tensions: "Norwegian *Ski-Idræt* appeared 'good,' 'true,' 'healthy,' and above all 'real,' something that was peculiarly Norwegian. Alpine skiing was 'social,' expensive, what detractors called 'hotel sport.'"[27]

Despite such critiques, Alpine skiing events were added as demonstration sports at the 1928 Games in St. Moritz, before becoming a permanent fixture of the Winter Olympic program in Garmisch-Partenkirchen in 1936. The hosting of the Games in these respectively Swiss and Bavarian resort towns foregrounded the typically elite nature of winter sport participants and the ways in which the Olympic movement had been co-opted to buttress "the commercial value of the winter sports."[28] The Nordiska Spelen were framed around their own nationalist and romanticized notions of an individual's connection to nature, yet was accessed only by predominantly elite, male participants. The Winter Olympics, however, as Renson observes, also "served to sell the tourist qualities of a winter resort as 'the place to ski.'"[29] The nature of the people attracted to such settings reflected the fact that "winter sports stayed in the years 1924–1930 what they had been before, namely an opportunity for a few wealthy tourists to spend an altitude vacation in more or less luxury hotels."[30]

There were other challenges in shoehorning winter sport culture into the Olympic movement. These included the principle of amateurism that was at the core of the Olympic ethos—not only that athletes were not to receive remuneration or compete for prizes, but also that sport was to be an avocation. Those compensated for their sporting prowess or expertise were, in Coubertin's configuration, to be excluded. Yet the Alpine economy, especially as it catered to the luxury tourist class, was based upon sporting experts attending to a wealthy clientele. The most skilled Alpine skiers who found employment as instructors were precluded from participating in Olympic events hosted in the villages they called home. Thus, Arnd Krüger observes the paradox that "those who made money from tourists by teaching them to ski were barred from competition as professionals; those who made money by providing them equipment or lodging were not."[31]

Debates over winter sport culture and Olympic ideals, especially surrounding skiing, would linger for half a century. By the late 1960s, then-IOC President Avery Brundage—a staunch believer in amateurism—expressed concerns with the practice of Alpine skiers who received sponsorship monies from ski manufacturers in exchange for using their equipment continuing to participate as amateurs. A 1971 threat from Brundage to ban skiers who continued to flout amateur rules from the following year's Winter Olympics in Sapporo led to a counterthreat of a boycott from many European ski federations. Though Brundage backed down, while announcing that skiers would not be allowed to display manufacturer logos during the Olympics, the issue came to a head in Sapporo when Austrian world champion Karl Schranz was expelled from the Games—the only skier punished for this apparent transgression.

The skiing controversy was only one issue that informed Brundage's growing distaste for what he felt was the increasingly commercial nature of the Winter Olympics. He argued that "sport must be amateur or it is not sport at all, but a branch of entertainment."[32] Brundage noted this on the eve of the second-ever Winter Games hosted by his home country, the 1960 Olympics in what is now Palisades Tahoe, California. Local organizers hired Walt Disney to design the spectacle and "the idea of a rustic, intimate Games" gave way to "giant snow creatures made of plaster" and "a 'western night' with a mock gunfight"—in essence, "the 'disneyfication' of the Games."[33]

Such a presentation was emblematic of the direction that the Winter Olympics began taking in the 1960s. The Games were dominated by the emergence of television coverage and the attendant desire to create telegenic spectacles. The 1956 Games in Cortina d'Ampezzo were the first

Winter Olympics to be televised, but it was the 1968 Olympics in Grenoble that, Renson argues, "marked the beginning of the media era in the Winter Games."[34] Developments such as these, in addition to his ongoing tensions with the Alpine skiing community, tested Brundage's patience with the Winter Olympics. Calling them the "Frostbite Follies"—for the professional nature of the participants, the increasingly commercial nature of the event, and his perception that the Games lacked widespread appeal (which may have reflected how uneasily outdoor winter pursuits fit within the internationalist and neoclassical ethos of the Olympics)—Brundage urged the IOC to remove the Winter Olympics from its program following the 1976 Games in Denver.[35]

Protest and Activism at the Olympic Games

Brundage appears at the forefront of some of the tensest moments in Olympic history. As IOC President he expelled from the 1968 Games in Mexico City two US sprinters, John Carlos and Tommie Smith, whose demonstration on the medal podium remains one of the most visible moments of protest at the Olympics. Four years later, in Munich, Brundage controversially insisted that the Games would "go on" after Israeli athletes who were being held hostage in the athletes' village by terrorists were killed, along with their captors, in a botched rescue attempt. Before he ascended to the IOC presidency, Brundage had been head of the American Olympic Committee (now the US Olympic & Paralympic Committee). It was in this capacity in 1934 that he had travelled to Germany. Increasingly prominent calls for a boycott of the 1936 Olympics that were being organized by Germany's Nazi government highlighted that regime's horrific treatment of Jews and other marginalized groups. Opponents to the Olympics being held in Germany questioned both who would be permitted to participate and whether attending the Games was tantamount to sanctioning Nazi beliefs and acts of violent oppression. High-profile calls for a boycott—including from the head of the Amateur Athletic Union in the United States—pushed Brundage to investigate. In what many have subsequently viewed as a public relations exercise, he declared his support for American participation in Berlin, using the moment as one of many opportunities to assert his view that sport and politics should be kept separate.[36]

Much of the historical memory of the "Nazi Games" focuses on the Berlin Olympics, although the initial calls for a boycott were directed at the Winter Games. Hosted by Germany as well, the 1936 Olympics in Garmisch-Partenkirchen were not only the first Winter Games to include

Alpine skiing on the official program, they were also one of the earliest moments of activism focused on the Olympic Games. This included athlete activism. Many of the athletes who later that year boycotted the Berlin Games committed instead to participate at the ill-fated People's Olympiad in Barcelona, which was canceled after the outbreak of what was to become the Spanish Civil War. But some winter sport athletes initially boycotted events in Garmisch-Partenkirchen, including Philippe de Rothschild, a French-Jewish bobsledder.[37]

Despite significant moments such as this, it is primarily since the 1960s that sporting events have most prominently been a focal point for important social protests. These have highlighted issues both within and beyond sport. While at times the concerns have been engendered by the organization of SMEs, at other moments the heightened attention garnered by such events provided resistance actors with an opportunity to promote their causes to a wide audience. Perhaps most prominently, as noted, the raised black-gloved fists of Carlos and Smith at the 1968 Olympics in Mexico City brought the domestic inequities faced by African Americans to an international audience, using the Games as a stage.

But if the 1960s and early 1970s saw a surge in activism connected to sport—from the actions of Muhammad Ali, Jim Brown, and Billie Jean King in the United States to antiapartheid activism connected with cricket and rugby tours of England and New Zealand—our contemporary moment has seen the resurgence of protest movements organized in and through sport. From American football player Colin Kaepernick "taking a knee" to prominent Australian athletes backing a campaign in support of legalizing same-sex marriage to Catalan independence movements advocating their cause at matches of high-profile teams, sport remains a highly visible and effective venue for advocating social and political causes, resisting corporatization, and holding governments accountable.

As a high-profile, wealthy institution that regularly taps into the public purse to hold its biennial event (alternating between "summer" and "winter" sports), the Olympic Games have with increasing frequency been the focus of much of this protest. As Jules Boykoff argues, "the Olympics are a contested terrain in two senses of the phrase: a location for athletic competition as well as a stage where athletes and protest movements raise in full public view the political issues that animate them."[38] Led primarily by social movement activists, anti-Olympic protests have focused on a variety of issues, from the significant public investment required to host the Games and the impacts of ancillary "development" on vulnerable populations, to the protection of civil rights and freedoms in the host country, to the occupation of traditional Indigenous lands and territories. When the

Olympics find themselves as the focal point of protest and activism, "this contestation is public, conflictual, and designed to use the stage of sport to spotlight marginalized positions and ideas that are not consistently entering the dominant political discourse."[39]

In this way, protest of the Olympic Games, as well as other SMEs, focuses on both issues related to on-the-field competition, often around equity and accessibility, as well as "larger issues outside the sphere of sports" because "the Olympic Games have a long history of jumpstarting political dissent away from the athletic field."[40] Boykoff notes that some of the earliest critiques of Olympic expenditures occurred in California in conjunction with the 1932 Los Angeles Games during the Great Depression. Helen Jefferson Lenskyj's larger catalog of Olympic resistance chronicles the ways in which local organizations—such as the Metro Atlanta Task Force for the Homeless (in anticipation of the 1996 Games) and Rentwatchers in Sydney (2000)—became increasingly attuned to the impact of Olympic development on underhoused communities.[41] The on-the-ground activism of such groups was mirrored by the monitoring of Olympic preparations by international NGOs and watchdog agencies. For example, the Centre on Housing Rights and Evictions (COHRE) offered an assessment of the 2008 Beijing Games and concluded that "over 1.25 million people were displaced due to Olympics-related urban redevelopment."[42]

Such efforts continue to inspire and inform anti-Olympic resistance. The increasing prominence of protest in and through SMEs has been accompanied by more detailed accounts of the nature of such activism. This has included thoughtful journalism such as Dave Zirin's account of resistance in Brazil to the 2014 FIFA men's World Cup and the 2016 Rio Olympics, as well as much of the in-depth reporting that accompanied the 2022 FIFA men's World Cup in Qatar.[43] Scholars have especially focused on the Summer Olympic Games. Case studies exploring the impact of and resistance to the Games include Lenskyj's look at the impact of Sydney 2000 and Boykoff's examination of activism at London 2012.[44] The 2012 London Olympics were the subject of a number of other analyses, such as Phil Cohen's chronicle of activism in East London, as well as Mark Perryman's reflection on the Olympic project.[45] Resistance to hosting the Olympics has become so well organized that, as noted earlier, major cities are foregoing the opportunity entirely or pulling out of the bid process once started. Successful anti-Olympic campaigns have been examined by Chris Dempsey and Andrew Zimbalist, and Boykoff's recent work considers continuing anti-Olympic resistance.[46] While evaluations of the Beijing 2022 Olympics are waiting to be written, in anticipation of the event, activists and scholars authored an account of China's human rights abuses.[47]

The Winter Olympic Games, although distinctly different in origin and impact from their larger summer cousin, have been the subject of fewer analyses (or have been, when considered, lumped in with the Summer Games or other SMEs). One of the members of the anti-Olympic coalition in Vancouver, Christopher Shaw, provided an account—and rationale— of the convergence of resistance movements leading up to 2010, while Boykoff's *Activism and the Olympics* includes not only London 2012 but also an examination of protest on the ground at the Vancouver 2010 Winter Games (a subject to which he returns in chapter 4).[48] Another post-Games analysis, by Robert Orttung and Sufian N. Zhemukhov, examines the 2014 Sochi Olympics hosted in Putin's Russia.[49] But the issues specific to the Winter Olympic Games—both locally and globally—have not been thoroughly explored. This collection is an effort to redress this imbalance.

Resisting the Winter Olympics

To more fully flesh out the history and continuing presence of protest at the Winter Olympics, this book is organized chronologically and includes eight case studies from an international roster of scholars. The collective analysis reflects debates that largely began in the 1960s and impacted Winter Olympic bids and Games from 1972 to the present. Yet, more than a march through time, these case studies reflect the successes and failures, commitments and concerns, and objectives and tactics of activists and social movements that have organized in opposition to the Winter Olympics and its impacts. They include Winter Olympic Games that did not happen and bids that failed; Games that took place but whose narratives were at the time or afterward impacted by protest and resistance; and finally, debates informing current or future bids, i.e., Games that might not take place.

While there was opposition to participation at Garmisch-Partenkirchen in 1936 and concern, especially within the IOC, over the increasing spectacularization of the Winter Olympics in the late 1950s and early 1960s, it was in the mid-1960s that frequent and organized opposition to the event emerged. That these developments intersected with contemporary civil rights campaigns, the nascent ecological (today environmental) movement, and other rights movements is significant but can also potentially be overstated. This anthology then captures both the evolution of protest at and through the Winter Olympic Games as well as the issues significant to activists (often local, but also global) at specific moments in time.

The first two chapters highlight the ways in which local concerns were informed by global issues. The influence of the ecological movement also demonstrated the emerging power of particular antidevelopment and antienvironmental preservation coalitions. These two case studies—one of a failed bid and the other examining the only time a successful bid city has turned down the Games—also demonstrate the First World circumstances and concerns emblematic of much Winter Olympic resistance.

In 1966, Banff/Calgary was making a third bid to host the Winter Olympics. This particular bid—for the 1972 Games—included Alpine events within the nearby Banff National Park. The development planned for the Games in Canada's oldest national park raised concerns for a number of conservation groups. As Russell Field details in chapter 1, despite the local interests supporting the bid, the oppositional campaign run by concerned citizens had an impact on IOC attitudes toward the bid. This was heightened when the leadership of the World Wildlife Fund also expressed its concerns over development within Banff National Park at a time when the Canadian federal government was articulating new policies for the administration of national parks.

The IOC chose Sapporo to host the 1972 Winter Olympics over Banff, and four years later selected Denver as the location for the 1976 Games. By November 1972, however, two and a half years after the IOC's decision, the citizens of Colorado rejected the Olympics (which were subsequently shifted to Innsbruck, Austria) in a plebiscite. The successful anti-Olympic opposition included environmentalists opposed to development of areas within the Rocky Mountains foothills and local politicians concerned with the cost to the public purse. Their campaigns, as Adam Berg details in chapter 2, were articulated through local media outlets, as were the pro-Olympic messages put forward by the Denver Organizing Committee. Berg argues that media representations of these competing positions are crucial to understanding the anti-Olympic campaign in Denver.

The next four chapters examine the Olympic Winter Games that proceeded—between 1988 and 2018—even in the face of organized resistance. In chapter 3, Christine O'Bonsawin recasts the failed Banff bid and the rejected-by-plebiscite Denver Games to foreground the territorial and environmental rights of Indigenous Peoples in her consideration of the 1988 Olympics in Mohkinstsis (Calgary). O'Bonsawin reiterates the environmental protections afforded to the Siksika, Kainai Piikani, Stoney-Nakota, and T'suu T'ina peoples in Treaty 7, which was negotiated and ratified in 1877. She argues that Indigenous voices of dissent were not only marginalized by Games organizers in Calgary, but that anti-Olympic campaigners also overlooked the ways in which the legal rights and environmental protections guaranteed by Treaty 7 could have supported opposition to the Olympics.

When the Winter Olympics returned to Canada (for the 2010 Vancouver Games, with many events also held at Whistler), one of the hallmarks of protests surrounding the Games was the "convergence" of social movements. In the twenty-two years between Calgary and Vancouver, actions in Chiapas, Mexico, and at the 1999 WTO meetings in Seattle, for example, had mobilized anti-globalization protesters. As Jules Boykoff observes, the protests in Vancouver focused on Indigenous rights, economic issues, and civil liberties. The Indigenous-led "No Olympics on Stolen Native Land" campaign took a leadership role, but anti-Olympic campaigns leading up to 2010 involved a wide array of actors. In chapter 4, Boykoff examines the relationships of such a diverse coalition through an exploration of spatial strategies and tactics, in particular by considering the ways in which anti-Olympic groups created a discursive space through which they could articulate their opposition to the Games and work together.

Vancouver was not the last Winter Games to see a convergence of anti-Olympic protest. In 2014, as Russia hosted a Winter Games in Sochi, a summer resort city on the Black Sea, activist causes attracted international attention, which at times overshadowed local reactions and interests. The former included international reaction to Russia's controversial anti-LGBTQ laws, protests aimed at raising awareness of the Circassian genocide, and demonstrations by the feminist punk band, Pussy Riot, who were attacked by Cossack security guards during the Games. Local concerns, however, highlighted the micropolitics of resistance. In chapter 5, Sven Daniel Wolfe examines the environmental concerns of villagers and communities in the vicinity of Sochi. Dissent at the local level focused on Olympic-related development. Wolfe finds that local residents were not anti-Olympic and that many had no issue with the Olympics taking place. Rather, as Russia touted the benefits of developing Sochi into a year-round resort city, local villagers wanted to ensure that they too shared in these benefits.

Anti-Olympic protestors and their allies in the social movements with which they are affiliated have a lot invested, personally and emotionally, in the causes they fight for. Yet, in all these instances of protests against, or at times through a Winter Olympics, the Games went on, the natural environment gave way to infrastructural development, and state funds were invested in support of these projects. Does this render activist efforts ineffectual? Should protesters view their actions as a failure? In chapter 6, Liv Yoon considers such questions in the context of protests mobilized against the development of Mount Gariwang for the 2018 PyeongChang Winter Olympics. Parts of what had been a protected area were earmarked for the Games' Alpine ski course. Elsewhere Yoon has documented activists' efforts to prevent this development, but in chapter 6, she considers what "success" and "failure" mean for activists, for the communities and causes that they represent, and for the Winter Olympics and other SMEs.[50]

The final two chapters consider recent Olympics bids that failed (or are ongoing) due to local opposition. Collectively, they reveal the shifting dynamics and power relations between the civic growth coalitions that have typically dominated the pursuit of SMEs and the social movements that have opposed such efforts. In 2013, 55 percent of Oslo residents voted in favor of their city pursuing a bid for the 2022 Olympics. Yet only a year later, the municipal government of one of the world's most prominent winter sport cities—and host of the 1952 Winter Olympics—pulled its support for the bid after the Norwegian national government opted not to guarantee federal funding. In chapter 7, Jan Ove Tangen and Bieke Gils examine the circumstances of this apparently sudden shift. While debates about costs and the use of the public purse were present, the specifics of the Oslo case highlighted both center-periphery tensions within Norwegian politics as well an increasingly contentious relationship between Norway and the IOC. Tangen and Gils make the case that these tensions reflect Norwegian moral values that stand at odds with the IOC's core values.

Another city with Olympic history, Sapporo, mooted a bid for the 2026 Games. A September 2018 earthquake in the region ended those plans. But 2019 elections brought to power a new governor in Hokkaido and a new mayor in Sapporo who collectively revived the idea—with an eye toward the 2030 Winter Games. Keiko Ikeda and Tyrel Eskelson contend in chapter 8 that the proponents of the 2030 bid have crafted a "recovery narrative" to advance their cause. Arguing that the Winter Games would contribute to the region's post-earthquake recovery follows a rhetorical strategy (labelled by critics as *Hukkō Gorin*) used by organizers of the 2020 Tokyo Games, who touted their event as part of Japan's renewal after the 2011 tsunami and subsequent Fukushima nuclear power plant disaster.

Ikeda and Eskelson assert that rather than advancing local or national narratives, Sapporo's bid should reflect international priorities, specifically UNESCO's 2015 Sustainable Development Goals (SDGs). They argue that SMEs such as the Winter Olympics need to reflect global concerns for improving economic, social, and environmental wellbeing. The Winter Olympics has faced (and continues to face) challenges to its relevance over issues of environmental stewardship, development, and increasing expenditure. These are not uniquely twenty-first century concerns, as the chapters that follow make clear. Despite the origins of the event as a celebration of Western and Northern wintertime sporting pastimes, the Winter Olympics and the protest and resistance its iterations engender has become an institution of global concern.

Notes

1. Cited in Human Rights Watch, "China: Ensure 2022 Olympics Won't Fuel Abuse," July 31, 2015, https://www.hrw.org/news/2015/07/31/china-ensure-2022-olympics-wont-fuel-abuse.

2. Minky Worden, "Human Rights at the 2022 Olympics," *New York Times*, 18 January 2018, https://www.nytimes.com/2015/01/19/opinion/human-rights-and-the-2022-olympics.html.

3. Nathan VanderKlippe, "Boycott Beijing Winter Olympics, Former Top Canadian Diplomat to Hong Kong Says," *Globe and Mail*, June 9, 2020, updated June 10, 2020, https://www.theglobeandmail.com/world/article-boycott-beijing-winter-olympics-former-top-canadian-diplomat-to-hong/; James Tapper, "MPs Urge British Olympians to Boycott 2022 Beijing Winter Games," *The Guardian*, February 6, 2021, https://www.theguardian.com/world/2021/feb/06/mps-urge-british-olympians-to-boycott-2022-beijing-winter-games.

4. Jules Boykoff, in "Toward a Theory of Sportswashing: Mega-Events, Soft Power, and Political Conflict," *Sociology of Sport Journal* 39, no. 4 (2022): 342–51, applies this concept to the Qatar 2022 FIFA men's World Cup.

5. See, for example, Shireen Ahmed, "Journalists Cannot Allow World Cup to 'Sportswash' Qatar's Human-Rights Abuses," CBC Sports, April 5, 2022, https://www.cbc.ca/sports/fifa-world-cup-sportswash-opinion-shireen-ahmed-1.6407923.

6. Cited in Anne Applebaum, "Boycott Beijing: The Olympics Are the Perfect Place for a Protest," *Slate*, March 24, 2008, https://slate.com/news-and-politics/2008/03/the-olympics-are-the-perfect-place-fora-protest.html.

7. All cited in Jon Schafer, "Beijing 2022. The Controversy Behind the Selection," Slowtwitch.com, November 9, 2015, https://www.slowtwitch.com/Opinion/Beijing_2022._The_Controversy_Behind_The_Selection.5474.html.

8. Niels de Hoog, "Rising Temperatures Threaten Future of Winter Olympics, Say Experts," *The Guardian*, January 25, 2022, https://www.theguardian.com/environment/ng-interactive/2022/jan/25/rising-temperatures-threaten-future-winter-olympics-games-global-emissions.

9. Eric Hobsbawm and Terence Ranger, eds., *The Invention of Tradition* (Cambridge: Cambridge University Press, 1983).

10. E. John B. Allen, *The Culture and Sport of Skiing: From Antiquity to World War II* (Amherst: University of Massachusetts Press, 2007), 186.

11. Ibid., 183.

12. Ibid., 18.

13. Cited in Ron Edgeworth, "The Nordic Games and the Origins of the Olympic Winter Games," *Citius, Altius, Fortius* 2, no. 2 (1994): 29.

14. Allen, *Culture and Sport of Skiing*, 183.

15. Arne Martin Klausen, "Norwegian Culture and Olympism: Confrontations and Adaptations," in *Olympic Games as Performance and Public Event: The Case of the XVII Winter Olympic Games in Norway*, edited by Arne Martin Klausen (New York: Berghahn Books, 1999), 28–29.

16. E. John B. Allen, *Historical Dictionary of Skiing* (Lanham, MD: Scarecrow Press, 2011), 145.

17. Allen, *Culture and Sport of Skiing*, 188.

18. Cited in ibid., 183, 188.

19. Ibid., 189.

20. Roland Renson, "The Cool Games: The Winter Olympics, 1924–2002," in *The Winter Olympics: From Chamonix to Salt Lake City*, edited by Larry Gerlach (Salt Lake City: University of Utah Press, 2004), 46.

21. Cited in Nadia Lekarska, "Olympic Congresses," *Proceedings of the International Olympic Academy, 34th Session*, edited by Konstantinos Georgiadis (Olympia: International Olympic Committee, 1995), 160.

22. International Olympic Committee, "Factsheet: The Olympic Winter Games," September 2014, updated October 14, 2021, https://stillmed.olympics .com/media/Documents/Olympic-Games/Factsheets/The-Olympic-Winter -Games.pdf.

23. Note that IOC Congresses and IOC Sessions are different. The latter are annual meetings; the former are convened to address issues of contemporary significance.

24. Andrew Denning, *Skiing into Modernity: A Cultural and Environmental History* (Berkeley: University of California Press, 2015), 112.

25. Ibid., 113.

26. Ibid., 117, 115.

27. Allen, *Culture and Sport of Skiing*, 194.

28. Renson, "The Cool Games," 48.

29. Ibid.

30. Pierre Arnaud and Thierry Terret, *Le rêve blanc: Olympisme et sport d'hiver en France* (Talence, France: Presses Universitaires de Bordeaux, 1993), 115, cited in Renson, "The Cool Games," 46.

31. Arnd Krüger, "The History of the Olympic Winter Games: The Invention of Tradition," in *Winter Games, Warm Traditions*, edited by Matti Goksøyr, Gerde von der Lippe, and Kristen Mo (Oslo: ISHPES, 1996), 116, cited in Renson, "The Cool Games," 47–48.

32. Cited in Renson, "The Cool Games," 56.

33. Renson, "The Cool Games," 56.

34. Ibid., 58.

35. Ibid., 61.

36. See, for example, Arnd Krüger, "United States of America: The Crucial Battle," in *The Nazi Olympics: Sport, Politics, and Appeasement in the 1930s*, edited by Arnd Krüger and William Murray (Urbana: University of Illinois Press, 2003), 44–69.

37. Swiss and many Austrian Alpine skiers also boycotted the Games over the IOC's decision to declare ski instructors professionals.

38. Jules Boykoff, "Protest, Activism, and the Olympic Games: An Overview of Key Issues and Iconic Moments," *The International Journal of the History of Sport* 34, nos. 3–4 (2017): 163.

39. Ibid.

40. Ibid., 166.

41. Helen Jefferson Lenskyj, *Inside the Olympic Industry: Power, Politics, and Activism* (Albany: SUNY Press, 2000). See also Helen Jefferson Lenskyj, *Olympic Industry Resistance: Challenging Olympic Power and Propaganda* (Albany: SUNY Press, 2008).

42. COHRE Center on Housing Rights and Evictions, "Mega Events," accessed February 15, 2024, https://web.archive.org/web/20121123053140/http://www.cohre.org/topics/megaevents.

43. Dave Zirin, *Brazil's Dance with the Devil: The World Cup, the Olympics, and the Fight for Democracy* (Chicago: Haymarket Books, 2014). Thoughtful journalism from the Qatar 2022 FIFA men's World Cup included Shireen Ahmed, "A Few Weeks in Qatar Forced Me to Unlearn Some of My Own Biases About Muslim Women in Sport" (CBC Sports, December 14, 2022, https://www.cbc.ca/sports/opinion-qatar-muslim-women-shireen-ahmed-dec14-1.6651263; Jules Boykoff and Dave Zirin, "The Big Winners of the 2022 World Cup? Qatar and Despots the World Over (and Messi)," *The Nation*, December 18, 2022, https://www.thenation.com/article/society/world-cup-winner-qatar/; Karim Zidan, "The Qatar World Cup Should Be a Watershed Moment in Sports Journalism," *The Guardian*, December 20, 2022, https://www.theguardian.com/football/2022/dec/20/qatar-world-cup-sport-journalism.

44. Helen Jefferson Lenskyj, *The Best Olympics Ever: Social Impacts of Sydney 2000* (Albany: SUNY Press, 2002); Jules Boykoff, *Activism and the Olympics: Dissent at the Games in Vancouver and London* (New Brunswick, NJ: Rutgers University Press, 2013).

45. Phil Cohen, *On the Wrong Side of the Tracks? East London and the Post Olympics* (London: Lawrence & Wishart, 2013); Mark Perryman, *Why the Olympics Aren't Good for Us, and How They Can Be* (New York: OR Books, 2012).

46. Chris Dempsey and Andrew Zimbalist, *No Boston Olympics: How and Why Smart Cities Are Passing on the Torch* (Lebanon, NH: University Press of New England, 2017); Jules Boykoff, *NOlympians: Inside the Fight Against Capitalist Mega-Sports in Los Angeles, Tokyo and Beyond* (Halifax: Fernwood, 2020).

47. Macintosh Ross et al., "Critical Commentary: A Call to Boycott the 2022 Beijing Olympic Games and Establish Minimum Human Rights Standards for Olympic Hosts," *Journal of Emerging Sport Studies* 6 (Winter 2021), https://doi.org/10.26522/jess.v6i.3589.

48. Christopher A. Shaw, *Five Ring Circus: Myths and Realities of the Olympic Games* (Gabriola Island, BC: New Society, 2008).

49. Robert Orttung and Sufian N. Zhemukhov, *Putin's Olympics: The Sochi Games and the Evolution of Twenty-First Century Russia* (London: Routledge, 2017). See also Helen Jefferson Lenskyj, *Sexual Diversity and the Sochi 2014 Olympics: No More Rainbows* (Basingstoke, England: Palgrave Macmillan, 2014).

50. Liv Yoon, "Mount Gariwang: An Olympic Casualty," PhD diss., University of British Columbia, 2019, http://hdl.handle.net/2429/69863.

CHAPTER 1

Banff 1972

Sportsmen, Conservationists, and the Debate over Banff National Park

RUSSELL FIELD

The national parks have been dedicated to the preservation of the natural heritage of our country. The Olympic movement is dedicated to the preservation of peace in the world. We cannot see a more fitting combination and a more suitable place than Banff National Park to foster these ideals by celebrating the Winter Games in its majestic surroundings.
—Sidney Dawes, 1965

Canada's international reputation for stewardship in wilderness preservation began in the late nineteenth century at the natural springs that became part of Banff National Park.[1] But the "natural" environment being protected there—an impulse driven in large measure to preserve the springs for human enjoyment—began an era that Tina Loo has characterized as "the making of a modern wilderness."[2] Central to this rhetorical project, indeed "the most important group in this story," were "the urban sportsmen for whom conservation policies were largely developed."[3] But by the time the Banff interests that Canadian International Olympic Committee (IOC) member Sidney Dawes alludes to above were bidding for the 1972 Winter Olympic Games, "sportsmen" found themselves on the opposite side of the parkland preservation debate with the scientific and conservation communities—in an era when, as Michael Egan notes, "the environmental movement gained widespread credibility by deferring to scientific expertise."[4]

Since the 1960s, concerns over the damage to the natural landscape and wildlife habitat caused by Olympic-related development have gained public attention. Protests over these issues accompanied the preparations for both the 2010 Winter Games in Vancouver/Whistler and the 2018 Games in PyeongChang (see chapters 4 and 6). A generation earlier, environmental protests not only circulated around Olympic Games, but successfully derailed Denver's hosting of the 1976 Winter Olympics (see chapter 2). Less well remembered are the protests surrounding the Olympic bidding cycle prior to the 1976 Games, when sport interests in Calgary and the nearby resort town of Banff, Alberta, vied to host the 1972 Winter Games with proposed Olympic sites to include development within the boundaries of Banff National Park. While the creation and use of Banff National Park has drawn the attention of historians, little has been written about the Banff protests, which took place from 1964–1966.[5] But their "success"—that is, in playing a role in the failure of the Banff group to secure the rights to host the Olympics—suggests a moment when the building of sport facilities gave way to conservation concerns.

Based primarily upon archival material drawn almost exclusively from the papers of men who were advocating on behalf of the bid, this chapter details how the use of national parks, and Banff National Park specifically, was at the heart of the debate over Canada's potential hosting of the 1972 Winter Olympics. These debates were informed by the comparatively recent revisions to the National Park Policy and influenced the approach that bid proponents took to address the concerns of conservationists. The subsequent struggles over the bid highlighted the privileged attitudes of white, male, middle-class sportsmen and conservationists, the latter fighting for the protection of wildlife and the preservation of "natural" wilderness for recreational uses, while the former saw the merits in developing parkland for competitive sport. While never articulated as such, it is easy to frame these as the concerns of white men for the nature of their leisure. The voices of Indigenous peoples were entirely absent as was any consideration of Indigenous rights. (Christine O'Bonsawin critiques the settler-colonial nature of these debates and considers the Banff bid, among others, from an Indigenous perspective in chapter 3.)

The classed nature of these debates was reflected in the tactics used throughout the bidding process. While direct action would become a hallmark of environmental protests in the 1970s and 1980s, the opposition campaign (and counterarguments) surrounding the Banff bid in 1964–1966 consisted primarily of letter-writing campaigns and lobbying. That these were successful is a reminder that, in the mid-1960s, the IOC was a considerably less powerful institution than it is in the twenty-first century. The organization, which lacked the funding that its late-twentieth century move toward global corporate sponsors has subsequently provided, found itself embroiled in a number of Cold War—related controversies that left it reluctant to engage in more local disputes. Moreover, there were clear class affinities between members of the Olympic movement and environmental groups, as evidenced by the friendship between IOC President Avery Brundage and World Wildlife Fund leader Peter Scott. This confluence of interests may have changed by the time of the ultimately unsuccessful protests surrounding the Vancouver and PyeongChang Games, but in 1966 they were well positioned to scupper the Banff bid for 1972.

Banff Bids for the Games

The Banff bid was put forward by a group called Olympic '72, whose directors represented the Calgary Olympic Development Association (CODA). A subsequent incarnation would secure the right to host the 1988 Winter Olympics, but the original CODA was formed in 1957 to put forward an exploratory bid for the 1964 Winter Olympics and then to contest more vigorously the 1968 Games.[6] The Calgary-Banff bid for the 1968 Games lost to Grenoble, 27 votes to 24 votes, at the 61st IOC Session held in Innsbruck in 1964.[7] In defeat, CODA pointed the finger at two individuals who would come to play a prominent role in the failure of their 1972 bid two years later: Dawes—whose competence was questioned and who it was felt was "probably never 100% behind [the] Banff bid"—and Brundage, who "did not favor Banff ... [while] his personal assistant, S. E. Mohammed Taher, was actively lobbying for Grenoble."[8]

In the aftermath of the Innsbruck IOC Session, CODA officials heard concerns over accommodations, the altitude of cross-country skiing courses, and restrictive liquor regulations in Banff, but no IOC members expressed apprehension about the development of the natural environment for Games venues. Local opposition to the 1968 bid consisted primarily of a lone letter from J. D. Anderson of the Banff Citizens' Committee, which Dawes described as "a very disagreeable letter," telling the IOC to "take your ski bums elsewhere."[9] Of the letter, IOC vice president, Lord Burghley, told Dawes to "bury it" and a CODA official reporting from Innsbruck attested that: "Personally I do not believe that the 'famous' letter made any difference in the outcome of the voting."[10] Regardless, environmental concerns over the use of Banff National Park as an Olympic site were not raised, nor did they derail the bid. Two years later, this was most certainly not the case.

Officials for CODA left Innsbruck disappointed by their narrow defeat, but optimistic about a future bid. "Several IOC members stated to me that they are very pleased to hear that Banff will bid again," noted the CODA

FIGURE 1.1. Ed Davis, on the far left, pictured in 1965 with other dignitaries at the proposed grounds of the Centennial Planetarium. Credit: City of Calgary Archives, CalACR-92-029-037.

staff person who had reported from Innsbruck. "This included some that had voted against us and they expressed 'that they wished they had voted for Banff.' This indicates the great deal of sentiment that still exists in the IOC for Banff."[11]

The Calgary Olympic Development Association immediately set about to win the right to host the 1972 Winter Olympics in Banff, receiving Canadian Olympic Association (COA) approval as the preferred Canadian site in late September 1964. There were a number of key players in the 1972 bid, including Brundage and Dawes. The Banff bid was supported by the COA, including president James Worrall, vice-president Frank Shaughnessy, and executive director Henk Hoppener. The bid itself, organized by Olympic '72, was led by Ed Davis (see figure 1.1), future Alberta premier Peter Lougheed, and Max Bell, publisher of *The Albertan* newspaper. In all, the Olympic '72 board included fourteen men and one woman, with only four of the fifteen members resident in Banff.[12] They were supported by staff members Hans Maciej and Ted Trafford.

In general, the Banff bid was pursued by some of Calgary's best-known civic boosters and sports enthusiasts. Not surprisingly, their efforts were supported by national and local winter sport organizations, such as the Calgary Ski Club.[13] Bid officials also sought formal support from federal government officials, in particular Prime Minister Lester B. Pearson and Minister of Northern Affairs and National Resources Arthur Laing, under whose authority national parks (including Banff National Park) were administered. For Worrall this was a fait accompli, as "the government endorsed and supported our application in 1964 and will do so again in 1966."[14] Indeed, bid supporters would tout the use of Banff National Park as a site for Olympic events as a positive and be surprised to learn that some felt otherwise.

Opposition Arises: "Incompatible with the Primary Function of National Parks"

While supporters of Banff as an Olympic host were optimistic about the bid's chances for success, early in 1965 they learned of growing opposition from a variety of local and national organizations. At least six Canadian groups announced their opposition to the bid: the Alberta Fish and Game Association, the Canadian Audubon Society, the Canadian Society of Wildlife and Fishery Biologists (CSWFB), the Canadian Wildlife Federation, the Edmonton Natural History Club, and the National and Provincial Parks Association of Canada (NPPAC). These were groups primarily concerned with parkland conservation and wildlife protection. For example, the Edmonton Natural History Club's "principal objective was to promote the study, enjoyment, and conservation of natural history . . . provide field trips, lectures, and exhibitions . . . encourage research, promote [the] establishment of natural areas, and cooperate with groups having related interests."[15]

Members of these groups often belonged to more than one organization. Dr. William Fuller was a zoologist at the University of Alberta and typical of many of the individuals involved in these conservation groups. He was a member of Edmonton Natural History Club, a member of the board of trustees of the NPPAC, and chair of the parks committee of the Canadian Audubon Society. It was Fuller who "took the initiative in getting the ANPPC [NPPAC] to intervene" in opposition to the Banff bid.[16] The NPPAC's board of trustees was indicative of the nature of opposition to the Banff bid, counting a nationally representative group of scientists, sportsmen, and business interests among the 22-person roster, all of whom were men and included a Toronto-based petrochemical consultant, the editor of a major Quebec newspaper, and an investment executive from Calgary.[17]

There was also an international dimension to the opposition. The American Society of Mammologists weighed in, but the most prominent voice came from the UK-based World Wildlife Fund and its founder, Peter Scott. He was entreated to join the cause by the CSWFB and the NPPAC.[18] The COA called Scott the "pope" of Canadian conservationists, who, as a figure in international yachting, was, Dawes worried, "a friend of Avery Brundage."[19] From the perspective of Olympic '72, "it would appear that Peter Scott has been taken in by some people who must have presented to him a completely unrealistic picture of Banff."[20]

As W. E. Swinton, chairman of the Canadian Audubon Society, noted in a letter to Prime Minister Pearson, opponents to the Banff bid believed that holding the Olympics in a national park "would be permanently destructive of important areas of the environment of Banff or any other national park and would be contrary to the long-term public good."[21] Although somewhat varied in their concerns, the arguments put forward by these different groups centered primarily on three objections to the development of sites within Banff National Park for Winter Olympic events. Firstly, allowing development to occur within the Park would be an abrogation of Canada's longstanding commitment to the preservation of parkland and wildlife habitat preservation. Olympic development, Scott argued, would be "an unhappy repudiation of long-term vision for short-term considerations," while Fuller contended that "if Canada compromises its national parks in this manner, one may expect serious repercussions on conservation on the provincial level, since our country has always been a leader in progress concerning conservation of natural wealth."[22]

Secondly, considering this view of Canadian stewardship, critics argued that permitting development within Banff National Park would set a poor example for the rest of the world. Again, it was Scott who articulated this argument—this time directly to Brundage—when he noted that the selection of the host city for the 1972 Winter Olympics could have "international repercussions." He argued: "The rest of the world looks on the United States and Canada as the pioneers of the National Park movement. The developing countries—for example in Africa—will say to themselves: 'If businesses interests in Calgary can persuade the Canadian government to alienate a part of their world famous Banff National Park for this purpose, then we can do the same when business interests demand parts of our parks.'"[23] Scott worried about "the example set to the smaller nations of encroachment—they will then make use of the Game preserves rather than keeping them for wildlife."[24]

Finally, opponents argued that the bid was led by local business leaders interested primarily in development and self-aggrandizement. For the Canadian Wildlife Federation, resistance to the bid was evidence that "the long, seesaw battle against commercial exploitation of Canada's National Parks is being fought more vigorously than ever," with reference even being made to the 1960 Winter Olympics in a northern California resort town, where the Games were a pretext to establishing a sport and tourism infrastructure (and Walt Disney was hired to plan the event's ceremonies).[25]

The initial tactics employed by the opponents of the Banff bid say much about their politics. These were scientists, academics, and conservationists who belonged to organizations grounded in the politics of middle-class social reform and vigorous debate. One of the key expressions of opposition were resolutions proclaimed by these various societies. At least three such motions were brought forward, debated, and passed at annual general meetings. The Canadian Audubon Society unanimously agreed, on February 6, 1965, that their organization was "irrevocably opposed" to the Olympics being held in Banff National Park.[26] Two months later, on April 3, at their annual meeting in Calgary, the CSWFB passed a similar motion, one dissenting vote short of unanimity, opposing the "extension of sports facilities in Banff National Park" for fear that the Olympics would "cause serious local changes in the environment" and were "incompatible with the primary function of National Parks."[27] The American Society of Mammologists also passed a similar motion.

There were also appeals to the public. The UK-based *Animals* ran an editorial in its August 17, 1965, issue which suggested that "all Canadian readers of ANIMALS, and any others who feel as we do about this state of affairs, should complain to the Minister concerned."[28] At the same time, many groups went to great pains to reiterate that they were neither anti-sport nor anti-Olympic, but simply opposed to the Games being held in a national park. While Scott noted of the proposed development that "it is to me quite unthinkable that it should be done in the name of the Olympic Movement," Fuller was clear: "I'm not against the Olympics."[29]

Nevertheless, opposition to the Banff bid was neither unanimous nor absolute among conservation groups. The CSWFB wavered as it noted that if a site alternate to Banff could not be found, then the Games' organizers should seek to locate facilities outside the Park and host events in a way that "minimize their adverse effects on the environment." Indeed, Dr. Louis Lemieux, CSWFB president and based in Quebec City, where he held a position with the wildlife management service of the provincial Ministry of Tourism, Fish and Game, wrote to Dawes, to let the Canadian IOC member know that "I think you may find that it [the CSWFB resolution] is not altogether negative."[30] Of another organization, Davis felt that their opposition "was more a 'matter of principle' than it is a strong feeling throughout the National Parks Association."[31] Other groups, in particular local sport and recreational clubs, as well as individuals, were more supportive of the bid in the face of the growing criticism. The Lake Louise Ski Club resolved at a club meeting to "offer its support to Olympic '72 in helping to get the Olympics and in organizing the Games if we get them."[32] Davis was moved to assert that "there are strong differences of opinion on the subject" of the impact of the Games on the Park. "Those who have had direct experience with the Banff National Park have no objection to its use for skiing and limited recreational purposes."

The Bid Committee Responds: "Ridiculous Statements about Imaginary Damage"

While bid organizers rejected the ways in which their proposed Olympic plans were framed by conservationists, they were just as quick to label the protesting organizations "minority groups" whose positions were grounded in "a lack of knowledge of the function of the Olympic Winter Games" and "based upon inadequate and to some extent, erroneous information."[33] The responses from Olympic '72 and the COA—both within the media, as conservation groups' motions became public knowledge, and in communications with federal government and IOC officials—addressed the primary objections raised by the bid's opponents: the impact of Olympic-related development within Banff National Park; the use of that parkland as recreational space; and the charges that bid officials pursued this development to serve their own self-interests.

The position of those associated with Olympic '72 and the COA was that protestors' "concern about the effect of the Games on wild life in the park is," as Worrall wrote to Dawes, "exaggerated."[34] It was on this issue that the bid's proponents were least able to empathize with "such people, as bird watchers and bear lovers, making ridiculous statements about imaginary damage that the Olympics at Banff might do their animal friends."[35] This rhetoric framed wildlife preservation as little more than zoo keeping, with the animals' primary role to be on display as living exhibits for human visitors to Banff National Park. Davis bemoaned "the rather silly arguments presented by the wildlife people," while Dawes asserted that "animals can be moved from one place to another by the Game Wardens using opened bales of hay and salt licks just as is done each summer along the Banff-Lake Louise road so that animals will stay there to be seen by motorists."[36] For Dawes, there was "no more heartwarming scene than to see little children feed young deer roaming at large."[37] Wildlife species were little more than a tourist attraction, with Worrall touting the bid by contending that "another attraction of the Banff National Park is the wild animals that visit every hotel and tourist lodge along the way."[38]

Dawes also noted that "every winter for many years," areas within Banff National Park had "been used by skiers . . . without disturbing the animals."[39] That areas within the Park were "already being substantially used for both recreational and competitive skiing, and there are already in existence accommodations and lift facilities" was a dominant narrative in the counterarguments put forward by the bid's proponents.[40] They noted that park attendance and skiing use figures prepared by the Department of Northern Affairs and National Resources supported this position.[41] Annually, "there are well over a million visitors passing through the park and stopping over from varying periods at Banff and Lake Louise, and they have been holding winter sports events there for years."[42] (See figure 1.2.) Thus, the argument went, the Olympics would not be an unusual use of the park. The expectation of six hundred thousand Olympic visitors was "well below the number of people that come to Banff every July and August."[43] Moreover, potential Olympic park users would only impact a fraction of the land preserved in the adjoining national parks in Alberta and British Columbia—Banff, Yoho, Kootenay, and Jasper—which represented an area of eight thousand square miles, half the size of Switzerland (this comparison was specifically directed at IOC officials, whose headquarters were in the Alpine nation). Less than 1 percent of this area would be taken up by development for the proposed Olympic sites.

"Surely," Worrall concluded in a letter to Prime Minister Pearson, "the national parks are also for the use and enjoyment of the people of Canada, and . . . skiers and other winter sportsmen are citizens and taxpayers the same as those who would preserve our wild life."[44] Indeed, the federal government and the province had "already expended a very considerable sum of money on studies, services, and actual cutting of trails, improvement of ski slopes, construction of roads, and other developments which will be necessary if we are awarded the Games."[45] The federal government's attitude toward park use and the development of parklands would become a central feature in the debate over the Banff Olympic bid. But, first, Worrall wanted to assure all concerned that "it is quite improper to suggest that the desire to hold the Olympic Winter Games in Canada was motivated by commercial interests." While many of the bid officials were "admittedly 'Calgary businessmen,'" their pursuit of the Olympics for Banff was not motivated by "self-aggrandizement, commercial interest, or the destruction of national parks." Rather, these were "fair-minded and

FIGURE 1.2. The 1937 Dominion Ski Championships in Banff. Recreational use of Banff National Park was well established by the 1960s. Credit: Provincial Archives of Alberta, A1503.

objective sportsmen . . . very strongly opposed to any commercialization of our national parks."[46]

As part of the strategy to address the "conservationist controversy," it was decided that senior Olympic and political officials in Canada would tackle these issues and that the operational staff of the Banff bid would do their best to distance themselves from these debates.[47] An initial tactic was to engage opponents of the bid in dialogue, in the hopes of changing their opinions by "attempting to get together at the conference table" for "a free discussion of all aspects" in an "attempt to convince the wildlife people that their fears are not justified."[48] There was a belief that reasoned arguments could overcome ecological passions and scientific assessments. Lougheed received a letter from the Chamber of Commerce in the southern Alberta city of Lethbridge about Fred Browning, who was being promoted to head the National Parks Administration in Western Canada and would be based in Alberta. The author noted that Browning was "under the influence of the Fish & Game people who violently fight anything that is an improve-ment in national parks" although his "whole life is devoted to maintaining the beauty and savageness of our National Parks. He should be sold on the fact that the Olympics will do NOTHING to infringe on these ideals . . . if a proper selling job is done on him starting immediately, he will see 'our' way in a minimum of time."[49] Similarly, an internal memo circulated among the directors of Olympic '72 concluded that A. P. Frame of the NPPAC: "is not so fanatical as many of the council and that, provided we can 'educate' him to some extent, we might develop a very real ally."[50]

Co-opting the opposition was the goal. Davis wrote Laing that, following "a long discussion," an opponent of the bid "has agreed to an interim truce, pending further conversations." Both Frame and Fuller were invited by Olympic '72 "to join our group in various capacities."[51] The former wrote to Brundage that discussions with Olympic'72 personnel had been "helpful of achieving a meeting of the minds."[52] By April 1966, late in the bidding process, Fuller agreed to serve on the bid's Facilities Committee.[53] Participation on working committees was, in Frame's estimation, a way to protect the interests of the NPPAC from within the hosting organization.[54] Such détente was not welcome in all circumstances, however. In December 1965, Maciej suggested that Fuller be invited to a debate on issues related to the Banff bid hosted by the Calgary Chamber of Commerce. Davis emphatically wrote "NO!" next to this suggestion on his copy of Maciej's memo.[55]

The "Conservationist Controversy" and the National Park Policy: "A Battle which Should Be Fought Elsewhere"

These efforts occurred in the context of a new National Park Policy. The balance between reserving natural landscapes for human recreation and preserving wilderness from development began to shift toward environmental preservation after the implementation of the 1930 National Parks Act, under the leadership of James B. Harkin, first commissioner of the Dominion Parks Branch.[56] But, in September 1964, Laing set out a new policy for national park use and development, which while not expressly preventing Olympic-related development could be interpreted as less than favorable toward the Banff bid.[57]

The minister advocated a balanced approach: "National park policy cannot . . . [be] based on one of two extremes, maximum preservation on one hand, or maximum public use and development on the other."[58] The policy argued that "development in a national park must be considered solely on the direct effect it will have on increasing the public's enjoyment and use of the national parks and on maintaining them as sanctuaries not only of nature but for nature."[59] Yet, this did not mean "that the government does not wish further development undertaken in the parks."[60] Importantly for the Banff bid, however, "the government does not intend that national parks attempt to meet every recreational need . . . In future, only such activities as photography, sightseeing, hiking, swimming, riding, skiing, nature observation, fishing and boating will be encouraged by the national parks branch."[61] As a result, recreational activities that "do not require a natural environment for their enjoyment . . . should be sought elsewhere."[62] In trying to strike this balance, Laing reiterated that any belief that a park should be "developed to its maximum potential by allowing it to become a series of private or commercial resorts . . . is a misunderstanding of the purpose of the national parks."[63] Yet, at the same time, the new policy highlighted the need for a "zoning system" to "best locate such development."[64]

It was on these issues—park use and zoning for recreational development—that Olympic '72 officials focused their lobbying efforts. While Laing asserted in the House of Commons that "the support for the Olympic winter games given by the government of Canada will be the same as that which we endeavoured to give when we were trying to get the games for 1968," Donald Cameron, a Senator from Banff, urged Davis that "there must be no letup in the pressure on the Minister to develop a reasonable and extensive policy for tourism and recreation in the National Parks."[65] In April 1965, Olympic '72 "agreed political action was necessary," leaving this to Davis and Trafford.[66] By the end of the year, it was clear to the directors of Olympic '72 that "the zoning of national parks has become a most urgent matter and should be pursued immediately with the new Minister [Laing]."[67]

Private discussions and backroom lobbying yielded, in the eyes of the Olympic '72 leadership, some important successes leading up to the IOC decision. Indeed, Davis noted for Brundage, that the "Executive of the National & Provincial Parks Association, after carefully studying the impact of the Games on the Park site, have made recommendations to the Federal Government which, if acceptable, would allow them to *endorse* the use of the site for the Games. These recommendations are simply that a portion of the parks area would be given a different zoning or designation than they now hold."[68] Olympic '72 and the COA attempted to take the now-public opposition of conservation groups and shift the debate away from Banff, with Hoppener noting for Richard Passmore of the Canadian Wildlife Federation that "clearly your concern is with National Parks Policy and . . . your public action is intended to bring about changes in that policy. You and other spokesmen for Canadian and foreign conservation and naturalist bodies are illustrating your case with the candidature of Banff for the 1972 winter Olympics."[69] The COA wanted to ensure that concerns about parks policy did not "reflect on the merits of the Banff application which continues to enjoy the full support of the Canadian government." Hoppener implored the Canadian Wildlife Federation to "let the Banff application go forward without further public controversy."[70] This reflected his conviction that "the naturalists, conservationists[,] etc." were fighting on principle:

> They know and privately admit that Olympic games would have not negative effect on the area—only a minute section of the national park—and could well make a positive contribution through facilities, hiking trails, lookout posts, etc., not to speak of decent hotel accommodation in and around Banff . . . In other words Canadian nature lovers appear to be fighting over Banff a battle which should be fought elsewhere.[71]

These efforts sought to shift the focus from the plans proposed by the Banff bid to the broader issue of park use and the articulation of public policy. The latter, so this argument went, was not the responsibility of Olympic officials and bid supporters but of the federal Department of Northern Affairs and National Resources. Thus, officials could reassure the IOC, Brundage in particular, that the administration of Banff National Park "is in the hands of our Federal Government who over the years have trained many competent guardians to take care of the interests of the people as well as to protect the wild life"[72] and "the preservation of wild life and the impact of the development of sports and recreation, not to mention the holding of the Olympic Games, is at all times very carefully considered by the said Department."[73] In turn, Prime Minister Pearson and the federal government reassured the IOC that it "gives support to the staging of international events," and "if it becomes established that a particular area of a park is best suited for such an event, and it is in the national interest such an event be held in Canada, then the National Parks should permit the intrusion."[74]

This support—even as the Olympics were framed as an "intrusion" into Banff National Park—was made tangible when, a month before the IOC was to meet in April 1966 to select the 1972 Games' sites, Laing sent essentially the same letter to the NPPAC, Canadian Audubon Society, and Canadian Wildlife Federation. He addressed the possibility of rezoning certain spaces as separate from the protected areas and suitable for development, rejecting this course of action "without a great deal more consideration." Nevertheless, there was "insufficient justification to link this question with the Olympics." It was his opinion that the Olympics would "cause no permanent and very little temporary impairment to the park," as they would "make use of existing facilities" and might even lead to developments that the Ministry would itself have pursued in the near future.[75]

Conservation groups were dismayed, with the *Wildlife News*, published by the Canadian Wildlife Federation, noting "there may be some doubt whether the pressure of these organizations will cause any reversal of policy." The Federation was not entirely put off, as "there can be no doubt that growing numbers of Canadians are determined to see the National Parks preserved as islands of natural environment protected from the kinds of development and exploitation which prevail elsewhere."[76] Regardless, the leadership of Olympic '72 was confident that their strategy for dealing with conversationists' objections had put them in a good position. Davis wrote to the other directors that "our chances for the 1972 Games appear to be very good, although unforeseen circumstances could arise between now and April."[77] They did.

Ramping Up the Pressure: "The Subject Is With Us Again"

As the April 1966 IOC Session approached, opponents of the Banff bid stepped up their efforts, making their opposition more vocal and more visible. Letter-writing campaigns extended beyond Canada and targeted Brundage and the IOC. Concern was expressed by federal officials, with a manager in the Department of Northern Affairs and National Resources writing the president of the CSWFB that "we are concerned that sending a communication of this nature to an international body such as the International Olympic Committee could very well adversely affect Canada's reputation abroad. Before any communication is sent beyond our borders, we ask that an official of your association get in touch with us so that all facets of this question can be fully explored."[78] Conservation groups forged ahead anyway, with their opposition becoming front-page news. A Canadian Press report publicized the concerns, asserting that "If the Olympics go into Banff in 1972 and some of the Park is destroyed . . . it may never be the same."[79]

News of these expanded tactics reached Canadian officials. Brundage wrote to both Worrall and Davis, informing them that he was being "deluged with letters of protest against the Banff site from Canadian citizens and organizations."[80] Maciej was left to lament to the Olympic '72 directors that "the subject is with us again."[81] While Gavin Henderson of the NPPAC had previously indicated to Olympic '72 that "our Association does not intend to protest officially the holding of the Winter Olympics in Banff," at their November 1965 meeting, the NPPAC decided to pursue "the most vigorous protest possible."[82] The Canadian Audubon Society had also shifted from writing letters to the prime minister to approaching the IOC directly.[83]

Olympic '72 and COA officials were increasingly concerned by and frustrated with the persisting opposition to the bid—even as they interpreted the new parks policy as supportive of their plans. Worrall wrote to Brundage in May 1965: "I would be less than truthful, however, if I were to say that we are unconcerned about this type of representation." In defending the COA's choice of Banff as the Canadian bid site, as well as the preparations of Olympic '72, Worrall felt it "difficult to be restrained" in the face of those groups that he felt were "grossly exaggerating any possible detrimental effects to wild life and the natural beauty of this area."[84] A week later, following letters of assurance from Dawes, Worrall, and Davis, Brundage reassured Canadian officials that they had "disposed of the adverse criticism of the project."[85]

While Worrall was expressing his frustrations to Brundage, Dawes noted for the COA president "the absolute necessity of having this matter cleared up" as "the persistent opposition of the World and Canadian Wildlife Associations will greatly confuse I. O. C. Members at any meeting at which they are called upon to vote on the venue for the next Winter Olympic Games."[86] This sense of urgency was widely shared as bid officials began their final push to win support. In response to the letters arriving on the desks of Brundage and other IOC members, the Banff organizers themselves decided to ramp up a letter-writing campaign, hoping that high-level assurances from Canadian officials would defuse the situation. In January 1966, Davis wrote to the prime minister's executive assistant suggesting that a letter from the premier to Brundage was necessary "to reaffirm the Canadian Government's support of Banff as an Olympic site."[87] At the same time, while characterizing "Wild Life people" as "such obstructionists," Dawes encouraged Brundage to "disregard letters from Wild Life and other persons complaining about our imaginary interference with the animals and be guided by our Prime Minister."[88] Less than a week later, Worrall wrote to Brundage, that while "we live in a democratic country and we cannot prevent people from expressing their views, no matter how illogical they may seem," there were "Canadians who would take advantage of our Olympic application to attempt to force a section of the Government of Canada into making certain policy decisions which these organizations apparently want."[89] These frustrations boiled over as Worrall wrote to Prime Minister Pearson two months before the IOC was due to make its decision, bemoaning that some Canadians were jeopardizing their own Olympic bid based upon "internal and, I suspect, minority opposition from certain groups within our own country."[90]

Nevertheless, the bid proceeded on the assumption that the matter of environmentalists' objections had been resolved in Brundage's eyes. Maciej prepared a lengthy brief on the nature and impact of the bid that was intended to address opponents' concerns and was shared with Canadian conservation groups as well as Scott of the World Wildlife Fund. Maciej noted, "it is our hope that this brief will remove many, if not all, of the misconceptions that exist concerning the holding of the Olympic Winter Games in Banff National Park."[91] This final effort at allaying concerns—even as those concerns over parkland development and wildlife endangerment were reduced to "misconceptions"—served instead as fodder for the bid opponents' final push to scupper any proposed interventions in Banff National Park. Scott returned his copy complete with detailed annotations. He also wrote Brundage days before the IOC Session to express the "deep concern that is felt by the world's nature conservationists at the possibility of holding the 1972 Winter Olympic Games in the Banff National Park." While in Canada "the project is highly controversial," the prospect of an Olympic Games in a national park had "international repercussions." Scott had listened to the counterarguments from COA and Olympic '72 officials, but "none justify the repudiation of the long-term vision of those who set aside this Park for the enjoyment of future generations as wild country, to be kept inviolate in perpetuity. I cannot believe that such a repudiation is any part of Olympic philosophy." And, indeed, this was the final arrow in the conservationists' quiver: opting for Banff would compromise "the absolute moral integrity of the Olympic Movement."[92]

As members gathered in Rome in April 1966 for the 64th IOC Session, they found waiting for them a telegram from a group of "residents[,] parents[,] and Canadian citizens" signaling their commitment to "protest the holding of [the] Olympic Games in National Parks for [the] sake of [the] future of National Parks in Canada and [the] world."[93] In light of the "sporadic outbursts by the Audubon Society and Wildlife people," Olympic '72 had maneuvered, ultimately unsuccessfully, "to have the actual Superintendent of the Park at the meeting."[94] Instead, Olympic '72 representatives were joined by COA officials and the mayor of Banff in making the case for the bid. After they withdrew, debate among IOC members focused on whether the town had sufficient accommodations in addition to concerns about the use of the national park. IOC member and president of the International Ski Federation, Marc Hodler, spoke highly of the existing facilities, while two African IOC members acknowledged the presence of tourists in their own countries' national parks.

Brundage remained firm. Despite its support from Prime Minister Pearson, the bid troubled the IOC president, who "could not set aside all the protests he had received which came from informed circles, universities and clubs." Just who opposed the bid mattered to Brundage, as he felt that the IOC could not "risk hostile demonstrations at the time of the Games."[95] When bids were considered, Brundage supplemented the Banff presentation by reading excerpts from a letter from the Edmonton Natural History Club, among the most incendiary of the entire campaign and one of the few to promise to "do everything possible to mobilize an effective protest before, during and after the event" if Banff were awarded the Games. Olympic '72 officials were furious that Brundage read this letter "to the IOC members just prior to the *voting*" and that "no opportunity [was] given to [the] Banff delegation for rebuttal."[96] The 1972 Winter Olympics were awarded to Sapporo.

Aftermath: "A Controversy of This Kind"

If environmental protests were highly visible, they were not the sole contributing factor to Banff's defeat. Although some of his colleagues believed that the conservationists' opposition "was the most important single factor in the rejection of the Banff application," Trafford reported to the Olympic '72 board that it would be "a gross oversimplification to believe that if we had beaten the wildlife group all would have been well."[97] Olympic '72 was competing not only against Sapporo and other candidate cities in 1966, but also, as suggested by Tina Loo, in the context of the changing relationship between "sports*men*" (emphasis mine) and the construction of the "natural" world. Without losing sight of "the class and racial aspects of the sportsmen's paradise," by the 1960s sportsmen were no longer playing a leading role in the advocacy for national parks usage.[98]

Brundage was criticized for his perceived preference for Sapporo and the perception that he had manipulated proceedings in Rome. Dawes was, nearly seven months in advance of the IOC decision, "quite convinced that Sapporo will get the games."[99] The media reported that the chances of Sapporo getting the Games were "very real" as Brundage was impressed "by the facilities offered in the surroundings of Sapporo and by the existing facilities." This served "to confirm the anxieties held on the subject of Banff," as did, for some critics, the IOC president's penchant for collecting East Asian art.[100] But there were other issues troubling Brundage and challenging the Olympic Movement in the mid-1960s, from the persistent struggle over how to deal with the apartheid government in South Africa to the Cold War challenges presented by two Chinas, Koreas, and Germanys, as well as NATO visa restrictions, and the confrontation offered by the 1963 Games of the New Emerging Forces and the entry of the developing world into international sport. In this context, Brundage felt that, where Banff was concerned, the IOC "cannot very well be blamed for not wanting to place itself in the middle of a controversy of this kind."[101] These were Canadian issues, yet the IOC president felt that "an argument of this kind" would have "international ramifications."[102]

While Canadian officials were none too pleased with Brundage's conduct, they were equally disappointed in the performance of their "own" representative on the IOC. As early as February 1965, there was concern among Banff bid proponents that Dawes would not be their most effective advocate as it was suspected that his preference for a Canadian Winter Olympic site was Garibaldi Provincial Park in British Columbia, which had been passed over by the COA in favor of Banff National Park. Lougheed noted that Dawes "was apparently hostile to the Banff bid and definitely in favour of the Garibaldi proposal." He asserted that Dawes "should give more than merely nominal support to the Banff bid and should, on behalf of Canada, make an enthusiastic effort to assist" in promoting the bid.[103] According to Worrall, Dawes was "quite confused on many issues but, at the same time, obstinately determined on other points." He was likely to be a "danger so far as our bid in Rome is concerned." In the same conversation, Worrall noted, Dawes consistently "extolled developments on Garibaldi."[104] Shaughnessy implored Dawes to work with him to respond to conservationists' claims, noting that "former winter sports officials like you and I should do all we can to ensure that the people that count are acquainted with the truth." He also took an opportunity to re-center Dawes' site preferences by arguing that "we all know that Banff is the only area in Canada that can attract the Olympic Winter Games at this time."[105]

Suspicions surrounding the promotion of Garibaldi as an Olympic site went beyond Dawes. When *Northwest Sportsmen Magazine* published anti-Banff bid editorials written by Jim Railton, Davis claimed that Railton's son was "active in the Garibaldi Olympic Development Assn."[106] Similarly, after Shaughnessy read of the Canadian Wildlife Association's opposition to the Banff bid, he was moved to inquire of Davis, "Are there any Garibaldi people in the Canadian Wildlife Association?"[107] The late entry of a Montreal bid into the competition for the 1972 *summer* Olympics also led to presumptions that opposition to the Banff bid was based upon east-west biases in Canadian sport. Nevertheless, Trafford was assured by the NPPAC that their objections were led by the organization's "Alberta representatives . . . [who] were among the most insistent" in their opposition to the Banff bid.[108]

Despite the perceptions of Brundage's obstruction and Dawes's ineffectiveness, the real challenge that Olympic '72 and the COA faced was to understand why their bid for the 1972 Games generated the opposition it did. As Worrall wrote to the prime minister:

It does seem rather strange that these protests come at this particular stage of development. The first application by a Calgary group to hold the Games in Banff was made in 1959, and the second and almost-successful application was made in February of 1964. There has been publicity about the application from coast to coast, in the press, on the radio, and on television. A great amount of time, effort, and money has been expended by interested persons and various levels of government [to] bring the application to its present stage, and we find it is a little difficult to understand why the alleged impact on the wild life of the park should be brought up at this particular time.[109]

All of which suggests that the landscape was more complicated than the bid's proponents conceived. Even as the bid lost to Sapporo, they were reassured by sportspeople around the world that they had been mistreated in the process. "I cannot tell you how disgusted all the Winter sports folk in this country," one English correspondent wrote, "are at the decision to hold the 1968 [sic] Winter Olympics in Japan."[110] As a result, the Olympic '72 postmortem focused primarily on the need to amend federal parks policy. Davis was hopeful, in defeat, that "various senior civil servants" would soon be "prepared to accept some method of zoning as a solution to the Parks problem." Regulatory change was, to his mind, the only solution to the conservation and wildlife problem. Lobbying the naturalists would be ineffective. "Experience has taught us that it is not possible to reason with these people," Davis reported to the Olympic '72 board, "[as] their belief is one of faith."[111]

Such faith held great purchase in the 1960s, which is one reason (beyond a weariness for public protest) why environmental issues, once raised, influenced Brundage and the IOC and gained such public exposure. The opposition of conservationists, absent only two years earlier when Banff lost to Grenoble, emerged alongside the nascent environmental movement in the aftermath of Rachel Carson's influential ecological warning, the 1962 book *Silent Spring*.[112] Advocacy for environmental protection was, as Eeva Berglund and David G. Anderson have argued, a particularly middle-class concern, and those so concerned were turning to the new breed of "public scientists or scientists activists" like Carson.[113] Environmentalism, Denton E. Morrison observes, "came as something of a relief to a movement-pummeled white, middle class. The environmental movement especially seemed to have potential for diverting the energies of a substantial proportion of young people . . . [toward what] at worst [was] clearly the safest movement in town."[114]

A decade later radical movements of the 1970s, such as Earth First! and high-profile organizations like Greenpeace, would lead Catherine

Caulfield to describe Canadian environmentalists as activists who "block-aded logging roads with fallen trees, boulders and their own bodies; buried themselves up to their necks in the paths of advancing bulldozers, and suspended themselves from trees, dangling a hundred feet off the ground for days at a time."[115] But in the mid-1960s, the *tactics* employed by the opponents of the 1972 Banff bid said much about their *politics*. These were scientists, academics, and conservationists who belonged to organizations grounded in the politics of middle-class social reform, committed to bring-ing about change through lobbying and vigorous debate. No roads were blockaded; no one chained themselves to the gates of Banff National Park. In a decade of profound and, for some, unsettling social unrest, with which Brundage and the IOC were all too familiar, resistance over environmental issues enjoyed, as Ramachandra Guha argues, "one clear advantage over the other movements: it was less divisive."[116]

Notes

The epigraph is quoted from a letter by Sidney Dawes to Avery Brundage dated May 25, 1965, on file in the James Worrall papers at the International Centre for Olympic Studies at Western University.

1. Kevin McNamee, "From Wild Places to Endangered Spaces: A History of Canada's National Parks," in Philip Dearden and Rick Rollins (eds.), *Parks and Protected Areas in Canada: Planning and Management*, 2nd edition (Toronto: Oxford University Press, 2002), 24.

2. Tina Loo, "Making a Modern Wilderness: Conserving Wildlife in Twen-tieth-Century Canada," *Canadian Historical Review* 82, no. 1 (March 2001): 2.

3. Ibid., 18.

4. Michael Egan, "Shamans of the Spring: Environmentalism and the New Jeremiad," in Karen Dubinsky et al. (eds.), *New World Coming: The Sixties and the Shaping of Global Consciousness* (Toronto: Between the Lines, 2009), 296.

5. The most thorough examination of the protests over the 1972 bid comes from Cheryl Williams, who explores the ways in which Banff National Park was alternately framed as a site of sport, tourism, and environmental pro-tection (Cheryl Williams, "The Banff Winter Olympics: Sport, Tourism, and Banff National Park," unpublished MA thesis, University of Alberta, 2011). Importantly, the resistance to the Banff 1972 bid is mentioned elsewhere in this volume (see chapters 3 and 8). The creation and use of Banff National Park has been the subject of popular histories, e.g., Eleanor Georgina Lux-ton, *Banff: Canada's First National Park*, 2nd edition (Banff: Summerthought Publishing, 2008). Scholars have explored the establishment and operation of the park, including, in particular, the impact on Indigenous peoples, e.g., Theodore (Ted) Binnema and Melanie Niemi, "Conservation and the Exclu-sion of Aboriginal People from Banff National Park in Canada," *Environmental History* 11, no. 4 (2006): 724–50; Courtney W. Mason, *Spirits of the Rockies:*

Reasserting an Indigenous Presence in Banff National Park (Toronto: University of Toronto Press, 2014). The construction of this "natural" landscape as a sporting space has been considered most fully by PearlAnn Reichwein, *Climber's Paradise: Making Canada's Mountain Parks, 1906 to 1974* (Edmonton: University of Alberta Press, 2014). Finally, both the geography of southern Alberta as well as national parks in Canada have been the subject of environmental historians, e.g., Christopher Armstrong, Matthew Evenden, and H. V. Nelles, *The River Returns: An Environmental History of the Bow* (Montreal: McGill-Queen's University Press, 2011); Sean Kheraj, *Inventing Stanley Park: An Environmental History* (Vancouver: UBC Press, 2013).

6. Ken McKee, "3 Calgarians in East Seek Support for Banff as Site of 1968 Games," *Globe and Mail*, March 2, 1961, 40; No. 2781, *Alberta Gazette*, 14 September 1957, 1595.

7. For an examination of the 1968 bid, see Heather Dichter, "Canadian Government Involvement in Calgary's Failed 1968 Winter Olympic Bid," *International Journal of the History of Sport* 38, no. 13–14 (2021): 1329–49.

8. Hans Maciej, "Report on the 61st Session of the International Olympic Committee—Innsbruck, Austria, January 26–28, 1964," film 136, Ed Davis papers, CODA Archives, Winsport, Calgary (hereafter "Davis papers").

9. A. Sidney Dawes to R. E. Spackman, May 19, 1964, file 136, Davis papers. Also cited in "Reasons Which Have Been Suggested for Adverse IOC Decision," prepared by B. M. McVicar, undated, file 136, Davis papers.

10. A. Sidney Dawes, "Meeting of the International Olympic Committee held January 28, 1964 at Innsbruck, Austria," file 136, Davis papers; Maciej, "Report on the 61st Session," Davis papers.

11. Maciej, "Report on the Tokyo Trip."

12. "Olympic '72 Board of Directors (elected 28 June 1965)," file 97, Davis papers.

13. David Mittelstadt, *Calgary Goes Skiing: A History of the Calgary Ski Club* (Surrey, BC: Rocky Mountain Books, 2005), 129–32.

14. James Worrall to Avery Brundage, May 26, 1965, Avery Brundage papers, International Centre for Olympic Studies, Western University (hereafter "Brundage papers").

15. Donna Clandfield, "Edmonton Natural History Club," in Brian Hitchon (ed.), *Preserving our Natural Environment: Celebrating the Centennial of the Edmonton Nature Club* (Edmonton: Edmonton Nature Club, 2009), 14. This club history makes no mention of the opposition to the 1972 Banff Winter Olympic bid.

16. Jean La Boissiere, "Vigorous Opposition to Banff's Candidateship as the Site for the '72 Olympic Games," *La Presse*, December 10, 1965, translation, file 151, Davis papers. Note: ANPPC is the acronym for the French-language name of the NPPAC.

17. "National and Provincial Parks Association of Canada executive," 1965, file 151, Davis papers.

18. Hans Maciej, "Reference: Opposition to Winter Games at Banff,"

Olympic '72 Board Meeting No. 17 minutes, Appendix E, May 17, 1965, file 32, Davis papers.

19. H. W. Hoppener to James E. Brown, February 8, 1966, file 151, Davis papers; A. Sidney Dawes to James Worrall, May 17, 1965, file 138, Davis papers.

20. E. H. Davis to James Worrall, May 17, 1965, file 118, Davis papers.

21. W. E. Swinton to Lester Pearson, February 25, 1965, James Worrall papers, International Centre for Olympic Studies, Western University (hereafter "Worrall papers").

22. Peter Scott to Avery Brundage, cited in Avery Brundage to Sidney Dawes, May 10, 1965, Brundage papers; cited in full in La Boissiere, "Vigorous Opposition," 10 December 1965, Davis papers.

23. Peter Scott to Avery Brundage, cited in Avery Brundage to Sidney Dawes, May 10, 1965.

24. Memorandum from Ed Davis to Hans Maciej, May 31, 1965, file 151, Davis papers.

25. "Conservation Groups Oppose Winter Olympics in Banff," *Wildlife News* [Canadian Wildlife Federation] 1, no. 2 (Spring 1965): 2.

26. Swinton to Pearson, February 25, 1965, Worrall papers.

27. Cited in *Canadian Wildlife and Fisheries Newsletter* 22, no. 2 (May 1965), Worrall papers.

28. Cited in confidential memorandum from Hans Maciej to Olympic '72 directors, "Re: Opposition to Use of Banff Park for Games," December 15, 1965, file 151, Davis papers.

29. Peter Scott to Avery Brundage, cited in Avery Brundage to Sidney Dawes, May 10, 1965; cited in Canadian Press wire report, February 11, 1966, file 151, Davis papers.

30. Dawes to Brundage, May 25, 1965, Worrall papers.

31. Ed Davis to James Coutts, January 5, 1966, file 104, Davis papers.

32. Lake Louise Ski Club to Ed Davis, January 28, 1966, file 2, Davis papers.

33. Dawes to Brundage, May 25, 1965, Worrall papers; H. W. Hoppener to Richard C. Passmore, February 18, 1966, file 151, Davis papers.

34. James Worrall to Sidney Dawes, May 14, 1965, Worrall papers.

35. Frank Shaughnessy to A. S. Dawes, February 22, 1966, file 151, Davis papers.

36. Davis to Worrall, May 17, 1965, Davis papers; Sidney Dawes to Avery Brundage, May 12, 1965, Brundage papers.

37. Dawes to Brundage, May 25, 1965, Worrall papers.

38. Worrall to Brundage, May 26, 1965, Brundage papers.

39. Sidney Dawes to Avery Brundage, May 31, 1965, Brundage papers.

40. Worrall to Brundage, May 26, 1965, Brundage papers.

41. B. I. M. Strong to Hans Maciej, February 25, 1966, file 154, Davis papers.

42. Worrall to Dawes, May 14, 1965, Worrall papers.

43. Dawes to Brundage, May 25, 1965, Worrall papers.

44. James Worrall to Lester Pearson, March 1, 1965, Worrall papers.

45. Worrall to Brundage, May 26, 1965, Brundage papers.

46. Ibid.

47. H. W. Hoppener to Hans Maciej, March 1, 1966, file 117, Davis papers.

48. Dawes to Brundage, May 25, 1965, Worrall papers.

49. Lethbridge Chamber of Commerce to Peter Lougheed, December 9, 1964, file 112, Davis papers.

50. Confidential memorandum from E. LeM. Trafford to Olympic '72 directors, December 29, 1965, file 151, Davis papers.

51. Ed Davis to Arthur Laing, March 1, 1966, file 112, Davis papers.

52. A. P. Frame to Avery Brundage, February 25, 1966, file 138, Davis papers.

53. E. Trafford to E. H. Davis, April 7, 1966, file 151, Davis papers.

54. A. P. Frame to E. Trafford, February 25, 1966, file 138, Davis papers.

55. Confidential memorandum, Maciej to Olympic '72 directors, "Re: Opposition," December 15, 1965, Davis papers.

56. McNamee; see also Thomas R. Dunlap, "Ecology, Nature and Canadian National Park Policy: Wolves, Elk, and Bison as a Case Study," in Rowland Lorimer, Michael McGonigle, Jean-Pierre Reveret and Sally Ross (eds.), *To See Ourselves/To Save Ourselves: Ecology and Culture in Canada* (Montreal: Association for Canadian Studies, 1991).

57. Only a week later, the COA decided that Banff would again be the proposed Canadian host city for the upcoming competition for the 1972 Winter Olympics.

58. Arthur Laing, "A Statement on National Park Policy," September 18, 1964, Queen's Printer and Controller of Stationery, Ottawa, p. 2, file 110, Davis papers.

59. Ibid.

60. Ibid.

61. Ibid, 3.

62. Laing, "A Statement on National Park Policy."

63. Ibid.

64. Ibid, 2.

65. *Hansard*, photocopied page, 11570, hand-dated February 25, 1965, file 104, Davis papers; Donald Cameron to Ed Davis, March 30, 1965, file 36, Davis papers.

66. B. M. McVicar letter to Olympic '72 directors, April 26, 1965, file 112, Davis papers.

67. Confidential memorandum, Maciej to Olympic '72 directors, "Re: Opposition," December 15, 1965, Davis papers.

68. E. H. Davis to Avery Brundage, March 2, 1966, file 138, Davis papers, emphasis original.

69. Hoppener to Passmore, February 18, 1966, Davis papers.

70. Ibid.

71. Hoppener to Brown, February 8, 1966, Davis papers.

72. Dawes to Brundage, May 12, 1965, Brundage papers.

73. Worrall to Brundage, May 26, 1965, Brundage papers.

74. Lester Pearson to W. E. Swinton, March 25, 1965, Brundage papers.

75. Arthur Laing to Walter M. Tovall, March 23, 1966, file 151, Davis papers.

76. "Conservation Groups Oppose Winter Olympics in Banff," *Wildlife News* [Canadian Wildlife Federation] 1, no. 2 (Spring 1965): 2.

77. Memorandum, E. H. Davis to Olympic '72 Directors, October 21, 1965, file 142, Davis papers.

78. C. P. Simr to W. Winston Mair, April 7, 1965, file 151, Davis papers.

79. Cited in Canadian Press wire report, February 11, 1966, Davis papers.

80. Avery Brundage to James Worrall, April 1, 1966, CIO VIL-1972-WCAND, Candidatures for the Olympic Winter Games in 1972, sous-dossier: Banff 1964–1966, Olympic Studies Centre, Lausanne, Switzerland (hereafter "OSC").

81. Confidential memorandum, Maciej to Olympic '72 directors, "Re: Opposition," December 15, 1965, Davis papers.

82. Cited in ibid.; also in confidential memorandum, Trafford to Olympic '72 directors, December 29, 1965, Davis papers.

83. Confidential memorandum, Maciej to Olympic '72 directors, "Re: Opposition," December 15, 1965, Davis papers.

84. Worrall to Brundage, May 26, 1965, Brundage papers.

85. Avery Brundage to James Worrall, June 3, 1965; also Avery Brundage to Ed Davis, June 3, 1965, Brundage papers.

86. A. Sidney Dawes to James Worrall, May 25, 1965, file 138, Davis papers.

87. Davis to Coutts, January 5, 1966, Davis papers.

88. A. Sidney Dawes to Avery Brundage, February 23, 1966, file 151, Davis papers.

89. James Worrall to Avery Brundage, March 1, 1966, file 151, Davis papers.

90. James Worrall to Lester Pearson, February 28, 1966, file 151, Davis papers.

91. Hans Maciej to Gordon J. Cummings, June 22, 1965, file 151, Davis papers.

92. Peter Scott to Avery Brundage, April 7, 1966, file 151, Davis papers.

93. CIO VIL-1972-WCAND, Candidatures for the Olympic Winter Games in 1972, sous-dossier: Banff 1964–1966, OSC.

94. Davis to Laing, March 1, 1966, Davis papers.

95. 64th Session of the International Olympic Committee, Rome, April 1966, Olympic World Library, https://library.olympics.com/Default/doc/SYRACUSE/43075/64e-session-du-comite-international-olympique-rome-1966-64e-session-of-the-international-olympic-com.

96. Handwritten note on copy of George H. La Roi to Avery Brundage, February 21, 1966, file 151, Davis papers, emphasis original.

97. Hans Maciej, "Report on the 64th Session of the International Olympic Committee held in Rome April 22–29, 1966," Davis papers, file 93, 7; Memorandum, E. Trafford to Olympic '72 Board of Directors, Re: Failure of the Banff Bid—April 26th, 1966, May 25, 1966, file 93, Davis papers.

98. Loo, "Making a Modern Wilderness," 12.

99. Noted in James Worrall to Hans Maciej, November 8, 1965, file 138, Davis papers.

100. Brundage cited in La Boissiere, "Vigorous Opposition," December 10, 1965, Davis papers.

101. Avery Brundage to John A. Fraser, May 16, 1966, CIO VIL-1972-WCAND, Candidatures for the Olympic Winter Games in 1972, sous-dossier: Banff 1964–1966, OSC.

102. Brundage to Zanchi, May 31, 1966, sous-dossier 2: Correspondence, avril–juin 1944, CIOPTBRUNDCORR/7066, OSC.

103. Peter Lougheed to G. Max Bell, February 18, 1965, file 138, Davis papers.

104. Worrall to Maciej, November 8, 1965, Davis papers.

105. Frank Shaughnessy to A. S. Dawes, February 22, 1966, file 151, Davis papers.

106. B. J. Bruce to Hans Maciej, February 15, 1966, file 2, Davis papers.

107. Shaughnessy to Davis, April 12, 1965, Davis papers.

108. Confidential memorandum, Trafford to Olympic '72 directors, December 29, 1965, Davis papers.

109. Worrall to Pearson, March 1, 1965, Worrall papers; Worrall makes a similar argument in correspondence with Dawes: Worrall to Dawes, May 14, 1965, Worrall papers.

110. J. D. Richardson to Ed Davis, September 12, 1966, file 142, Davis papers.

111. Ed Davis, "Report to Olympic '72 directors," May 26, 1966, file 93, Davis papers.

112. Rachel Carson, *Silent Spring* (Boston: Houghton Mifflin, 1962).

113. Eeva Berglund and David G. Anderson, "Introduction: Towards an Ethnography of Ecological Underprivilege" in David G. Anderson and Eeva Berglund (eds.), *Ethnographies of Conservation: Environmentalism and the Distribution of Privilege* (New York: Berghahn Books, 2003), 1–15.; Egan, 297–98.

114. Cited in Ramachandra Guha, *Environmentalism: A Global History* (New York: Longman, 2000), 81.

115. Cited in ibid., 87.

116. Ibid., 80.

CHAPTER 2

Denver 1976

Framing the Battle Over
Whether to Host a Winter Olympics

ADAM BERG

In May 1970, the International Olympic Committee (IOC) awarded the 1976 Winter Olympic Games to the city of Denver, Colorado. However, about two and half years later, citizens of Colorado voted affirmatively on a ballot measure that barred their state from spending a single dollar on the event. As a consequence, Denver's Olympic organizers lost access to federal funding as well. The Denver Organizing Committee (DOC), constituted and supported by many of Colorado's most powerful individuals and institutions, thus had no choice but to rescind its offer to host "the youth of the world." Denver won the right to host—but then relinquished—the Olympics.

This chapter explores the machinations behind the contested "framing" undertaken by both proponents and opponents of "Denver '76." It shows that local newspapers worked explicitly with the DOC to promote having the Games in Colorado. At the same time, it highlights how influential partners and tactful methods enabled anti-Olympics forces to "represent" the Olympics and outdo an alliance of business elites and popular media.

Growth Machines, Newspapers,
and Framing Contests

Behind the bid to host the Denver Games stood what sociologist Harvey Molotch terms a "growth machine."[1] This was a collection of powerful businesspeople and allied politicians who, despite any differences, achieved mutual benefits from their particular city's or region's overall expansion.[2] For business interests, growth meant customers, commerce, and higher values for fixed assets such as land. Local politicians also took part and reaped rewards. Support for growth not only made economic sense from the perspective of city halls. It ensured backing from the above-referenced influencers. It could also enable positive publicity. In the drive to host the Olympics in Denver, machine elements came most directly from local banks, utility providers, construction companies, the ski industry, and city- and state-level elected officials.[3] All looked to profit from depictions of Denver as a modern, upscale metropolis; increases in tourism statewide; and the channeling of public resources to those ends.[4]

Moreover, as Molotch predicts, local newspapers proved a paradigmatic growth machine contributor. The reason for this is that the nature and direction of development mattered little to them. As the population of a city increased, local dailies became more read and more valuable. One could argue, as Molotch points out, that newspapers served as "the most important example of a business which has its interests anchored in the aggregate growth of a locality." "The newspaper has no ax to grind," Molotch opines, "except the one ax which holds the community elite together: growth." As a result, newspapers generally took "prime responsibility" for fostering "growth enthusiasm."[5]

Indeed, within Denver's popular print media—namely, the *Denver Post* and the *Rocky Mountain News*—when it came to the Olympics, the presence of "framing" appeared apparent. As media scholar Robert Entman explains, framing refers to the way journalists inevitably select and highlight certain ideas, events, people, or issues—and not others—to promote coherence and meaning, often in the form of a "particular problem definition, causal interpretation, moral evaluation, and/or treatment recommendation."[6] In this case, the Denver papers created excessively optimistic portrayals about the prospect of the Mile High City becoming an Olympic host and depicted Olympics opponents as selfish, ill-informed naysayers. Yet, this was an intentional bias. Coverage in the *Post* and *Rocky* along with sources found in DOC archives reveals that there were explicit pacts made between Colorado's Olympic leaders and the media outlets.

On the other hand, what political scientist Sidney Tarrow calls an "event coalition" emerged to challenge the DOC's plans. This coalition included Mexican Americans and African Americans concerned about affordable housing in the city, white middle-class environmentalists worried about unsightly structures and overcrowding in the foothills west of Denver, and Coloradans troubled by the possibility of wasteful public spending. Furthermore, carefully planned criticism about costs introduced by two state-level politicians, skeptical interrogation from an incoming editor and journalist at the *Rocky Mountain News,* and shrewd anti-Olympics advertising and performances coordinated by grassroots operatives reframed the sport spectacle as an undemocratic and self-interested publicity stunt.

With an impressive array of resources and strategies, opponents engaged savvily in a "framing contest." They created images to counter the views propagated by Colorado powerbrokers, fashioned certain understandings of the Games and themselves, and thereby buttressed anti-Olympics grievances.[7] Following political scientist and Olympic scholar Jules Boykoff, the fate of Denver '76 confirms that the dynamics of "mass media coverage are crucial in understanding activism vis-à-vis the Olympics."[8]

The Denver Papers Support the Bid

In June 1963, recently elected Colorado Governor John Love announced a plan to bid for the 1976 Winter Games. Shortly thereafter he formed the Colorado Olympic Commission, which later became the Denver Organizing Committee. This group undertook the task of bidding to host the event. As this endeavor began, pro-Olympics sentiment extended up the chain of command at Denver's major newspapers. The editors of both the *Denver Post* and the *Rocky Mountain News*—Palmer Hoyte and Jack Foster, respectively—served as advisors going into the DOC's 1967 proposal to the United States Olympic Committee (USOC). Then, with USOC support in hand, as the DOC prepared to submit its final plans to the IOC, Hoyte and Foster became official bid team members.[9]

The bid organizers thus felt no apprehension about asking the newspapers to share all Olympic-related news releases that they received from abroad. Nor did they feel the need to conceal the profit motive underlying such a request. As one bidder wrote to Hoyte and Foster, "We want to be in the best possible position to know what to expect if the infighting for this multimillion dollar plum begins to get rough."[10]

In turn, writers at the presses parroted tales of Olympic preparedness and prestige. As *Denver Post* journalist Cal Queal characterized things in 1964, "Gov. John Love has launched an international mission that could bring one of the world's greatest sports attractions to Colorado." In Queal's words, "Colorado has the raw material and the know-how to stage a first-class Olympiad . . . the finest Olympics in history."[11] In 1966, writing from the perspective of all Coloradans, the *Rocky Mountain News* similarly editorialized, "We boast the best snow in the nation—and the world" and "would like to be the [w]orld's winter showcase. We're keeping our skis crossed."[12]

These optimistic portrayals remain a constant in the years leading up to the IOC's selection. When the *Denver Post* reported a year later on the Interski Congress held by ski industry boosters in Aspen, it told of how "Officials see the congress, with the resulting worldwide publicity and influx of visitors . . . as a major boon to the economy." The paper then

added that the event was a stepping stone to an even more effective promotional tool. The *Post* continued, the "Olympic implications" of hosting the Interski "could, in the long run, be even more vital."[13] After the
1968 Winter Olympic Games took place in Grenoble, France, *Denver Post*
sport reporter Jim Graham proclaimed in equally sanguine fashion, "on
our black and white set, the spectacle of the finest winter sports athletes
from 38 nations in the colorful parade sent shivers down my spine . . . I
wish every man, woman, and child in Colorado could envision through
the magic of a time machine the 1976 Winter Olympics here in our own
Centennial State."[14]

If there were ever any doubt, it again became evident that the major
Colorado newspapers accepted the presumed virtues of hosting the Olympics when Governor Love, Denver Mayor Thomas Currigan, and fellow
bidders traveled to the 1968 Grenoble Winter Games. While Currigan
explained that they went to "lobby" for Denver to become an Olympic
host, journalist Alan Cunningham of the *Rocky Mountain News* endorsed
the venture. "You might expect criticism when the mayor and the governor set out for a junket to France in the midst of frenzied city and state
business," Cunningham commented. "But Gov. Love and Mayor Currigan
will have the blessings of most of their constituents when they depart on
separate flights Wednesday for Grenoble." The two leaders, Cunningham
reasoned, would be trying "to persuade members of the International
Olympic Committee that the site for the 12th winter games eight years
from now should be Colorado."[15] The *Rocky Mountain News* sports section
editor, Chet Nelson, affirmed as well during the 1968 Winter Games: "the
benefits" of holding the event in Colorado "will last long into the future."[16]

As the IOC selection approached, dominant portraits highlighting the
benefits of the Olympics continued to go unchallenged within the Colorado popular press. When the bid team left for Amsterdam in May 1970 to
present its final proposal to the IOC, the *Denver Post* promised its reader-
ship that the "1976 Winter Games would be a definite plus for the Denver
area." We wish "the Denver committee well," the paper exclaimed, "and
hope theirs is a successful trip."[17]

Local Politicians Bring the Question
of Costs into the Narrative

During and following the bid, however, opposition to aspects of the
DOC's plans began to emerge. In the city, Mexican American and African American residents voiced disquiet about their lack of inclusion in
urban planning and started advocating for the DOC to make affordable

housing options an outcome of having the spectacle in Denver. To the west of the Mile High City, in the foothill towns of Evergreen and Indian Hills, exurban townspeople objected to the Nordic events, ski jumping, the luge, and the bobsled events scheduled for their area. Once the IOC named Denver as its host, these middle-class, environmentally oriented concerns became an uproar.[18]

Meanwhile, two state-level representatives began to raise questions about the DOC's projected price tag. Richard Lamm and Robert Jackson served together in the Colorado House and on the Colorado Audit Committee at the ages of thirty-one and forty. As Audit Committee members fresh to the legislature, they came to realize that the DOC had underestimated its probable expenses. In truth, nobody really knew what the Games would cost. With the event set for Denver, the efforts of Lamm and Jackson to divulge this information became key to breaking the rosy image that the *Denver Post* and *Rocky Mountain News* had constructed of the Games thus far.[19]

A series of interviews with Lamm provides insight into how he and Jackson went about achieving that outcome. Due to the passage of time and the fallibility of memory, it is impossible to give the exact timing of events, but with the assistance of newspaper accounts, a likely chronology emerges. In January 1971, the DOC prepared to speak before Colorado's Joint Budget Committee (JBC). The Olympic organizers intended to offer their justification for a recent $310,000 request from the state. Beforehand, Lamm reached out to JBC members and passed along information about the Olympics' probable cost and the DOC's lack of detailed plans. Lamm and Jackson hoped that, upon seeing this material, their fellow legislators would come to the same realization as they had. The DOC was significantly "low balling" Olympic expenses.[20]

In particular, Republican Joe Shoemaker ran with the baton. The DOC came to the meeting with a well-rehearsed presentation, but Shoemaker repeatedly interrupted it. How much money would the DOC need exactly? What would it spend the money on? Where precisely would requisite financial supplies come from? Shoemaker asked for specifics and DOC members proved unable to answer.[21]

Along with underplaying costs to suit IOC preferences, the DOC had selected unrealistic event locations in its initial proposal. Thus, at this time, it did not know where many of the winter sport contests it meant to hold would take place, let alone how expensive they would be.[22] Months after the JBC presentation, a top advisor to Denver's current Mayor, William McNichols, took part in a gathering between the DOC and Colorado's representatives in Washington, DC. Together they aimed at strategizing how to obtain federal dollars for the Games. As this aide informed McNichols afterward: due to several "contradictions and changing of figures . . . I think it must be concluded . . . the DOC still does not have a valid handle on revenues and cost."[23]

Standing before the JBC, the DOC thus stood tongue-tied. And, as the *Denver Post* reported in an article titled "Colorado Olympic Plan Termed Too General," the JBC recommended the state withhold financial support for the moment. The paper also quoted Shoemaker, who explained the decision by asserting, "I don't think the homework has really been done in terms of funding." Acknowledging the Colorado legislature had previously provided a "blank check," Shoemaker counseled the DOC, "you've reached the point in time where it's got to be done according to the same (budget request) standards we apply to everyone else."[24] As Coloradans now learned through the local paper, there was reason to doubt the veracity of DOC cost estimates and, in turn, promises that the Olympics would bring overall prosperity.

Furthermore, for Lamm and Jackson, this was but the first shot of a larger anti-Olympics attack. One week later, with uncertainty regarding the DOC's projections in focus, Jackson made news again, albeit this time more transparently. He announced he was going to introduce a bill to bar state funds from going to the DOC for good. As the *Denver Post* recounted, Jackson alleged the $310,000 the DOC asked for was "a small part of the iceberg." "I can't see putting money into a sport [such as the Olympics] . . . when there are higher priorities such as education, environmental protection, and benefits to the elderly." Jackson exclaimed, "if we're going to change our minds, this is the time to do it."[25] A few days later, Lamm stated his support of Jackson to the *Post*, repeating that the Denver Olympics would not be worth the cost to Colorado taxpayers.[26]

Jackson's proposal to end state funding of the DOC never got out of committee.[27] Yet, as elected officials, in the following weeks they proved able to repeat their concerns for public consumption. Jackson told Queal of the *Post*, "I don't think anyone knows how much the Olympics will cost and I'm certain nobody knows exactly where the money's coming from." Likewise, Lamm asserted to the *Post* that although he and Jackson had voted in favor of the Olympics in 1967, "We had no idea what it was going to cost." "If wisdom comes late," Lamm surmised, "that doesn't mean reject it."[28]

Then, when the DOC returned to Colorado's capitol building in late February 1971 to update a joint session of the Colorado House and Senate on its plans, it once more arrived ill prepared. Rather than provide specifics, the group went in intending to emphasize simply that there could be no question about whether Denver should host the Olympics.[29] "We have the games for 1976," the DOC's Chairman of Finance and Business Relations avowed. "There's no moral or proper way that this fact can be reversed or refuted . . . Our job now—yours and mine—is to stage these games the best way possible."[30] The *Post* and the *Rocky* covered the DOC presentation. Thus, its readers also learned that Jackson listened and remained incredulous. "We deserve better," he told the DOC speakers.[31] Additional representatives similarly began to see the Olympics in this critical light and express their perspectives. According to House Democrat Wayne Knox, as Coloradans again read in the *Post*, the DOC's presentation was nothing but "one hour of propaganda."[32]

About two months later, in April 1971, Lamm and Jackson presented what they must have known would be a series of symbolic amendments to the state's annual appropriations bill. One meant to stop state funding of the DOC for the current year. Another set a spending limit, making the money allocated in the current bill the last of the state's Olympic investment. A third gave the state power to review and sanction all Olympic expenditures. None of the amendments passed.[33] Though several fellow Democrats in the Colorado House began to follow Lamm's and Jackson's lead, making Olympic spending a somewhat partisan issue, most of Colorado's political leadership showed no desire to let the Winter Games slip through their grasp.[34] Still, the two legislators continued to work to infuse the idea into the public sphere that investing in the Olympics Games was risky and not worthwhile for everyday people.

The DOC and the Press Respond

The idea that Colorado citizens would question the DOC's Olympic intentions seemed to shock boosters and state leaders. But after the emergence of Lamm and Jackson, the DOC and its supporters realized they needed to answer their Olympic foes. As one DOC member put it, Denver's Olympic planners felt "constantly under attack" from environmentalists in "Evergreen," "minorities" in the city, and policymakers on "the Joint Budget Committee."[35] By midway through 1971, the organizers therefore directed their attention to what was fast becoming a genuine public relations battle.

Along with several other tactics designed to appear responsive to fiscally and environmentally apprehensive citizens, the DOC began working hand in hand with the *Post* and the *News* to create pro-Olympics representations.[36] As DOC meeting minutes described, both of Denver's major newspapers began apprising the DOC of "extensive research" for "a series of constructive articles." By acknowledging that the *Post* and the *Rocky* conducted "research" meant from the outset to be "constructive," the DOC exposed the intention of the Colorado newspapers to bolster its image amid a rising public backlash.[37]

The newspapers also condemned Lamm and Jackson, portraying them as baseless political agitators. After the two representatives came out against the Games at the start of 1971, the *Post* responded by taking shots at urban housing advocates, exurban environmentalists, and Jackson, asserting that the "1976 Winter Olympics have been awarded to Denver and it is inconceivable that the community would allow that fact to be negated." The *Post* continued, the "award of the prestigious event . . . looms large in the history of the city and state . . . it should not suffer lack of support merely because it provides a convenient lever for some to use in an effort to pry concessions for their interests." "To follow Jackson's advice," the paper professed, "would be a disastrous and stupid mistake."[38]

When Lamm and Jackson went to the Denver City Council requesting city residents be given the chance vote on whether to host the Games, the *Rocky Mountain News* likewise went on the offensive. "The almost unbelievable flap thrown up by a handful of state legislators . . . to renege on Denver's successful bid for the 1976 Olympics is the rawest kind of political pandering," the newspaper exclaimed. "We certainly hope that [the] City Council ignores that ridiculous demand." Acknowledging criticisms about costs and environmental damage, the *News* retorted, "We don't buy either . . . Tourism is the state's second biggest cash crop. To hold off priming the pump of attraction would be like a beet farmer not fertilizing his field." "The environmental pitch," the paper went on, "is almost too ridiculous to take seriously."[39] As the *Rocky* concluded in a separate piece pointed at Jackson, "We . . . trust that other legislators with less concern for political grandstanding will take a look at the facts, weigh the probabilities and possibilities, and then act without [a] closed mind, such as Jackson exhibits."[40]

All the while, DOC conferred with Denver's most prominent media sources. In early March 1971, DOC contributor Norm Brown, the Vice President of Marketing for the powerful Boettcher and Company investment firm, met with the editors of the *Post* and the *Rocky*, as well as executives from major television stations KOATV, KZL, and KBTV. The "purpose of this meeting," Brown explained in a memorandum to Colorado National Bank Vice President and DOC member Donald Magarrell, was to give "to the executive level of the major media in Denver some . . . insight into the DOC, the problems and solutions the DOC is encountering and trying to work out." Brown clarified, this "will allow these management people to possibly head off certain elements of the press that could be destructive."[41]

Most Denver media bosses fell in line. The *Post*, for one, remained devoted to fostering positive views of the 1976 Winter Olympics.[42] When the newspaper did a series of stories on the discontent of environmentalists living in the foothills, it consulted the DOC for "suggestions" and "accuracy."[43] By April 1971, as Brown informed fellow DOC members, the *Post* cleared all its stories on the Olympics with him.[44] Both main newspapers would provide generally favorable coverage in the final months before the referendum, while television stations deliberated with pro-Olympics forces and provided the DOC free ad space.[45] As DOC members themselves speculated, broadcasters remained behind the Olympics, eyeing the profits that coverage of the Games would bring.[46] For the moment, when it came to Denver's most widely consumed media outlets, the DOC could safely assume few would object to the commercial value of hosting the sport extravaganza.

The *Rocky Mountain News* Legitimizes the Opposition

With backing from Denver media, the DOC probably felt the path to hosting the Olympics remained under control, even if it had become bumpier than expected. However, around this time, the *News* came under new leadership. Michael Howard, an heir to the Scripps-Howard newspaper fortune, took over as editorial manager. The young and wealthy scion, surely with more freedom and less to lose, permitted his paper to take a more critical look at the Games. Howard had attended the gathering with Brown and other media kingpins. Yet, as Brown told Magarrell afterward, "Mike, being younger, still has some doubts and thinks we were trying to curtail the press."[47] Indeed, Howard would permit his paper to undertake the kind of coverage that the DOC wished to avoid.

During the week of April 4, 1971, the *Rocky* published a six-part series on the Denver Olympics written by investigative journalist Richard O'Reilly. It became a vital ingredient in the Denver Olympics' demise. O'Reilly had just begun working at the paper in January, charged by Howard to "come up with something" new to explore. When O'Reilly saw the DOC's bid books submitted to the IOC, he found his first story.[48]

As he recalled, the books "had this beautiful steep mountain covered with snow, which I recognized as a place called Mount Sniktau." An avid skier, O'Reilly had driven past the mountain many times traveling to distant resorts. He knew "that it was always bare in the winter." Sniktau "was a windblown place and whatever snow fell just blew right off," O'Reilly recounted; "I thought this is nonsense. That's not going to be an Alpine site."

The DOC knew full well that Sniktau could never host the downhill races but listed it in its proposal because it recognized the mountain's proximity to Denver would please IOC voters.[49] As a DOC representative admitted to O'Reilly, the Olympic bidders had actually airbrushed snow onto the image of Sniktau that the journalist observed in the DOC bid books.[50]

Like many Coloradans, O'Reilly held positive views of the Winter Games in general. "My opinion of the Olympics," O'Reilly remembered, "was high."[51] He thus undertook his investigation intending to clear up what the DOC needed to do to make the Denver Olympics a success. In this respect, he fit the profile of a common growth machine editorialist. He called for "good planning" and "technical expertise" and in moments became skeptical of a particular business or project. He did not, though, mean to stop the Olympics or commercial growth broadly.[52]

Perhaps this is why the DOC did not appear suspicious of O'Reilly's work, granting him multiple interviews with many of its contributors and even admitting to the doctored picture of Sniktau. Nonetheless, O'Reilly also spoke with the leading anti-Olympics environmentalist from the westward foothills, as well as Lamm and Jackson. He even sought input from organizers of the 1960 Squaw Valley Olympics. O'Reilly then framed the Games as an issue with two embellished but reasonable enough sides. "Its opponents say the event will ruin our fragile mountain ecology, while its boosters say it will be the best thing ever to happen to Colorado . . . The truth," O'Reilly posited, "undoubtedly lies somewhere in between."[53]

O'Reilly downplayed the overall objections of environmentalists in his series, noting that although "some trees will be cut and some mountain slopes will be carved up to prepare for the games . . . the damage will be far less than that caused by normal mountain area construction and exploitation over the next five years." The crowds, he observed, would be big, but no greater or more inconvenient than a Denver Broncos' football game. O'Reilly's series also gave credence to the DOC's view that the Games would promote tourism and become a source of local and national pride.[54]

Even so, O'Reilly provided reasons to doubt the benefits of hosting the Games and for trusting the DOC. Most noticeably, he revealed the DOC airbrushed snow onto a picture of Sniktau to gain the IOC's approval. He cited multiple DOC members admitting the mountain was not an ideal Alpine site.[55] He likewise noted that the DOC probably could not hold cross country events in the foothills because of a lack of snow there. The climate in the area, O'Reilly additionally observed, would make it challenging to keep frozen the seventeen million gallons of water needed for the luge and bobsled courses. As his reporting indicated, the DOC's placement of these events was another ploy to win over the IOC, making it seem the contests could remain closer to the central city than geographical and climatologi-cal realities allowed. O'Reilly similarly recognized it would be difficult to displace University of Denver students and turn their dorm rooms into an Olympic Village, as the DOC offered.[56] Moreover, examining the 1960 Palisades Tahoe Olympics as a precedent, he noted that those Games cost thirteen times more than initially predicted, while many facilities built for the event had since proven useless, an outcome not unlikely for Denver.[57] Finally, acknowledging that ambiguity remained over final event locations and that the DOC's unsure cost estimates had already risen from $14 mil-lion to as high as $25 million, O'Reilly concluded, "there's no way at this point to know how much of that taxpayers will have to provide."[58]

Although Olympics opponents had been struggling to make these points for months, even years, O'Reilly's articles legitimized the information. They probably also brought it to many Coloradans for the first time. Many had not heard of the extent to which the DOC lied to the IOC. Though Lamm and Jackson raised questions about costs, the Denver media had not treated their criticism as serious up to this point—quite the opposite. As Lamm thus described, until "a gentleman named Dick O'Reilly from the *Rocky Mountain News* came along, no one in the whole media even questioned the assumption that holding the 1976 Olympics in Colorado would be a cornucopia of benefits."[59] But now, although balanced and intended to motivate careful preparations, O'Reilly's articles reinforced the warnings of Lamm and Jackson and damaged the integrity of Olympic organizers. As one reader penned to Denver Mayor McNichols, O'Reilly provided "quite a jolt . . . for a change the public has been presented with fact, rather than fiction."[60]

O'Reilly also provided Olympics future opponents with a ready arse-nal. In the words of Meg Lundstrom, a key anti-Olympics protester: "I don't know that we could have done what we did without his series. His series cast such a bright light on the whole DOC operation . . . That was the basis of all of our literature initially and we used it heavily later on in the campaign . . . In some ways, I don't know if anything would have hap-pened without that series."[61] Sam Brown, another leading Denver Olympics objector, reiterated that O'Reilly's articles proved "absolutely central to making the case" against the event.[62]

CCF Introduces Itself

Against this backdrop, in late 1971, Lamm met with one of the most suc-cessful anti–Vietnam War organizers in the nation, Sam Brown. Just twenty-nine years old, Brown had helped guide antiwar Senator Eugene

McCarthy's 1968 New Hampshire Primary race against sitting President Lyndon B. Johnson, where McCarthy lost by only seven points, 42 percent to 49 percent, leading Johnson to withdraw from the race.[63] Then, in 1969, Brown oversaw the Vietnam Moratorium, a nationwide strike intended to exert pressure on the Nixon administration to finally pull American troops out of Southeast Asia. With two million people participating, it was the largest mass demonstration in American history.[64] Brown next moved to Colorado to focus his attention on a book about the antiwar movement. There, he became involved in Oklahoma Senator Fred Harris's campaign for the Presidency, another chance to put in power an opponent of the war. When Brown's writing and Harris's run both stalled, at Lamm's urging, he turned his attention to the Denver Olympics. Thus, Lamm, Jackson, Brown, and about a dozen others formed a group called Citizens for Colorado's Future (CCF). The CCF's expressed goal was to stop the Games.[65]

Notably, four other liberal-minded political operatives in their mid-twenties joined Brown in forming and leading CCF: Meg Lundstrom, John Parr, Tom Nussbaum, and Dwight Filley (see figure 2.1). Like Brown, three of the four were new to the Centennial State. With Lamm and Brown as strategic guides, the foursome ran CCF's day-to-day operations. They did the grunt work, collecting petition signatures, creating and disseminating campaign materials, organizing volunteers, and ultimately politicking to push through the passage of the measure that blocked public funding of the Games. In doing so, however, they made sure to frame themselves as restrained, reasonable, and respectful. As Filley described, "we were clean, but we weren't exactly wearing coats and ties . . . we got our spelling right and our documents looked good . . . but we were still almost counterculture."[66]

When they made public pronouncements, the young CCF organizers made sure to present as left-leaning professionals, dressing well, showing rigor and discipline, creating polished, well-written publications, and even spending extra money on high-quality stationery.[67] At the same time, as much as possible, Lamm and Jackson served as CCF's spokespeople. As "recognized authority figures," Filley explained, they "gave a lot of credibility that would have otherwise been beyond the pale."[68] In Lamm's own words, he became the group's "titular head."[69]

In this vein, when the group raised money to place a full-page advertisement in the *Post*, in line with a tactic suggested by Brown in a book he wrote on grassroots organizing, the ad's sponsors included prominent leaders and groups from the Colorado community—lawyers, well-known environmentalists, Lamm, Jackson, and the Sierra Club. The actual CCF organizers, who carried less social standing, went unnamed.[70] Similarly, in

FIGURE 2.1. Dwight Filley (left) of Citizens for Colorado's Future explains the organization's strategy for the 1972 ballot initiative on city and state funding of the 1976 Winter Olympics. Credit: The Denver Public Library, Western History Collection, Call #WH2129-2018-373.

CCF's first letter to potential supporters, the foursome running the anti-Olympics campaign did not sign as the senders. Rather, more established and diverse Coloradans Paul Hamilton, Ruth Weiner, and John Zapien took the lead—an African American Representative in the Colorado House, a white college professor and environmentalist, and a Mexican American heading the Legal Aid Society in Denver, respectively.[71] Only Zapien became a regular CCF participant following this opening missive.[72]

This again followed a Brown recommendation. "You must get local people deeply involved in the campaign or organization in a public and visible way," Brown advised. "You should not be the person who opens a storefront, has a press conference, talks to the press. You should find ways to make yourself secondary to local personalities." Even if the homegrown contributor "is rarely in," Brown implored, "it's tremendously important that visibility be from a local standpoint."[73]

CCF Frames the Games

While CCF framed itself as moderate, trustworthy, and with connections to Colorado, it also presented a particular vision of the DOC—as a self-interested and fundamentally antidemocratic body. On January 2, 1972, the headline of CCF's initial ad read: "Sell Colorado? Olympics '76? AT WHAT COST TO COLORADO?"[74] Questions with answers implicating the corruption and greed of Denver's Olympic enterprise followed.

The first question the advocates posed in the *Post* was: "Who Pays?" To which CCF answered: "YOU do." This suggested that every potential reader of the paper and thus every person in the state would foot the Olympic bill. The CCF then highlighted how the DOC originally placed the price tag of the Denver Games as low as $8–10 million, but now predicted a cost of about $28 million. The ad pointed out as well that the 1968 Winter Olympic Games in Grenoble, France, cost a quarter of a billion dollars, while the 1972 Summer Olympics in Munich was slated to cost West Germany over half a billion. Given these huge discrepancies, CCF listed the "actual cost" of the Denver Games at: "$?" The group also pointed to "HIDDEN COSTS," such as highway construction, sewage expansion, military personnel and equipment, and other government services for which the DOC did not account.[75] According to CCF, the DOC not only underestimated the pending taxpayer contribution, it purposefully concealed it.

Why would the DOC do this? "For what?" "For whom?" and "Who profits?" the CCF ad rhetorically asked. The "what" was "a 10-day spectacular of winter sports in artificial snow in highly-engineered technologically contrived structures." To the question of "who" all this was for, CCF responded: the IOC and DOC. According to the ad, the IOC was "a self-appointed, self-perpetuating board of men who rule the Olympics," while the DOC was "a self-appointed coterie of political and business figures who privately made public decisions of broad and lasting effect on Colorado."[76] In CCF's portrayal, this "coterie" ignored and even undermined citizen input to hold a sport event for its self-interest.

Furthermore, CCF tried to make it clear that these "self-appointed" powerholders neglected Coloradans of diverse backgrounds. Following the question of "who profits," CCF provided an additional set of queries. "How many black and Chicanos will be on sports teams?" "How much low-income housing will really result?" "What quality environment will result from this kind of hard sell of Colorado's beauty?"[77] The inferences seemed to be that hosting the Olympics would not be a good thing for Mexican Americans and African Americans in Denver nor environmentally concerned suburban and exurban inhabitants, who by this time were in open defiance of the DOC. None of them would see genuine benefits.

The group then complemented its presentation by listing two sets of "Priorities" and their corresponding prices. One list included a bobsled, a luge, a speed skating rink, a ski jump, and an Alpine facility. The other made note of Colorado's budget for water pollution, air pollution, handicapped children, and venereal disease. For example, CCF pointed out that whereas a new speed skating rink would cost $6,673,000, Colorado only spent $512,874 to remedy smog-filled air.[78] As CCF rendered it, the Games would take vital resources away from other, more important, and neglected public needs.

Finally, CCF asked, "How?" How could such a misguided event be thrust upon Colorado's citizens? The answer reveals the crux of the view the group meant to popularize. CCF claimed the people of the Centennial State were victims of a systematic usurpation of democracy. "NO state referendum has ever been held on . . . the Olympics," CCF professed. "ALL meetings of the Denver Organizing Committee (DOC) are held in secret," CCF bemoaned, "with press and public barred."[79] As the ad also underlined, "NO cost-benefit analysis has been made, by either city or state, on the desirability of holding the '76 Winter Olympics in Colorado, or the desirability of population increase, urban growth, and the mountain development that will follow worldwide publicity."[80]

The group thereby accused the DOC and its backers of hiding costs, disregarding the preferences of numerous citizens, and perpetuating policies for self-aggrandizement. As Brown claimed in a *New Republic* cover story published around the same time, titled "Snow Job in Colorado," the Winter Olympics is "sport of the rich paid for by the poor in order to promote real estate and tourism."[81] By various means, CCF continued to project these narratives of the DOC and the Olympics.[82]

Toward the end of the Denver Olympics debate, the DOC, in response, turned to the rhetoric of Olympism combined with American exceptionalism to make its case, asking Coloradans to consider the intangible value of promoting global harmony through sport. Denver Olympics opponents might argue that Colorado would be better off with state money going to health care, education, environmental protection, or affordable housing. Nevertheless, former mayor and Olympic supporter Thomas Currigan asserted, while "all of these things are good . . . It is ridiculous to make this kind of comparison." From Currigan's point of view, it was "impossible to measure the worth and the long-range benefits of the Olympics in dollars." "How do you measure the worth of people-to-people diplomacy? How do you measure the Olympics as an instrument of peace, as a way to foster understanding between peoples?" he asked. As Currigan contended, "Goodwill through fair competition, mutual respect, universal ideals and striving for excellence … simply cannot be measured in dollars and cents."[83] When Lamm, Jackson, and CCF suggested the state focus on other more pressing local concerns, Colorado's Olympic ideologues could respond that the invaluable purposes of the Winter Games outweighed it all.

In the month before the November election in which Coloradans voted against hosting the event, Olympic proponents leaned upon such framing via 176 ads in over fifty Colorado newspapers, 190 television commercials, and 1,274 radio announcements.[84] "International sports provide one of the most permanent and unifying links between the people of the world," a pro-Olympics promotion began; "Recognition of this fact comes when one sees athletes from 128 nations participating in the Olympic Games." Referring to the ultimate vote on whether to host the event, supporters urged: "When Coloradans go to the polls November 7 to vote on Amendment 8 [on blocking public funding of the Olympics] all the world will watch and learn what we of this state feel about the ideals and objectives [that] the Olympics encompass."[85]

On the other hand, CCF and its allies stuck to their messaging and worked mostly from the bottom up. CCF produced an estimated 550,000 copies of its own anti-Olympics pamphlet, which it disseminated through approximately five thousand volunteers. In the pamphlet, CCF alleged, "The groups planning and promoting the Olympics are dominated by a business and financial elite which comprise a virtual *Who's Who* of wealth, power and influence in Colorado" with "numerous instances of substantial conflicts of interest." "Just about everyone who profits from a crowd," the anti-Olympic activists argued further, contributed to the Olympic cause. Although "certain sectors of the business community always clear big profits from games," CCF contended, these were "profits the taxpayer must subsidize." "[N]o government has ever made enough money from the Olympics to cover the money put into it," the opponents stressed.[86]

While Lamm and Jackson went on television and radio to explain Olympic drawbacks, CCF's younger operatives assigned volunteers to blocks, neighborhoods, precincts, and districts to distribute campaign literature door-to-door.[87] The CCF instructed fellow Olympic opponents on how to interact with likely voters and how to organize more volunteers. As the fateful anti-Olympics vote drew near, CCF continued to advise volunteers on ways to increase foot soldiers and on what materials and directives to pass along. The week of the election, they encouraged followers to hold anti-Olympics signs at voting sites, pass out its anti-Olympics tracts, or "simply park a car with [anti-Olympics] bumper stickers on it near the polling place." Such bumper stickers read: "The Olympics Are Taxing," "Save Our Money, Save Our Mountains—Stop the Olympics," and "Recycle the Olympics to Squaw Valley."[88] Through these methods, CCF made its case against the Games, reached a broad audience, and embodied the grassroots organization it purported to be—one that listened to and cared about the everyday inhabitants of the Centennial State.

Contesting a Growth Machine— Local Media Alliance and Defeating an Olympics

At the outset, it may have seemed that engaging in a framing contest with the DOC would have been a tall task. The popular media was on the DOC's side. Yet, CCF and other Olympics opponents revised how many Coloradans read the Denver Games. With ease, CCF collected the requisite petition signatures to place a measure to bar state funding on Colorado ballots (see figure 2.2). Then, following its all-out grassroots drive, on November 7, 1972, results showed 537,400 voted "yes" while 358,906 voted "no" on constitutional "Amendment Number 8."[89] With the amendment passed, the state of Colorado was legally disallowed from funding the 1976 Denver Olympics. By placing state monies out of reach, local citizens effectively chose to banish the Games. Citizens for Colorado's Future wanted to make sure Olympic expenses were not passed onto Denver alone, so it gathered signatures and placed a similar initiative on the city ballot. Denverites also voted in favor, preventing Denver City Hall from spending any money on the event.[90] The multimillion-dollar pro-growth advertising project supported by Colorado's governor, Denver's mayor, Denver newspapers, and the city's and state's most powerful businesses was finished.

The battle over framing Denver '76 did not only take place through representations within the printed press. In addition, several interested parties—such as affordable housing advocates and environmentalists—moved toward more obstinate anti-Olympics positions on their own and eventually agreed to support CCF's effort to end the Games completely. Still, for over two years, many citizens learned about and assessed the event with the *Denver Post* and the *Rocky Mountain News* as their main sources of information. One may speculate that winning the battle over how to frame the referendum within print media was necessary—though not sufficient for stopping the world's premier winter sport spectacle.

In this regard, several factors seem pertinent in understanding how opponents were so successful. For one, the DOC's overconfidence and mismanagement helped. The organizer's public projections fluctuated and rose, as their lies to the IOC and lack of detailed planning surfaced.

FIGURE 2.2. A billboard encourages voters to reject public funding for the 1976 Winter Olympics. Credit: The Denver Public Library, Western History Collection, Call #WH2129-2018-374.

Olympics proponents lost credibility. Lamm and Jackson, meanwhile, carried forth their criticisms with an air of authenticity accrued through their positions as established politicians. When Lamm called on Coloradans to "build fiscal sanity," many apparently listened.[91] Indeed, the backlash to their anti-Olympics advocacy from the *Post* and the *Rocky* did not, ultimately, extend to the Colorado populace in general, as evidenced through the November vote and the fact that Coloradans elected Lamm governor two years later. Instead, Lamm and Jackson aligned with, strengthened, and perhaps shaped opinions against the Games. Besides this, the hold of the DOC on the popular press fractured. The *Rocky Mountain News* more or less broke ranks. Howard assigned O'Reilly to the Olympic story and then to cover all things Olympics through the November election. Additional reporting from O'Reilly would continue to stir doubt in the DOC's dependability.[92] In March 1972, as CCF began its petition drive for the anti-Olympics initiative, Howard himself penned a front-page article centered on a *News* poll that showed almost seventy percent of Colorado citizens favored holding a statewide ballot on Olympic outlays.[93] Finally, with these factors already working to its aid, CCF tactfully inserted a middle-of-the-road populist persona for itself and an unfavorable understanding of the mega-event and the organizers behind it. It was with a vulnerable adversary in the DOC, support from elected officials, questioning journalists from a prominent paper, and skillful organizers at the helm that opponents reframed and helped dismantle Denver's Olympic cauldron before it could even be built.

Notes

1. Harvey Molotch, "The City as a Growth Machine: Toward a Political Economy of Place," *American Journal of Sociology* 82, no. 2 (1976): 309–22.

2. "Growth" or "development" here refers to general increases in economic activity, production, and consumption, as well as technological innovation, industrialism, materialism, and consumerism. This is how most Americans have historically understood the terms. See Robert Collins, *More: The Politics of Economic Growth in Postwar America* (New York: Oxford University Press, 2000).

3. Major players included the Public Service Company of Colorado, the Mountain State Telephone Company, the Colorado National Bank, associates of the Colorado ski industry, consecutive mayors of Denver, and the governor of Colorado. For a more detailed account of the growth machine behind the 1976 Denver Olympics, see Adam Berg, *The Olympics that Never Happened: Denver '76 and the Politics of Growth* (Austin: University of Texas Press, 2023), especially chapter 3.

4. For an excellent account of the emphasis on tourism promotion in Colorado, see William Philpott, *Vacationland: Tourism and Environment in the Colorado High Country* (Seattle: University of Washington Press, 2013).

5. Molotch, "The City as a Growth Machine," 315; John R. Logan and Harvey L. Molotch, *Urban Fortunes: The Political Economy of Place* (20th Anniversary Edition) (Berkley: University of California Press, 2007), 70–73.

6. Robert W. Entman, "Framing: Toward Clarification of a Fractured Paradigm," *Journal of Communication* 43, no. 4 (1993): 51–58, quote at 52.

7. William Gamson, "Bystanders, Public Opinion, and the Media," in *The*

Blackwell Companion to Social Movements, edited by David A. Snow, Sarah A Soule, and Hanspeter Kriesi (London: Blackwell Publishing, 2004), 245.

8. The theoretical approach described in this paragraph is greatly influenced by Jules Boykoff, *Activism and the Olympics: Dissent at the Games in Vancouver and London* (New Brunswick, NJ: Rutgers University Press, 2014), 29–30. Also see Doug McAdam, John D. McCarthy, and Mayer N. Zald, "Introduction: Opportunities, Mobilizing Structures, and Framing Processes—Toward a Synthetic, Comparative Perspective of Social Movements," in *Comparative Perspectives on Social Movements: Political Opportunities, Mobilizing Structures, and Cultural Framings*, edited by Doug McAdam, John D. McCarthy, and Mayer N. Zald (New York: Cambridge University Press, 1996), 6; and Robert D. Benford and David A. Snow, "Framing Processes and Social Movements: An Overview and Assessment," *Annual Review of Sociology* 26 (2000): 615–17.

9. Denver Organizing Committee, Denver Organizing Committee's Response to Questionnaire for Bid Cities, April-May 1967, Folder 1, Box 1, Denver Organizing Committee for the 1976 Winter Olympics Records, Denver Public Library, Denver, Colorado (hereafter DOC DPL); Denver Olympic Committee Roster, Folder 23, Box 99, William McNichols Papers, Denver Public Library (hereafter WMP DPL); William H. McNichols Jr. to Palmer Hoyt, 22 July 1969, Folder 8, Box 100, WMP DPL; Richard M. Davis, Denver Organizing Committee Meeting Minutes, September 11, 1969, Folder 9, Box 100, WMP DPL, Denver, Colorado. "Mayor Expands Olympic Panel," *Denver Post*, September 17, 1969, 3.

10. Laura Lee Katz Olson, *Power, Public Policy and the Environment: The Defeat of the 1976 Winter Olympics* (PhD Diss., University of Colorado, 1974), 117; also see box S4151, Administrative Records of the Denver Organizing Committee, Colorado State Archives and Records, Denver, Colorado (hereafter ARDOC CSAR).

11. Cal Queal, "Winter Olympics 1976," *Denver Post*, February 6, 1964, 62.

12. "Winter Olympics for Colorado," *Rocky Mountain News*, 16 December 1966, clipping, Folder 25, Box 99, WMP DPL.

13. Charlie Meyers, "Interski Meet Called Olympics Forerunner," *Denver Post*, January 6, 1967.

14. Jim Graham, "Olympic Pomp 'Seen in Colo.,'" *Denver Post*, 7 February 1968, 74.

15. John Morehead, "Olympic Pitch Set by Denver," *Denver Post*, January 11, 1968, 28; "Coloradans Carry Bid for Olympics to Grenoble," clipping, 31 January 1968, Folder 25, Box 99, WMP DPL; Alan Cunningham, "Love, Currigan: Flying to Olympic Site," *Rocky Mountain News*, January 31, 1968, clipping, Folder 2, Box 99, WMP DPL.

16. Chet Nelson, "The Winter Olympics," *Rocky Mountain News*, circa February 1968, clipping, Folder 25, Box 99, WMP DPL.

17. Bick Lucas, "Good Luck, Denver, On Winter Olympics," *Denver Post*,

3 May 1970, clipping, Folder 2, Box 6, Mountain Area Protection Council Records, Jefferson County Archive, Golden, Colorado (hereafter MAPC JCA).

18. Berg, *The Olympics that Never Happened*, for Mexican American and African American advocacy for affordable housing see chapter 5; for exurban environmentalists see chapter 6; for Lamm's and Jackson's questioning see chapter 7.

19. Ibid., see chapter 8; for verification that no one knew the nature of Olympic costs, see chapter 4.

20. Richard Lamm, telephone interview with author, May 9, 2016, notes and recording in author's possession.

21. Fred Brown, "Colorado Olympic Plan Termed Too General," *Denver Post*, January 4, 1971, 14.

22. Ted Farwell to DOC Board, Letter, December 9, 1971, Folder "Board of Directors," Box S4130, ARDOC CSAR; G. D. Hubbard, Jr. to DOC Executive Council, Letter, January 6, 1971, Folder 28, Box 1, DOC DPL; Technical Division to the DOC Executive Committee, Report No. 1, January 14, 1971, Folder 2, Box 2, DOC DPL.

23. John Henry to Mayor, Letter, August 19, 1971, Folder 7, Box 104, WMP DPL.

24. Shoemaker quoted in Brown, "Colorado Olympic Plan Termed Too General."

25. "Bill Planned to Bar Funds for Olympics," *Denver Post*, January 10, 1971, clipping, Folder 65, Box 6, Protect Our Mountain Environment, Stephen H. Hart Library, Denver, Colorado (hereafter POME SHHL).

26. "Many Pay, Few Gain: Legislators Challenge Olympics for Colorado," *Denver Post*, January 15, 1971, 24.

27. Colorado H. B. 1156, 48th General Assembly, 1st Session, 1971, Colorado State Archives and Records, Denver, Colorado (hereafter CSAR).

28. Lamm and Jackson quoted in Cal Queal, "Yes, They Want no Olympics," *Denver Post*, February 7, 1971, 7.

29. Richard M. Davis, Denver Organizing Committee Board of Directors Meeting Minutes, February 18, 1971, Folder 19, Box 1, DOC DPL.

30. Leonard Larsen, "Games Must Go On, Solons Told," *Denver Post*, February 26, 1971, 3. For the DOC's preparation for the joint session, see Richard M. Davis, Denver Organizing Committee Board of Directors Meeting Minutes, February 18, 1971, Folder 19, Box 1, DOC DPL; Robert Olson, "Outline of Presentation to Joint Session of the Legislature, Thursday, February 25, 1971—11 a.m.—State House Chambers," February 18, 1971, Folder 13, Box 1, DOC DLP.

31. Larsen, "Games Must Go On, Solons Told."

32. Knox quoted in Larsen, "Games Must Go On, Solons Told."

33. Olson, *Power, Public Policy and the Environment*, 223–24.

34. Ibid., 242–46.

35. Technical Division to the DOC Executive Committee, Report No. 1, January 14, 1971, Folder 2, Box 2, DOC DPL.

36. For the DOC's additional tactics, see Berg, *The Olympics that Never Happened*, chapter 7.

37. Richard M. Davis, Denver Organizing Committee Board of Directors Meeting Minutes, February 18, 1971, Folder 19, Box 1, DOC DPL.

38. "Sniping Clouds the Olympics without Solving Any Problems," *Denver Post*, January 12, 1971, 18.

39. "Sabotaging the Olympics," *Rocky Mountain News*, January 27, 1971, 38.

40. "Looking on the Blind Side," *Rocky Mountain News*, February 27, 1971, clipping, Folder 68, Box 6, POME SHHL.

41. Norm Brown to Don Magarrell, Memorandum, "Re: Media Executive Advisory Committee Meeting on March 8th 1971 at the DOC offices between members of the DOC staff and Mr. Charles Buxton, Bill Hornby and John Rogers of Denver Post; Mike Howard of the Rocky Mountain News; Don Faust, General Manager, KOATV Hugh Terry and Sheldon Peterson, KLZ Al Flanagan, President of Mullins Broadcasting (KBTV)," March 11, 1971, Folder 39, Box 1, DOC DPL.

42. "Right Steps Taken to Brighten Outlook for 1976 Winter Games," *Denver Post*, April 2, 1972, 25.

43. Richard M. Davis, Denver Organizing Committee Board of Directors Meeting Minutes, March 18, 1971, Folder 19, Box 1, DOC DPL.

44. Staff Meeting Minutes, April 2, 1971, Folder 44, Box 2, DOC DPL.

45. Al Knight, "Pro-Olympic Unit Apparent Recipient of Free KBTV Ads," *Rocky Mountain News*, October 25, 1972, 5; "KBTV to Provide Airtime to CCF," *Denver Post*, November 3, 1972, 44.

46. Olson, *Power, Public Policy and the Environment*, 201–2.

47. Norm Brown to Don Magarrell, "Memo, Re: Media Executive Advisory Committee Meeting on March 8th 1971 at the DOC offices between members of the DOC staff and: Mr. Charles Buxton, Bill Hornby and John Rogers of Denver Post; Mike Howard of the Rocky Mountain News; Don Faust, General Manager, KOATV Hugh Terry and Sheldon Peterson, KLZ Al Flanagan, president of Mullins Broadcasting (KBTV)," March 11, 1971, Folder 39, Box 1, DOC DPL.

48. Richard O'Reilly, interview with author, Pasadena, California, June 1, 2016, notes and recording in the author's possession.

49. For more details on this see Berg, *The Olympics that Never Happened*, chapter 3.

50. O'Reilly interview.

51. Ibid.

52. Logan and Molotch, *Urban Fortunes*, 72–73.

53. Richard O'Reilly, "Olympics—Good or Bad in Colorado?," first installment of the Olympics and Colorado series, *Rocky Mountain News*, April 4, 1971, 1, 5, 8. Much of what O'Reilly reported (including problems with Evergreen and Sniktua) was reported two months earlier in *Sports Illustrated*; see Roger Rapoport, "Olympian Snafu at Sniktau," *Sports Illustrated*, February 15,

1971, 60–61. However, Rapoport's article did not seem to reach Coloradans as effectively as O'Reilly's series.

54. Richard O'Reilly, "Benefits of Olympics are Disputed," sixth installment of the Olympics and Colorado series, *Rocky Mountain News*, April 9, 1971, 8.

55. Richard O'Reilly, "Olympic Alpine Conflict Brewing," fourth installment of the Olympics and Colorado series *Rocky Mountain News*, April 7, 1971, 6, 8, 18.

56. Richard O'Reilly, "Snags Arise in Olympic Site Selection," third installment of the Olympics and Colorado series, *Rocky Mountain News*, April 6, 1971, 8, 22.

57. Richard O'Reilly, "60 Winter Olympics Cost Skyrocketed," second installment of the Olympics and Colorado series, *Rocky Mountain News*, April 5, 1971, 8, 16.

58. Richard O'Reilly, "Olympic Cost Estimates Vary Widely," fifth installment of the Olympics and Colorado series, *Rocky Mountain News*, April 8, 1971, 8, 18.

59. Richard Lamm, "Promotional Pollution: The Case for Not Holding the 1976 Winter Olympics in Colorado," speech transcript, February 12, 1972, Folder 2, Citizens for Colorado's Future, Denver Public Library, Denver Colorado (hereafter CCF DPL).

60. R. A. Smith to William McNichols, Letter, April 9, 1971, Folder 4, Box 101, WMP DPL.

61. Meg Lundstrom, telephone interview with author, March 30 and May 19, 2016, notes and recording in the author's possession.

62. Sam W. Brown, telephone interview with author, April 11, 2016, notes and recording in the author's possession.

63. Tom Wells, *The War Within: America's Battle over Vietnam* (Berkeley: University of California Press, 1994), 223–26; with Brown heading Youth for McCarthy, McCarthy won Democratic Presidential Primaries in Wisconsin, Pennsylvania, New Jersey, Illinois, and Oregon; see also "Vietnam: A Television History; Interview with Sam Brown, 1982," 08/11/1982, Open Vault from GBH, accessed March 11, 2024, http://openvault.wgbh.org/catalog/V_A55BE 9295E024182AD926622157A9791.

64. Wells, *The War Within*, 328–31, 370–79.

65. Sam W. Brown interview (2016); Lundstrom interview.

66. Dwight Filley, telephone interview with author, May 21, 2016, notes and recording in the author's possession.

67. Lundstrom interview; Tom Nussbaum, telephone interview with author, April 6, 2016, notes and recording in the author's possession.

68. Filley interview.

69. Lamm interview (2016); Lundstrom interview; Sam W. Brown interview (2016); Norman Udevitz, "Cost of Olympic Games Debated," *Denver Post*, September 29, 1972, 42.

70. Brown suggests this strategy in Sam W. Brown Jr., *Storefront Organizing: A Mornin' Glories Manual* (New York: Pyramid Books, 1972), 62.

71. Paul L. Hamilton, Ruth Weiner, and John Zapien to Friend, Letter, January 1, 1972, Folder XII, Reel 110, Winter Games 1976, Denver, Col. Organizing Committee (1972), Avery Brundage Collection, International Olympic Committee Archives, Lausanne, Switzerland (hereafter ABC IOCA).

72. Sam W. Brown, telephone interview with author, June 24, 2020, notes and recording in the author's possession; Richard Lamm telephone interview with author, June 22, 2020, notes and recording in the author's possession.

73. Brown Jr., *Storefront Organizing,* 29.

74. "Sell Colorado? Olympics '76? AT WHAT COST TO COLORADO?" advertisement in the *Denver Post,* January 2, 1972, 41.

75. Ibid.

76. Ibid.

77. Ibid.

78. Ibid.

79. Ibid.

80. Ibid.

81. Sam W. Brown Jr., "Snow Job in Colorado," *New Republic,* January 19, 1972, 15–19, quote at 18.

82. For more on this strategy, its impact, and the formation of CCF, see Berg, *The Olympics that Never Happened,* chapter 8 and chapter 10.

83. Thomas Currigan, Speech, March 1972, Folder 12, Box 102, WMP DPL.

84. "Colorado for the '76 Olympics Newspaper Recap," Report, October 12, 1972, Folder 7, Box 104, WMP DPL; Frye-Still Inc. Media Department, "Coloradans for the '76 Winter Games Broadcast Schedule," October 13, 1972, Folder 7, Box 104, WMP DPL.

85. H. C. Kimbrough, "Coloradans for the 1976 Olympics," Folder 3, Box 102, WMP DPL.

86. "Who Will be Profiting?" *The Colorado Destiny,* September 2, 1972, CCF DPL.

87. Ron Wolf, "Yes, We Have No Olympics," *Straight Creek Journal,* November 21, 1972, 3.

88. Dwight Filley, Meg Lundstrom, and John Parr to Friend, Letter, November 2, 1972, Folder "Citizens For Colorado's Future," Box 2, Richard Lamm Collection Stephen H. Hart Research Center; Dwight Filley, Meg Lundstrom, and John Parr, Citizens for Colorado Newsletter, June 25, 1972, Box 5, Folder 50, CCF DPL; for Brachman, see Lundstrom interview.

89. Norm Udevitz, "Voters Reject Funding for '76 Olympics," *Denver Post,* November 8, 1976, 1, 3; "Asks IOC to Retain Denver as '76 Site," *Chicago Tribune,* November 14, 1972, C1.

90. Udevitz, "Voters Reject Funding for '76 Olympics."

91. Richard Lamm, "Promotional Pollution: The Case for Not Holding the

1976 Olympics in Colorado," speech transcript, February 12, 1972, Folder 2, CCF DPL.

92. For example, see Richard O'Reilly, "DOC Mulls Ways to Cut TV Cost," *Rocky Mountain News*, February 10, 1972, 5.

93. Michael Balfe Howard, *"News* Survey Indicates Heavy Support for Olympic Referendum," *Rocky Mountain News*, March 13, 1972, 1.

CHAPTER 3

Mohkinstsis (Calgary) 1988

Settler Colonial Roots of Olympic Environmentalism and the Disavowal of Indigenous Rights

CHRISTINE O'BONSAWIN

In the Siksika language, Mohkinstsis refers to the area where the Bow and Elbow Rivers meet. As Siksika elder Miiksika'am (Clarence Wolfleg) explains, Mohkinstsis served as an important navigational area, place of medicine gathering, and center of exchange for many years. It continues to be a place of great importance to the people of Siksikaitsitapi (Blackfoot Confederacy) and other Indigenous nations.[1] Mohkinstsis is commonly known today as Calgary, Alberta, Canada. The history of Indigenous presence on these territories goes back thousands of years—to the creation of Siksikaitsitapi and other Indigenous peoples on these territories and surrounding regions. Settler history on and around Mohkinstsis is considerably shorter, generally dating back to the late nineteenth century when the first Europeans established permanent structures on the banks of the Elbow River. As this chapter explores, the arrival of the 1988 Olympic Winter Games at Mohkinstsis a mere century after the coming of the earliest permanent settlers to the territory further complicates the settler colonial history of this place.

In recent years, scholars have made significant contributions to Olympic environmental history, recognizing that environmental concerns were important and, at times, contested aspects in Olympic history. Unfortunately, the historical record remains generally silent on Indigenous peoples' experiences, interests, and legal rights. Consultation of empirical and secondary sources reveals that Indigenous histories, perspectives, and (acknowledgement of) their legal rights remain absent in Olympic environmental history. This absence is certainly not due to Indigenous peoples' lack of concern for the welfare of their territories and their own prosperity. Rather, it is owing to the fact that a significant number of Indigenous peoples have been forcefully (often violently) removed from their lands, politically silenced, and ultimately replaced by (invasive) settler populations that have engaged in destructive environmental behaviors. The dispossession of Indigenous lands and the subjugation of the original peoples are critical aspects of Olympic environmental history that have been largely forgotten, overlooked, purposely excluded, or all of the above. This chapter revisits the Olympic Winter Games at Mohkinstsis by first exploring the seeming absence of Indigenous peoples in organizing Winter Olympics hosted on Turtle Island (i.e., North America) in the first half century of these Games, specifically 1932–1976, and the response of settler environmentalists to Olympic-related environmental threats posed to these Indigenous territories. Second, this chapter underscores the near–decade long opposition of settler environmentalists from the late 1950s to 1966 to hosting the Winter Games at Mohkinstsis, arguing that these individuals and entities operated according to a settler colonial logic that failed to see the presence of Indigenous peoples (historically and presently) and disregarded their inalienable human and legal rights. Finally, this chapter assesses the (in)actions of Olympic organizers and settler environmentalists in the organizing years of the 1988 Winter Games at Mohkinstsis. Although Olympic organizers and settler environmentalists were at diametric odds, both sides engaged in settler colonial practices that ultimately resulted in the further dispossession and alienation of Indigenous peoples from their territories.

Foregrounding an Indigenous Presence in Olympic Environmental History, 1932–1976

There is little to no evidence to suggest that Indigenous peoples participated in organizing Winter Olympics hosted throughout Turtle Island in the first half century of these Games, specifically 1932–1976, or that Indigenous peoples were directly impacted—either positively or negatively—by the hosting of these Games on their territories. Their absence in Olympic history is of significant concern. Failures to see Indigenous peoples (historically and presently) and their absence from written history is embedded within processes of settler colonialism, which "structures political and social life through the ongoing appropriation and occupation of Native land, and is culturally enforced through practices that actively obscure or erase Indigenous peoples—an effort to complete via ideological and cultural means that work [to correct] earlier failed attempts at total physical genocide."[2] As Rita Dhamoon reasons, settler colonialism is not a contained, unchanging, historical phenomenon. Rather, it is "temporal and ongoing, dynamic, and continuous," involving socioeconomic, cultural, ideological, and political practices, discourses, institutions, and actors.[3] It pervades settler colonial societies and functions in the politics, laws, and cultures of national and international institutions, including the Olympic movement. Because the central goal of settler colonialism is the ongoing dispossession and appropriation of Indigenous territories and resources—by and to the benefit of settlers—it is a fundamental theoretical basis for thinking about environmental relations, environmental racism, and colonial ecological violence.[4] It is an important theoretical framework that has been neglected in the environmental history of the Olympic Games.

As suggested throughout this book, because of the nature of winter sport and its associated geographies, from an environmental standpoint, the Winter Olympics require further attention and perhaps greater scrutiny because of the many harmful effects posed to natural landscapes. According to Stephen Essex and Brian Chalkley, "The construction and operation of event facilities for the Winter Olympics in remote rural regions can have considerable physical and aesthetic implications for natural and seminatural landscapes within the region. The installation of large structures and the use of chemicals, such as ammonia for artificial freezing, represent two examples of obvious Olympic intrusions into fragile environments."[5] As this growing body of literature illustrates, the Winter Olympics have introduced substantial threats to remote and ecologically sensitive regions.[6] In recent years, Olympic studies scholars have made significant contributions to this history, recognizing that since the inception of the Winter Games, "environmentalists" have frequently opposed the hosting of the Games, often citing ecological concerns for vulnerable and natural landscapes.

In the context of Turtle Island, these environmental Olympic histories remain largely incomplete and arguably inaccurate because they are epistemologically bound with settler colonialism. The actions of supposed environmentalists in early Olympic history were contingent on the genocide, dispossession, and alienation of Indigenous peoples from their territories and a refusal to acknowledge that the landscapes these settlers became so emphatically attached to were (and remain) the places Indigenous peoples have cared for and called home since time immemorial. This form of logic derives from settler colonialism that fails to see Indigenous peoples as contemporary members of the world—past and present—and as people who possess inalienable human and legal rights. As J. M. Bacon reasons, "Even deeply committed environmentalists with a stated commitment to place often have difficulty when it comes to questions that touch upon the settler-colonial structuring of those very places they are committed to. This results not only from widespread erasure [of Indigenous peoples] but also from the settler-colonial roots of U. S. environmentalism."[7] An examination of Winter Olympic Games held on Turtle Island between 1932 and 1976 suggests that the roots of settler colonialism, too, pervade Olympic environmentalism. Accordingly, this discussion foregrounds an Indigenous presence, recognizing that although they did not participate in the formal planning and hosting of these Winter Games, they remain a central part of this history, mainly as it concerns settler claims over their territories and the survivance of Indigenous peoples and nations.

The 1932 Winter Olympics at Wawôbadenik ("White Mountains")

The 1932 Lake Placid Games were held in a small village in the Adirondack Mountains in what is now known as the State of New York. These territories are often acknowledged as Haudenosaunee (Iroquoian-speaking peoples), specifically Kanien'kehá:ka (Mohawk) hunting territories. However, the history of these territories is more complex as they were regularly occupied and cared for by multiple Iroquoian *and* Algonquian-speaking peoples in both the pre- and post-contact periods. As Melissa Otis explains, "this space was much more than 'just a hunting territory,' a phrase that allowed, and in some instances still allows, Euro-Americans to see this landscape, and others similar to it, as empty and free to exploit and appropriate."[8] Several Iroquoian and Algonquian-speaking peoples have a word in their language for this region. For example, the Kanien'kehá:ka refer to the Adirondacks as Tso-non-tes-ko-wa ("the mountains") or Tsiiononteskowa ("big mountains") and the Abenaki refer to it as Wawôbadenik ("white mountains"). Considering past and present relationships Iroquoian and Algonquian-speaking peoples have to this place, Wawôbadenik[9] may be understood to be what Otis has termed, a *location of exchange*, a place that has always involved multifaceted, entangled, and reciprocal relationships between these Indigenous nations and their territories.[10]

In many ways, the history of Indigenous-settler relations throughout these territories belongs to a broader global history of European imperial conquest beginning in the fifteenth century. European colonists justified their unlawful conquests of territories throughout the world based on a set of beliefs about their superiority over Indigenous peoples. Following such doctrines, settler colonists began to claim and eventually impose governmental, political, and commercial control over Indigenous peoples and their territories.[11] The political, legal, and economic fabric of the United States and other settler colonial states worldwide, including Canada, continues to be shaped by such racial and religious beliefs. As to Wawôbadenik, European settlers did not arrive in large numbers in this region until the mid- to late nineteenth century mainly because of its cold and sometimes inhospitable climate and quickly established resource extraction industries, such as lumbering and mining, thereby disrupting Indigenous peoples' ability to carry on fully with their own resource economies. Tourists arrived in Wawôbadenik in earnest after the US Civil War (1861–1865), in conjunction with an increase in American leisure time and disposable income, and the completion of the first rail line into the region in 1871. Significant depletion of natural resources and the influx of permanent settlers and tourists by the late nineteenth century prompted state legislators to take on a conservation role.[12]

In 1892, the State of New York created the Adirondack State Park. In 1894, half of the park's acreage was protected within the state constitution as "forever wild." Article VII, section 7 of the constitution recognized that this vast portion of the Park, known as the Adirondack Forest Preserve, "shall forever be kept as wild forest lands. They shall not be leased, sold or exchanged, or be taken by any corporation, public or private nor shall the timber thereon be sold, removed or destroyed."[13] In establishing legal protections over the Park, state officials helped to establish, as Jonathan Alzalone contends, "a modern wilderness playground" for the growing number of permanent settlers and tourists arriving in the region, many in pursuit of outdoor play, recreation, and sporting opportunities.[14]

The decision to bid for the 1932 Winter Olympics was prompted, in part, by the region's growing popularity as a winter sporting destination as well as a growing desire to encourage economic development, through tourism, in response to the significant decline in heavy industry throughout Wawôbadenik by the 1920s. In January 1929, four months before the Games were awarded to Lake Placid, state lawmakers began plans to construct Olympic facilities, introducing a bill to authorize the construction of the bobsled run within the "forever wild" protected area of the Adirondack Park. The Association for the Protection of the Adirondacks (AfPA), a local environmental group, challenged the bobsled bill, formally titled Chapter 417 of the Laws of 1929. In January 1930, the Supreme Court of New York, Appellate Division upheld their challenge, declaring the bill unconstitutional largely because the proposed location required the clearcutting of approximately 2,500 trees protected under state law as a natural landscape within the park boundary. The Court of Appeals upheld this decision in March 1930,[15] concluding, "However tempting it may be to yield to the seductive influences of outdoor sports and international contests, we must not overlook the fact that constitutional provisions cannot always adjust themselves to the nice relationships of life."[16] In the end, the bobsled site was built at South Meadow Mountain, later renamed Mount Van Hoevenberg, requiring the removal of significant trees, earth, and rock to build the 1.5-mile track.[17]

The bobsled controversy associated with the 1932 Winter Games is an important aspect of Olympic history. As Peter M. Hopsicker asserts, it "should be credited as the first major environmental protest of any Games in modern Olympic history."[18] Although certain natural areas were safeguarded, specifically in the Adirondack Forest Preserve, the Games catalyzed economic growth and recreational development throughout Wawôbadenik. More permanent settlers and tourists arrived in the years following the Games, ultimately leading to the transformation of the landscape and a repurposing of the region into a human-centered environment developed for mass sport and recreation.[19] In the process, Iroquoian and Algonquian-speaking peoples became further displaced from Wawôbadenik and the places where they had long experienced multifaceted, entangled, and reciprocal relationships. This displacement further contributed to the illusion that Algonquian and Iroquoian people were vanishing from this region, a concept often applied to Indigenous peoples, particularly in the Northeast, to justify Euro-American claims to their lands through a settler denial of an Indigenous future on these territories.[20]

The 1960 Winter Olympics at Da?aw
(The Lake)

By the mid-1930s, winter sports had gained in popularity. In the context of the Winter Olympics, this meant more participating countries, resulting in more athletes, officials, media personnel, and spectators travelling to the Games. Between 1936 and 1960, Winter Olympics organizers faced greater infrastructural demands, leading to increased Olympic-induced ecological destruction. Advancements in ski-hill technology throughout the 1940s and 1950s, for example, meant that organizers needed to procure up-to-date equipment, such as snowmaking and grooming machines and chair lifts and gondolas, requiring significant alterations to the landscape and placing further stresses on the natural resources. Further, the swelling number of participants meant increased transportation needs. Organizers in larger host cities quite often needed to move participants from the Olympic Village, usually situated in the city center, to faraway events in distant locations, often in short time frames. Conversely, organizers in

FIGURE 3.1. DaɁaw, Wá·šiw territory, 2022. Credit: Christine O'Bonsawin.

smaller cities typically needed to move the growing number of participants in and out of isolated mountainous regions. The short- and long-term environmental impacts following the 1960 Olympic Winter Games, held in a small remote area in eastern California, offer critical insights into the extent of Olympic-induced ecological destruction as a consequence of hosting the Winter Olympics.

The Palisades Tahoe (formerly S**** Valley[21]) ski resort in the Lake Tahoe region of California served as the main site of the 1960 Olympic Winter Games. Palisades Tahoe lies on the eastern flank of the Sierra Nevada Mountain Range, home of the Wá·šiw people (commonly referred to as the Washoe Tribe), who have occupied and cared for these territories since time immemorial (see figure 3.1). The Wá·šiw people have long referred to Lake Tahoe as DaɁaw (the lake).[22] According to Wá·šiw creation stories, DaɁaw is the center of the Wá·šiw world, geographically and spiritually, containing many sacred sites, and its waters have forever breathed life into the surrounding land, plants, fish, birds, animals, and people.[23] Settlers began to flood the Lake Tahoe region, commonly referred to as "the valley," in the early 1850s, specifically California-bound gold seekers who used the area surrounding Da?aw as a place of respite before ascending the Sierra Nevada mountains.[24] Settler encroachment on these territories over the next century not only threatened Wá·šiw language and culture, but it also led to the destruction of significant ecosystems that the Wá·šiw people had cared for since time began.[25]

Modest ski resort development was underway in the Lake Tahoe region by the late 1940s and early 1950s. In fact, before unexpectedly receiving the rights to host these Winter Games, Palisades Resort, in 1954, consisted of one chairlift, two rope-tows, and a dirt road. As Brian Friel suggests, "[i]t was the first time that the Olympics had not been awarded to a city, but to a piece of real estate."[26] Following its selection to host the 1960 Games, there was a boom in ski resort infrastructural growth at Palisades Resort and throughout the area, which continued for the next three decades. This infrastructural explosion was supported by the State of California, which revived an old state bill previously committing $1 million to the 1932 Los Angeles Summer Olympics.[27] This state contribution helped to expedite the dramatic transformation of the valley, resulting in the construction of spectator centers, athlete dormitories, multiple arenas, a police station, and systems for electricity, water, heating, and sewage. In the end, more than 250,000 visitors travelled to Palisades Tahoe for the Olympic Winter Games. Numerous ski resorts opened throughout the Lake Tahoe basin throughout the 1960s and 1970s, leading to increased infrastructural demands and resulting in the construction of a new interstate highway in 1964 to facilitate the movement of tourists flooding to the valley. By the mid-1960s, conservationists were actively seeking wildlife protections for those species at risk due to increased fishing, hunting, deforestation, and water pollution throughout the Lake Tahoe region.[28]

Researchers associated with the University of California, Davis Tahoe Environmental Research Center (TERC) explain that when heavy development began at the outset of Olympic organizing, in the mid-1950s, developers did not understand the importance of filtration systems within natural wetlands surrounding freshwater lakes. Further, in June 2021, the research center concluded that the algal growth rate in Lake Tahoe had quadrupled since 1959.[29] When addressing the question of environmental problems facing Lake Tahoe presently, TERC researchers reason that the selection of the Lake Tahoe region for the 1960 Winter Olympics certainly gave it global publicity and greatly increased visitor traffic to the basin, and similar to so many natural landscapes throughout the world, human impacts have gradually taken their toll.[30] As the Wá·šiw people rightly

contend, "[t]he demand on the natural resources by the immigrant population depleted much of [the natural environment]. The logging industry
denuded the forests . . . to support the mining industry and towns that
sprang up everywhere. The fisheries of Lake Tahoe once bountiful with
the native cutthroat trout had been reduced to nothing."[31] In a relatively
short period, the Wá·šiw world had changed forever, largely stimulated
by what Conor Villines characterizes as "the Olympic onslaught."[32]

The 1976 Winter Olympics (Not) In/On
Ute, Cheyenne, and Arapaho Territories

One of the best-known examples of environmental protest in Olympic
history is Denver, Colorado's withdrawal from hosting the 1976 Winter
Games, largely owing to what residents claimed to be environmental concerns and fears about ecological impacts on fragile mountainous regions.
(Adam Berg discusses these protests in chapter 2.) The City of Denver
sits on the territories of the Nunt'zi (Ute), Tsitsistas (Cheyenne), and
Hinonoeino (Arapaho) nations. Approximately fifty other tribal nations,
including the Lakota, Kiowa, Comanche, Apache, Paiute, Zuni, and Hopi,
to name just a few, have been interwoven with one another over the centuries and the vast territories that were eventually appropriated into the
State of Colorado.[33] The confluence of the Platte River and Cherry Creek,
for example, has long been an important location for trade, information
sharing, and future planning, having been visited by Indigenous peoples
and nations for thousands of years for purposes of ceremony and in celebration of community, family, and allies.[34] The forceful dispossession
of Indigenous peoples from their territories in the Denver and broader
Colorado regions commenced in the mid-nineteenth century with the
California Gold Rush (1848–1855) and later Colorado Gold Rush (1858),
commonly known as the Pikes Peak Gold Rush. The influx of gold seekers
and settlers to the region throughout the 1840s and 1850s resulted in the
founding of the city of Denver in 1858 and the creation of the Colorado
Territory in 1861 (with statehood finalized in 1876). As Andrew R. Goetz
and E. Eric Boschmann explain, around this period:

> Native Americans were 'vanquished' from the plains, as justified by racist
> ideologies, in order to remove obstacles of progress and develop com-
> mercial agricultural activity that diversified Denver's economy. The
> Sand Creek massacre in 1864 was the most horrific anti-Indian event
> in which over 160 Cheyenne and Arapaho, mostly women and children,
> were killed during a nightmare military ambush.[35]

After ratifying several mostly one-sided treaties and agreements (1849–1873), Indigenous peoples were pushed to the borderlands and forcefully relocated to faraway reservations. Many of their children were abducted and sent to Indian boarding schools.[36]

A growing number of settlers moved into the region in the late nineteenth and early twentieth centuries, transforming the city from a dusty, brawling mining camp into the finance, transportation, and communication hub for the Rocky Mountain region. By the mid-twentieth century, with further environmental degradation following military and federal development, city planners remained steadfast in their determination to bring a "city beautiful" vision to Denver, "usher[ing] in a new image of outdoor recreationalism, environmental consciousness, and personal attachment to place."[37] Nonetheless, as Abby Hickcox argues, this form of greenwashing of cities and places within Colorado creates a space for racist and classist assumptions to reside unnoticed or unquestioned, thus, hiding the landscapes' social histories of race and class privilege. "Power relations are stamped onto material landscapes through their physical management. This management then becomes common sense, hiding its social histories."[38] Analysis of Colorado's conservation history reveals that it is premised on white subjectivities and couched in rhetoric of environmental preservation and the dangers of population growth. Denver's withdrawal from hosting the 1976 Olympic Winter Games must be understood within such frameworks, recognizing that the brand of environmentalism attached to this protest movement was premised on racist and classist assumptions that went largely unnoticed.

Most historians frame Denver's abandonment of its hosting obligations as a pivotal moment in history when environmental consciousness outwardly permeated Olympic realms. However, as Adam Berg details in chapter 2 of this volume, opposition to these Games was spearheaded by predominantly white middle- and upper-class suburbanites who desired to protect not the environment per se but rather the physical and aesthetic details of residential life and the property value of their homes. However, when voicing their concerns to Olympic organizers and the public, they understood the need to cite something other than their own privileged racial and class positions, compelling them to associate their interests with environmental questions, including concerns about deforestation, water contamination, and soil erosion.

The absence of Indigenous peoples from Olympic environmental history perhaps comes as no surprise. As the above examples demonstrate, the actions of these supposed environmentalists were premised on both a settler colonial logic and the drastic inequalities between settlers and

Indigenous peoples, thus resulting in the further dispossession and appropriation of Indigenous territories.[39] Concepts such as "empty spaces," "wilderness," "natural beauty" are some of settler colonialism's most enduring symbols, suggesting territories to be empty and devoid of humans, which quite literally is dependent on the erasure of Indigenous peoples.[40] It is dependent on white subjectivities and failures to recognize the multifaceted, entangled, and reciprocal relationships Indigenous peoples have forever enjoyed with their territories. As the above examples demonstrate, environmentalism in early Olympic history had less to do with the environment and more to do with racial and class-centered motives, such as maintaining structures of white privilege and individual class interests, and thus, settler colonialism.

Treaty 7 First Nations, Colonial Conservationism, and Failed Olympic Bids

Our understanding of environmentalism today is shaped mainly by global expansion following the Second World War and the politicization and radicalization of environmental action during the late 1960s and 1970s. As Olympic environmental scholar John Karamichas reasons, "In this context, environmentalists saw the Olympic Games and other megaprojects as extremely negative developments for the preservation of the natural environment, and they acted accordingly to prevent them from happening."[41] Concerning the Winter Games specifically, throughout the 1960s and 1970s, rapid infrastructure growth, expanding real estate markets, and advancements in resort technologies coincided with increased attention toward preserving natural spaces, catalyzing growing environmental concerns by people around ski resorts.[42] As previously discussed, there are several examples of environmental advocacy in the first half century of the Winter Olympics; nonetheless, the most significant opposition, arguably, came from environmentalists who helped to successfully avert three consecutive Olympic bids developed by the business elite of southern Alberta.

The Olympic Winter Games were awarded to Calgary and held at and around Mohkinstsis on Treaty 7 territory in 1988. Historical scholarship on this event mainly concentrates on organizational efforts beginning in 1981, after the Games were awarded and the eventual hosting of these Olympics in 1988.[43] In assessing environmental racism and the disavowal of Indigenous rights, this chapter takes a more expansive view, recognizing that efforts to bring the Games to the Calgary and Banff region began in 1957 with the formation of the Calgary Olympic Development Association (CODA), which remained mostly active until 1981, when the Games were eventually awarded to Calgary following its fourth bid attempt.[44] The IOC mostly credited the determination of environmentalists throughout the Calgary and Banff regions as the main reason for its rejection of CODA's three consecutive Winter Olympic bids for the 1964, 1968, and 1972 Games. The actions of these environmentalists were, too, contingent on the dispossession and alienation of Indigenous peoples from their territories, a settler refusal to acknowledge that the landscapes they had become so emphatically attached to were (and remain) the places Indigenous peoples have cared for since time immemorial, and their failure to see Indigenous peoples as possessing inalienable human and legal rights. In this case, settler environmentalists disregarded and thus neglected their Treaty 7 responsibilities.

Treaty 7 was negotiated and ratified in September 1877. At this time, representatives of five Indigenous nations, including Siksika, Kainai, Piikani, Stoney Nakoda, and Tsuut'ina, met with Crown commissioners on Siksika territory—at Blackfoot Crossing—to negotiate a treaty that would ensure their peaceful coexistence on the lands now known as southern Alberta. It is fair to suggest that the promises made between these politically autonomous collectives represent "a noncolonial, reciprocity-activated, inter-political relations, where multiple co-present, cooperating, and co-witnessing beings [agreed to] live together respectfully without any of them problematically subordinated to others. All retain their distinction and difference."[45] The exchange of promises at Blackfoot Crossing were bound ceremonially, thus requiring that relations and guarantees be revisited and renewed frequently and necessarily. According to Treaty 7 elders, "the memory of that occasion is vivid among our people and the story has been told many times among the Niitsitapi (the real people) throughout the years since that time . . . In our languages there is no word for treaty; the event is simply remembered as istsist aohkotspi or iitsinnaihtsiiyo'pi (the time when we made a sacred alliance)."[46] Regrettably, as Treaty 7 elders make clear, since the confirmation of this sacred alliance, "The promises have not been properly fulfilled."[47]

Whereas Crown representatives documented in writing their understandings of promises made at Blackfoot Crossing, including the erroneous claim that Indigenous nations agreed to surrender their land, Siksika, Kainai, Piikani, Stoney Nakoda, and Tsuut'ina oral histories corroborate that they were willing to *share* their lands with arriving settlers. As Crowfoot, speaking chief of the Siksika, famously proclaimed at the time of negotiation, "We cannot sell the lives of men and animals, and so, we cannot sell the land. It was put here by the Great Spirit and we cannot sell it because it does not really belong to us."[48] From their epistemological perspectives, the land—in its ecological totality—was inalienable, and thus could not be surrendered.[49] For example, First Nations negotiators industriously negotiated land protections into the treaty, denying newcomers subsurface rights. Siksika elders Augustine Yellow Sun (b. 1898) and Jim Black (b. 1893) agreed that First Nations representatives insisted on what land could and could not be used by settlers, explaining that "two feet for post holes and one foot, or the length of a shovel blade, for ploughing. The rest of the earth was not sold; neither as the water or 'black rock' [i.e., coal and oil]."[50] For well over a century, Treaty 7 First Nation elders have confirmed that indeed the land was not surrendered: "In the oral histories passed down from generation to generation, their understanding of what happened at Blackfoot Crossing remains consistent. According to the research, this is true whether elders were interviewed in the 1920s, 1930s, 1960s, or 1990s. The elders have said that Treaty 7 was a peace treaty; none of them recall any mention of a land surrender."[51]

In settler colonial political discourse, the word treaty has become debased. As such, historical treaties have come to serve the "coloniality of power" that works to constrain freedom to conform to a particular power arrangement, reinforcing boundaries around peoples, animals, nonhumans, air, lands, and waters. They have come to be seen as one-sided contracts that take away, with finality, from Indigenous peoples. As Brian Noble contends, historical treaties, including Treaty 7, "have come to characterize settler-Indigenous relations under Euro-Canadian settlement, individualist-focused common law, Westphalian confederation, and expansive capitalism, where the expectation is that the dominance of the settler-polity and its proprietary ambitions must and will prevail."[52] In this context, environmental opposition to the hosting of the Olympic Winter Games in southern Alberta is examined, recognizing that Treaty 7 not only contains explicit environmental protections but that the supposed environmentalists opposing the Calgary and Banff bids were operating in a particular colonial power arrangement. By reinforcing boundaries around peoples, animals, nonhuman entities, air, lands, and waters, these environmentalists could potentially resist Olympic expansive capitalism and, thus, advance their own (white) interests in settler colonial Canada.

Scholars, including Russell Field in chapter 1, have effectively taken up the near three decade—long failure to secure the Winter Games for Calgary and Banff, calling attention to environmental controversies and political interferences afflicting the three bid processes in 1964, 1968, and 1972.[53] The histories of the three failed Calgary/Banff bids are predictably entangled in a more extensive political history concerning environmental politics and protections of national parks, specifically Banff National Park.

On the one hand, scholars appropriately call attention to the fact that national parks are indeed colonial spaces that were (and are) instrumental in sustaining settler colonial objectives.[54] On the other hand, scholars of Olympic environmental history position such dissent from environmentalists, including those opposing the Calgary/Banff bids, as instrumental to the eventual integration of environmentalism within the Olympic movement.[55] Narratives that position national parks, such as Banff, as important conservation sites are increasingly prominent aspects of Olympic environmental history. Yet, they remain epistemologically bound to the environmental principles of settler colonialism because they actively work to obscure the history of Indigenous land dispossession as well as enduring settler interests in such territories.

In 1887, ten years after signing Treaty 7, Rocky Mountains Park, now Banff National Park, became Canada's first designated national park, spanning 673 square kilometres. In 1902, its borders were extended to encompass 11,400 square kilometres. In his important work on colonial encounters in Banff National Park, Courtney W. Mason details how the park's creation posed immediate threats for local Indigenous populations. Although Indigenous hunting and land subsistence practices were protected by virtue of Treaty 7, in the immediate years following its ratification, settlers came to see these legal protections, and Indigenous peoples themselves, as impediments to their access to lands, including pristine and natural spaces.[56] In fact, the government set on a path to create its first federally protected area, now Banff National Park, not because it aspired to safeguard vulnerable ecosystems and wildlife, but rather because it desired to secure those lands perceived to be of geological and proprietary value. In this case, settler "discovery" of mineral hot springs in the mid-nineteenth century and ensuring private interest disputes spurred the government into action in its desire to take possession of this promising tourist center. One of its first steps was to restrict Indigenous access to these areas and, thus, the territories so central to their physical and cultural survival. Tyrannical colonial policies of the day, such as the pass system, the legalized abduction of Indigenous children, and police surveillance functioned to limit an Indigenous presence within the park. Indigenous people were officially excluded from the park in 1895—through the first wildlife regulations in Canada's national park history—because they purportedly posed a threat to large game mammals.[57] In truth, Indigenous hunting practices threatened the sport hunting priorities of settlers, who hunted for trophies rather than food and survival, and further jeopardized the government's creation of a tourist and recreational paradise. As Mason appropriately reasons, "Although this [history of Banff National

Park] is a less glamorous account than some historians have put forward, few conservation principles shaped these decisions because the park was originally created to centralize control of the lands and restrict access to the region."[58] Through the guise of conservationism, settlers began to *create* their own uninhabited wilderness spaces, proclaiming that these spaces required their protection. They have since vehemently protected such places.

In chapter 1, Russell Field explains how the 1972 bid occurred at a time of increased environmental awareness, whereas in the 1960s, settler conservationists feared that construction projects in Banff National Park would alter the landscape, citing threats to vulnerable ecosystems and wildlife, such as elk, deer, and mountain sheep. Conservationists included individuals like Hal Eidsvik, a national parks planner, who suggested hosting the Olympic Games within a national park boundary compared to outright thievery. "You [cannot] walk into somebody's house and say, 'Hey, [we are] going to build this in your house.' No, the final authority of what was going to be developed and where it would be developed rested with the [Park] branch, the minister, literally, but certainly not with the Olympic Development committee."[59] The irony herein is that the Park branch was neither the lawful owner nor authority of the metaphorical house erected, albeit illegally, on Treaty 7 territory.

Field goes on to explain how Sapporo's selection over Banff to host the 1972 Olympic Winter Games is attributed mainly to the misgivings of IOC members who feared the dissent of environmentalists who sought to strengthen environmental protections in and around Banff National Park. Further, it might be said that the bid failure was predicated on what Harvey Locke has claimed to be "the great reawakening of Canadian civil society in the 1960s," a time when Canadian civil society awoke from its long, neglectful slumber concerning protected areas (Second World War to the 1960s).[60] To be sure, Locke understands "civil society" to refer to "the public when it acts as individual citizens or through nongovernmental organizations for public-spirited reasons, and is distinct from other social grouping such as government, business, or family. (It does not include aboriginal groups, who are a form of government)."[61] This characterization of civil society, to the exclusion of (a narrowly understood realisation of) Indigenous collectives, reflects conventional colonial mindsets. It is not enough that Indigenous peoples were physically removed from these places of "natural beauty," but that conservationists continue to justify their indifference to Indigenous peoples in their arguably misguided efforts to protect endangered spaces and species. As Dina Gilio-Whitaker (Colville Confederated Tribes) corroborates, when settler environmentalists "reiterate narratives about pristine national park environments, they are participating in the erasure of Indigenous peoples, thus replicating colonial patterns."[62]

The 1988 Winter Games at Mohkinstsis and the Controversy Over Wataga ipa (Mount Allan)

Following three consecutive bid failures, CODA went into a decade-long dormancy. Bid activities resumed in 1978 when predominantly local businessmen from Calgary revived the volunteer organization to bid for the 1988 Olympic Winter Games.[63] In its candidature file, CODA made the bold promise to build mostly new venues throughout Calgary and the adjacent region known as Kananaskis Country.[64] At the bid stage, CODA proposed to build "new venues to overcome Calgary's lack of winter sports facilities, arguing that Canada's inventory of facilities would increase if Calgary was awarded the Games." This was certainly a well-devised strategy in appealing to IOC sensibilities. On September 30, 1981, at the 84th IOC Session in Baden-Baden, West Germany, CODA—on its fourth attempt—secured the confidence of IOC members who voted in favor of Calgary over Falun, Sweden and Cortina d'Ampezzo, Italy. It perhaps comes as no surprise that Indigenous peoples, specifically Treaty 7 First Nations, remained outsiders to Olympic organizational efforts and environmental controversies in the ensuing years. Their absence from these seemingly critical matters regarding their territories raises particular concerns, especially given that Calgary was chosen during a time of sweeping legal and political changes as it concerns Indigenous rights in settler colonial Canada.

A close reading of Calgary's candidature file reveals that CODA outwardly misrepresented certain aspects of the bid in what appears to have been a tactical organizing strategy used to circumvent environmental opposition and ultimately secure Calgary's selection.[65] As explicitly stipulated in the bid book, "Mount Sparrowhawk and Mount Shark are the mountains selected as sites for the downhill, slalom and giant slalom events."[66] Although the Olympic bid was based on a development proposal for Mount Sparrowhawk and Mount Shark in the Spray Lakes Area of Kananaskis Country, following Calgary's selection, the province of Alberta announced that there would be a selection process to determine a suitable Alpine site that met IOC and Fédération Internationale de Ski (FIS) requirements.[67] Considering CODA's previous bid failures, it was a well-devised strategy to purposefully deceive members of the IOC and the public at large by providing misinformation on the proposed Alpine site. In 1982, Aplan Recreation, a private consultant, was hired to analyze potential Alpine sites. Following its investigation, Aplan endorsed Mount

Allan as the most appropriate site, resulting in immediate objections from environmentalists.[68]

Mount Allan is located approximately ninety kilometers west of Mohkinstsis, on the eastern slope of the Canadian Rockies, situated outside the eastern boundary of Banff National Park. This region has always been of central importance to Stoney Nakoda, who have long used the area's resources to make a living, often encamping, hunting, and gathering throughout the vast territory.[69] Stoney Nakoda people's right to engage in these practices is embedded in their own systems of governance, which require the renewal of relationships and responsibilities to the land and nonhuman relations, frequently and necessarily. An integral part of maintaining these relationships and promoting a continuing healthy relationship among animals, the environment, and people is the carrying out of ceremonies, songs, and dances.[70] Their "[s]tories recount relationships and communications among the animals and the Stoney Nakoda and serve as life teachings describing how to survive in balance with nature and one another."[71] The grizzly bear, for example, is revered as a highly spiritual being among Stoney Nakoda people. They have lived with the grizzly (as well as other animals) for thousands of years, acquiring deep knowledge about their need for space, their territorial ways, and their sacred areas. One of the names used by Stoney people for the mountain commonly known today as Mount Allan is Wataga ipa, meaning "grizzly hill point."[72] The word in Nakoda for grizzly is wataga: the "hill point" or mountain has long been an important habitat for grizzly populations.

The settler history of this region typically begins in 1859 with the arrival of the Captain John Palliser expedition, which travelled into Siksikaitsitapi (Blackfoot Confederacy) territory, eventually reaching Stoney Nakoda lands.[73] At this time, Palliser chose the name Kananaskis, purportedly the name of a Cree warrior, Kin-e-a-kis, despite not being in Cree territory.[74] For a brief period, Kananaskis Country was included in the Rocky Mountain National Park (1902–1911), before being transferred to the provincial government in 1930. In 1948, the mountain long known to Stoney Nakoda people as Wataga ipa was appropriated to Mount Allan, in honor of Dr. John Allan, former head of the Department of Geology at the University of Alberta.[75] Following the conservation movement of the late 1950s through 1970s, the province established various parks throughout the region, identifying the need to protect the watershed and provide resource development, tourism, and recreation opportunities. In 1978, Alberta premier Peter Lougheed established Kananaskis Provincial Park (now Peter Lougheed Provincial Park) in Kananaskis Country. The Alberta Fish and Wildlife Division immediately identified the Mount Allan area as a highly vulnerable wildlife habitat, resulting in a 1979 written agreement with the Department of Tourism that the area would not be developed.[76] The written agreement now stood in the way of a decision concerning Mount Allan's suitability as an Olympic site.

On November 9, 1982, the newly formed organizing committee for the Calgary Winter Games—Olympiques Calgary Olympics (OCO'88)—announced that Mount Allan had been chosen as the Alpine venue site (see figure 3.2).[77] According to OCO'88 Chairman Frank King, Mount Allan proved to be "a cheaper site, more consistent with the policy of our partner, the government of Alberta."[78] Despite its seeming economic and commercial viability, environmentalists were amongst the first to voice their objections to the selection of Mount Allan. In reference to the province's 1979 written agreement concerning the vulnerability of wildlife habitat at Mount Allan, environmentalist Brian Horejsi concluded that "[t]he solution to this dilemma proved to be simple—ignore the agreement—and so it was that the people of Alberta saw the first in a series of betrayals by elected people entrusted with safeguarding the province's wildlife heritage."[79] Environmentalists mainly were concerned for the large herd of bighorn sheep that wintered on Mount Allan, with further considerations for other wildlife, such as elk, mule deer, wolf, grizzly and black bear populations in the area. Archival review indicates that throughout the organizing years, IOC President Juan Antonio Samaranch, like Avery Brundage some twenty years earlier, received a barrage of letters from concerned individuals and environmental organizations, locally, nationally, and globally. Olympic insiders responded in a characteristic fashion, shifting responsibility from one Olympic organizational body to the next. By 1985, OCO'88 had a mostly pre-scripted response letter for all environmental-related criticism, explaining that environmental affairs were the responsibility of the province and, in condescending fashion, suggested that "Once these facts *are understood by yourself* we are confident that your concerns will be laid to rest."[80] A copy of the letter in the archival repository has affixed to it a yellow sticky note recommending to organizing committee members, "Let's use the same approach for every one!"[81] While the focus of this chapter is not to analyze the interactions between settler environmentalists and Olympic officers, this example demonstrates that in their efforts to resist Olympic expansive capitalism, settler environmentalists did so according to their own colonizing frameworks, failing to observe the long presence of Indigenous peoples, Indigenous traditional ecological knowledge, including knowledge of wildlife such as the grizzly, and the legal framework that allowed (and allows) for the settlement by others of Treaty 7 territory.

FIGURE 3.2. Construction on Wataga ipa (Mount Allan). Credit: City of Calgary Archives, XV Olympic Winter Games Olympic Photograph Collection fonds, Binder 01, Image oco-01-110-04-0587.

A comprehensive review of archival materials, including letters, news source materials, and planning documents, confirms that at no point did Olympic organizers or environmentalists consider the legal rights of Treaty 7 First Nations. Specifically, there is no mention of Treaty 7 nor acknowledgement that throughout the years of Olympic organizing, the treaty rights of Indigenous and settler peoples were reaffirmed through the patriation of Canada's supreme legal instrument—its constitution—on April 17, 1982. The first part of the Constitution is dedicated to the *Charter of Rights and Freedoms,* with Section 25 affirming that "The guarantee in this Charter of certain rights and freedoms shall not be construed as to abrogate or derogate from any aboriginal, treaty or other rights or freedoms that pertain to the aboriginal peoples of Canada."[82] Section 35 of the *Constitution Act* is dedicated to the "Rights of Aboriginal Peoples of Canada"; subsection (1) acknowledges that "The existing aboriginal and treaty rights of the aboriginal peoples of Canada are hereby recognized and affirmed."[83] Although this was the legal and political framework Olympic organizers were operating in throughout the planning years, it seemingly had no bearing on the organizing efforts for these Olympic Winter Games.

A review of archival records confirms that organizers remained apathetic to Indigenous land rights—that is, until a relatively small Indigenous nation from Treaty 8 territory in northern Alberta brought their treaty claims to the forefront of Olympic organizing. To briefly summarize, in 1985, member of Muskotew Sakahikan Enowuk, commonly known as Lubicon Lake Cree Nation, called for a boycott of the 1988 Olympic Winter Games in a tactical move to bring national and global attention to their 85-year outstanding treaty claim. By the 1970s, petroleum companies had invaded Lubicon territory, actively destroying their way of life.[84] In fact, two of the petroleum companies invading Lubicon territory were official sponsors of these Olympic Games. Lubicon dissent was of notable concern, compelling organizers to consider the formal involvement of Indigenous people in the organizing of the Games. In typical colonial, paternalistic fashion, organizers anticipated that Indigenous people could serve important cultural roles, including that of tourist attraction. For example, in early deliberations about Indigenous involvement, OCO'88 president Bill Pratt claimed, "You'll probably see more Indian people together at the opening ceremonies than you've ever seen . . . because the Europeans are crazy about [Indians]."[85] The creation of the Native Participation Program was confirmed in late 1987—less than a year and a half before the Games were scheduled to open—and was responsible for organizing events to be held within the purview of the cultural program of these Winter Olympics.[86]

As the years went on and Lubicon pressure on the organizing committee and governments mounted, leaders of Treaty 7 First Nations—to varying degrees—expressed support for Lubicon land rights and further frustration with the tokenistic nature of Indigenous involvement. In the rare instances when economic opportunities were discussed, they were usually denounced rather quickly. For example, in considering potential economic opportunities available to Stoney peoples, Mark Lowey of the *Calgary Herald*, again in typical colonial paternalistic fashion, explained that "Mount Allan, venue for the Olympic downhill events, is in Kananaskis Country—not on an Indian reserve. The closest Indian band is the Stoneys, who at the turn of the century signed a treaty with Ottawa and obtained a reserve at Morely. Some Stoneys will be performing traditional native dances during Olympic ceremonies" (see figure 3.3).[87] In the end, the involvement of Treaty 7 First Nations was mostly an organizational afterthought, resulting mainly in their precarious placement in opening and closing ceremony performances involving stereotypical clashes between "cowboys and Indians." As otipemisiwak/Métis scholar Jennifer Adese avows, "the tropes of the cowboy and Indian are indeed the 'nation's most passionate, embedded form of hate talk.' Ceremonial displays such

FIGURE 3.3. Bird's eye view of Alpine ski runs on Wataga ipa (Mount Allan).
Credit: City of Calgary Archives, XV Olympic Winter Games Photograph
Collection fonds, Binder 01, Image oco-01-110-04-0498.

as [the Calgary ceremonies] really only serve as 'grim reminders of the
weak attempts by Canadians to conceal historical oppressive relations
between cultures, a rather hideous past, and a tension-filled present.'"[88]
Stereotypical displays such as these also serve the central goals of settler colonialism, which is the further dispossession and appropriation of
Indigenous territories and resources by and for the benefit of settlers.

Conclusion

There is little to no evidence suggesting Indigenous peoples participated
in organizing and/or hosting the Winter Olympics in the first half of the
twentieth century or that they were impacted by the hosting of the Games
on their territories. Early Olympic environmental history on Turtle Island,
and associated discourse, are premised on the actions and perspectives of
settler environmentalists who relied on familiar conceptual frameworks of
landscapes as comprising "empty spaces." Settler environmentalists' failure to see Indigenous peoples, and Indigenous people's deep connections

to these places, is quite literally dependent on the physical (often violent) removal of such peoples from the lands they have occupied and cared for since time immemorial as well as their erasure from settler consciousness. It operates to dispossess Indigenous peoples of their territories further. The prospect of Olympic expansive capitalism, environmental damage, and the further dispossession of Indigenous territories became a reality for Treaty 7 First Nations in the 1960s when politicians and business-men attempted, on three occasions, to bring the Games to Mohkinstsis and its surrounding areas. Those environmentalists credited with hav-ing thwarted the three consecutive bids did so through a "coloniality of power" framework, thereby failing to uphold their legal responsibilities to Treaty 7. The 1988 Olympic Winter Games were eventually awarded to Calgary in 1981, in a period of sweeping legal and political transformation in Canada, seemingly unbeknownst to Olympic organizers and settler environmentalists. As explained by the late Lazarus Ta Daa Wesley of the Stoney (Bearspaw) Nation, esteemed Stoney Nakoda elder, knowledge holder, and lifelong advocate of treaty rights, "at the time [1877] nothing was ever mentioned about cutting up the land here and there into recre-ational areas and provincial parks, etc. The government didn't tell them it would be doing this. It is because of these special areas, we can't go hunting. In the Kananaskis valley we can't hunt because it is now a park . . . The government says you can hunt. You have the right to hunt, but there is nowhere to hunt."[89] Suffice to say, at the time of treaty negotiation, nothing was ever mentioned to First Nations about cutting up the land here and there into recreational and elite sporting spaces that would serve the interests of predominantly affluent settlers and their international guests. And while settler environmentalists were undoubtedly at odds with politicians and Games' organizers, in the end, the colonizing frameworks that all these groups were operating within resulted in the strengthening of boundaries around people, animals, nonhumans, air, lands, and waters, and, ultimately, the further dispossession of Treaty 7 territories.

Notes

1. CFN Productions, "Elder Clarence Wolfleg Miiksika'am: Warrior, Leader and Teacher," January 19, 2022, YouTube video, https://youtu.be/d63exSlxSrc.

2. J. M. Bacon, "Settler Colonialism as Eco-Social Structure and the Produc-tion of Colonial Ecological Violence," *Environmental Sociology* 5, no. 1 (2019), 59.

3. Rita Dhamoon, "A Feminist Approach to Decolonizing Antiracism: Rethinking Transnationalism, Intersectionality, and Settler Colonialism," *Feral Feminisms* 4 (2015), 32.

4. Bacon, "Settler Colonialism as Eco-Social Structure," 59.

5. Stephen Essex and Brian Chalkley, "Mega-Sporting Events in Urban and Regional Policy: A History of the Winter Olympics," *Planning Perspectives* 19 (2004), 206.

6. See Essex and Chalkley, "Mega-Sporting Events," 201–32; Jean-Loup Chappelet, "Olympic Environmental Concerns as a Legacy of the Winter Games," *The International Journal of the History of Sport* 25, no. 14 (2008), 1884–1902; and Helen Jefferson Lenskyj, "The Winter Olympic: Geography is Destiny?" in Helen Jefferson Lenskyj and Stephen Wagg (eds.), *The Palgrave Handbook of Olympic Studies* (London: Palgrave Macmillan, 2012), 88–102.

7. Bacon, "Settler Colonialism as Eco-Social Structure," 61.

8. Melissa Otis, "'Location of Exchange': Algonquian and Iroquoian Occupation in the Adirondacks Before and After Contact," *Environment, Space and Place* 5, no. 2 (2013), 8.

9. In this paper, I refer to this territory in my Abenaki language as Wawôbadenik.

10. Otis, "'Location of Exchange,'" 9–11.

11. For more information on the Doctrine of Discovery and Manifest Destiny, see Robert J. Miller, "American Indians, The Doctrine of Discovery, and Manifest Destiny," *Wyoming Law Review* 11, no. 2 (2011), 330–31.

12. Jonathan Alzalone, *Battles of the North Country: Wilderness Politics and Recreational Development in the Adirondack State Park, 1920–1980* (Amherst: University of Massachusetts Press, 2018), 12.

13. Alzalone, *Battles of the North Country,* 16.

14. Alzalone, *Battles of the North Country*, 13.

15. George M. Lattimer, compiler, *Official Report: III Olympic Winter Games, Lake Placid, 1932* (Lake Placid, NY: III Winter Olympic Games Committee, 1932), 159–61.

16. *Association Protection Adirondacks v. MacDonald*, 253 N. Y. 234, 170 N. E. 902 (N. Y. 1930).

17. Peter M. Hopsicker, "Racing with Death: The Not-So-Ordinary Happenings of the 1932 Lake Placid Olympic Bobsled Events," *Journal of Sport History* 41, no. 1 (2014), 80.

18. Peter M. Hopsicker, "Legalizing the 1932 Lake Placid Olympic Bobrun: A Test of the Adirondack Wilderness Culture," *Olympia* XVIII (2009), 113.

19. Alzalone, *Battles of the North Country*, 34.

20. Melissa Otis, *Rural Indigenousness: A History of Iroquoian and Algonquian Peoples of the Adirondacks* (Syracuse, NY: Syracuse University Press, 2018), 214.

21. It was announced in September 2021 that the resort had abandoned its racially derogatory name, recognizing that the word "squaw" has been used as a slur, historically and presently, by settlers to refer to Indigenous women and girls. After decades of deliberations and consultations with Washoe tribal members, community officials announced that the name would be changed to Palisades

Tahoe. See Monique Beals, "Squaw Valley Ski Resort Announces New Name After Criticism," *The Hill*, September 13, 2021, https://thehill.com/news-by-subject/other/571994-squaw-valley-ski-resort-announces-new-name-after-criticism.

22. According to Wá·šiw language speakers, Tahoe is a mispronunciation of Daʔaw. As these speakers point out, the anglicized name of the lake is nonsensical because it simply translates to lake, lake. See Ezra David Romero, "It's Not Just a Ski Report: From Tahoe to Carson, Indigenous People Say Names Misrepresent Them," CapRadio, July 21, 2020, https://www.capradio.org/articles/2020/07/21/its-not-just-a-ski-resort-from-tahoe-to-carson-indigenous-people-say-sierra-names-misrepresent-them.

23. Christine Gordon, "Where Wašiw is Spoken: The Washoe Tribe Is Passing Its Unique Language On and Up," *American Indian* 20, no. 2 (2019), https://www.americanindianmagazine.org/story/where-wasiw-spoken.

24. David C. Antonucci, *Snowball's Chance: The Story of the 1960 Olympic Winter Games* (Lake Tahoe, CA: Art of Learning Publishing, 2010), 7.

25. Gordon, "Where Wašiw is Spoken."

26. Brian Friel, "The Future of Squaw Valley and Alpine Meadows," theses in partial fulfillment of a Bachelor of Arts degree at Pomona College (2015), *Pomona Senior Theses*, Paper 126, 9, https://scholarship.claremont.edu/pomona_theses/126/.

27. Conor Villines, "The California Ski Boom: Tourism, Urban Growth, Environmentalism, and Social Diversity in Sierra Nevada Ski Areas, 1960–1980," *Footnotes* 3 (2019), 97.

28. Villines, "The California Ski Boom," 106.

29. Tahoe Environmental Research Center (TERC), "Environmental Issues Facing Lake Tahoe," in chapter 4 of the Docent Manual, "Science and Research at Lake Tahoe" (version 10, updated September 2022), https://tahoe.ucdavis.edu/sites/g/files/dgvnsk4286/files/inline-files/Docent%20Manual%20Chapter%204%20-%20Science%20&%20Research.pdf; you can also find a link to the chapter at the Docent Program page, accessed March 13, 2024, https://tahoe.ucdavis.edu/docents.

30. TERC, 25.

31. "Washoe History: A Brief Summary," Washoe Tribe, accessed March 13, 2024, https://washoetribe.us/aboutpage/4-Page-washoe-history.

32. Conor Villines employs this expression when describing significant transformations throughout the region following the 1960 Olympic Winter Games. See Villines, "The California Ski Boom," 97.

33. Alanya Alvarez, "Denver City Council to Read Indigenous Land Acknowledgement Following Pledge of Allegiance," *Colorado Politics*, October 27, 2020, updated November 9, 2020, https://www.coloradopolitics.com/denver/denver-city-council-to-read-indigenous-land-acknowledgement-following-pledge-of-allegiance/article_8f2585c8-185c-11eb-83f9-7be9e58de513.html.

34. Aldora "Dodie" White Eagle, "Auraria Campus Land Acknowledgement," University of Colorado Denver, https://www.ucdenver.edu/offices/

diversity-and-inclusion/about-us/land-acknowledgement#ac-aurarias
-establishment-1.

35. Andrew R. Goetz and E. Eric Boschmann, *Metropolitan Denver: Growth and Change in the Mile High City* (Philadelphia: University of Pennsylvania Press, 2018), 4.

36. Treaties that cover parts of Colorado include the Treaty of Abiquiú (1849), Treaty of Fort Laramie (1851), Treaty of Fort Wise (1861), Conejos Treaty (1863), Medicine Lodge Treaty (1867), Little Arkansas Treaty (1868), Ute Treaty of 1868, Brunot Agreement (1873). See Elliot West, *Contested Plains: Indians, Goldseekers, and Rush to Colorado* (Lawrence: University of Kansas Press, 1998).

37. Goetz and Boschmann, *Metropolitan Denver*, 15.

38. Abby Hickcox, "Green Belt, White City: Race and the Natural Landscape in Boulder, Colorado," *Discourse* 29, no. 2 (2007), 242.

39. Bacon, "Settler Colonialism as Eco-Social Structure," 59.

40. Andrew Baldwin, "Ethnoscaping Canada's Boreal Forest: Liberal Whiteness and its Disaffiliation from Colonial Space," *The Canadian Geographer* 53, no. 4 (2009), 432.

41. John Karamichas, *The Olympic Games and the Environment* (London: Palgrave Macmillan, 2013), 32.

42. Villines, "The California Ski Boom," 105.

43. For example, see Kevin B. Wamsley and Michael Heine, "Tradition, Modernity, and the Construction of Civic Identity: The Calgary Olympics," *Olympika* 5 (1996), 81–90, and Kevin B. Wamsley and Michael Heine, "'Don't Mess with the Relay—It's Bad Medicine': Aboriginal Culture and the 1988 Winter Olympics," in *Olympic Perspectives: Third International Symposium for Olympic Research*, edited by R. K. Barney, S. G. Martyn, D. A. Brown, and G. H. MacDonald (London, ON: International Centre for Olympic Research, 1996), 173–78.

44. XV Olympic Winter Games Organizing Committee, "XV Olympic Winter Games: Official Report," 1988 (Calgary, AB: Calgary Olympic Development Association, 1988), 51, https://library.olympics.com/Default/doc/SYRACUSE/43821/rapport-officiel-des-xves-jeux-olympiques-d-hiver-xv-olympic-winter-games-official-report?_lg=en-GB.

45. Brian Noble, "Treaty Ecologies: With Persons, Peoples, Animals, and the Land," in *Resurgence and Reconciliation: Indigenous-Settler Relations and Earth Teachings*, edited by Michael Asch, John Borrows, and James Tully, 315–42 (Toronto: University of Toronto Press, 2018), 319.

46. Treaty 7 Elders and Tribal Council with Walter Hildebrandt, Dorothy First Rider, and Sarah Carter, *The True Spirit and Original Intent of Treaty 7* (Montreal: McGill-Queen's University Press, 1996), 4.

47. Treaty 7 Elders et al., *The True Spirit*, vii.

48. Jim Thunder, "Voices from Our Past: Crowfoot Valued Land more than Gov't Money," *Windspeaker* 5, no. 9 (1987), 35.

49. Noble, "Treaty Ecologies," 320.

50. Treaty 7 Elders et al., *The True Spirit*, 144–45.

51. Treaty 7 Elders et al., *The True Spirit*, 323–24.

52. Noble, "Treaty Ecologies," 322.

53. See, Heather L. Dichter, "Canadian Government Involvement in Calgary's Failed 1968 Olympic Bid," *The International Journal of the History of Sport* 38, no. 13–14 (2021), 1329–49; Cheryl Williams, "The Banff Winter Olympics: Sport, Tourism, and Banff National Park," MA thesis, Faculty of Physical Education and Recreation, University of Alberta, 2011; and Russell Field, "Banff 1972: Sportsmen, Conservationists, and the Debate over Banff National Park," chapter 1 in this collection.

54. For example, see Courtney W. Mason, "Colonial Encounters, Conservation, and Sport Hunting in Banff National Park," in *Sport and Recreation in Canadian History*, edited by Carly Adams 77–100 (Champaign, IL: Human Kinetics, 2020) and PearlAnn Reichwein, *Climbers Paradise: Making Canada's Mountain Parks, 1906–1974* (Edmonton: University of Alberta Press, 2014).

55. For example, see Chappelet, "Olympic Environmental Concerns,"1889, and Anthony Gino Del Fiacco and Madeleine Orr, "A Review and Synthesis of Environmentalism within the Olympic Movement," *International Journal of Event and Festival Management* 10, no. 1 (2018), 69.

56. Mason, "Colonial Encounters," 85.

57. Mason, 83–90.

58. Mason, 94.

59. Hal Eidsvik, National Parks Planner (January 13, 2011), as cited in Williams, "The Banff Winter Olympics," 77.

60. Harvey Locke, "Civil Society and Protected Areas: Lessons from Canada's Experience," *The George Wright Forum* 26, no. 2 (2009): 113.

61. Locke, "Civil Society and Protected Areas," 101.

62. Dina Gilio-Whitaker, *As Long as Grass Grows: The Indigenous Fight for Environmental Justice, from Colonization to Standing Rock* (Boston: Beacon Press, 2019), 93.

63. "XV Olympic Winter Games: Official Report," 51.

64. Calgary Olympic Development Association (CODA), *Calgary Canada*, official bid file of Calgary for the Olympic Winter Games in 1988 (Lausanne: International Olympic Committee, 1981), 78–95, https://library.olympics.com/Default/digital-viewer/c-56437.

65. For example, see Brian L. Horejsi, "Bighorn Sheep, Mount Allan, and the 1988 Winter Olympics: Politics and Biological Realities," *Proceedings of the Fifth Biennial Symposium, Northern Wild Sheep and Goat Council, 1986* (Missoula, MT, April 14–17, 1986), 313–24; and Michelle Nicole Murray, "Alberta Ski Resorts on the Eastern Slopes and Environmental Advocacy: Conservation Politics and Tourism Development in Kananaskis Country, 1980–2000" (MA thesis, University of Alberta, 2018).

66. *Calgary Canada*, 51.

67. Murray, "Alberta Ski Resorts," 39.

68. Murray, 48–49.

69. Stoney Consultation Team—Stoney Tribal Administration, "Stoney Nakoda Nations Cultural Assessment for the "Enhancing grizzly bear management programs through the inclusion of cultural monitoring and traditional ecological knowledge," report prepared for Environment Canada, 10, accessed March 13, 2024, https://a.storyblok.com/f/112697/x/aac0e71d75/stoney-nakoda-nations-cultural-assessment-for-the-enhancing-grizzly-bear-management-programs-through-the-inclusion-of-cultural-monitoring-and-traditional-ecological.pdf.

70. Stoney Consultation Team, "Stoney Nakoda Nations Cultural Assessment," 13.

71. Stoney Consultation Team, 16.

72. Murray, "Alberta Ski Resorts," 39.

73. Irene M. Spry, "Captain John Palliser and the Exploration of Western Canada," *The Geographical Journal* 125, no. 2 (1959), 163–64.

74. Alberta Parks, "Kananaskis Country—History," updated November 6, 2018, https://www.albertaparks.ca/parks/kananaskis/kananaskis-country/information-facilities/history.

75. Murphy, "Alberta Ski Resorts," 39.

76. Horejsi, "Bighorn Sheep, Mount Allan," 318–19.

77. Alberta Olympic Secretariat, *Mount Allan Master Plan: Summary Information Document* (Edmonton, AB: Alberta Olympic Secretariat, 1984), 1, https://archive.org/details/mountallanmaster00albe/page/n1/mode/2up.

78. "Row Brewing over Calgary Olympics Downhill Ski Site," *The Citizen*, April 27, 1983, 50.

79. Horejsi, "Bighorn Sheep, Mount Allan," 319.

80. See the letter from Frank King to Celia Lindblom, August 1, 1985, XV Olympic Winter Games Communications Group Fonds, Series II Communication Group, Sub Series: General Files, Box 4, File: Environmental Concerns, 1985–1986, The City of Calgary Archives (emphasis added).

81. King to Lindblom.

82. *Canadian Charter of Rights and Freedoms,* s. 25, Part 1 of the *Constitution Act,* 1982, being Schedule B to the *Canada Act 1982* (UK), 1982, c 11.

83. *The Constitution Act,* 1982, s. 35, being Schedule B to the Canada Act 1982 (UK), 1982, c 11.

84. For more information on Lubicon history and controversy concerning the Olympic Games, see Dawn Martin-Hill, *The Lubicon Lake Nation: Indigenous Knowledge and Power* (Toronto: University of Toronto Press, 2008) and Darlene Ferreira, "Oil and Lubicons Don't Mix: A Land Claim in Northern Alberta in Historical Perspective," *Canadian Journal of Native Studies* 12, no. 1 (1992): 1–35.

85. Wendy Smith, "Indians Told They're a Games Attraction," *Calgary Herald*, February 11, 1985, B2.

86. Communication, Skyes F. Powerderface (Coordinator, Native Liaison) to European journalists (September 21, 1987), XV Olympic Winter Games Communications Group Fonds, Series II. Communication Group, Sub Series: General Files, Box 4, File: Natives, 1985–1987, The City of Calgary Archives.

87. Mark Lowey, "Errors on Games Send Klein to Europe," *Calgary Herald*, October 20, 1987, B1.

88. Michael Yellowbird, "Toys of Genocide: Icons of American Colonialism," *Wicazo Sa Review* 19, no. 2 (2004), 43, quoted in Jennifer Adese, "Colluding with the Enemy? Nationalism and Depictions of 'Aboriginality' in Canadian Olympic Moments," *American Indian Quarterly* 36, no. 4 (2012), 491.

89. Treaty 7 Elders et al., *The True Spirit*, 90, 335.

CHAPTER 4

Vancouver 2010

A Convergence of
Protest Movements

JULES BOYKOFF

As I ambled briskly down East Cordova Street in Vancouver in February 2010, making my way from a meeting in Japantown to an interview with an anti-Olympics activist at a coffee shop in Gastown, I spotted a gaggle of reporters filming a seemingly random storefront. As I approached, I realized that the object of their attention was not random but scandalous, at least in the eyes of Vancouver Olympics boosters. The journalists were assembling a story on a controversial mural at the Crying Room Gallery, installed by local artist Jesse Corcoran, that depicted the Olympic rings as four frowning faces and one smiling face spraypainted on a large piece of plywood (see figure 4.1). Under the spell of the Olympic state of exception, staff from the City of Vancouver requested in December 2009 that the art be removed for violating the "2010 Winter Games Sign Designation and Relaxation Bylaw" passed by the city in the runup to the Olympics. This "Sign By-Law" outlawed placards, posters, and banners that were not "celebratory," though people were allowed to display a sign "that celebrates the 2010 Winter Games, or creates or enhances a festive environment and atmosphere." In short, the ordinance criminalized anti-Olympic signs and provided Canadian authorities with the right to remove such signs, even if it meant entering private property to seize them after a 24-hour warning period. The fine for breaking the bylaw ranged from $500 to $2,000 for each offense.[1] The special, Olympics-induced law raised eyebrows among activists and civil libertarians. To them, it appeared the Canadian Charter of Rights and Freedoms was being temporarily suspended in the name of a sports mega-event. After an outcry from artists, activists, and civil liberties groups, the City of Vancouver backpedaled, asserting that the

FIGURE 4.1. Jesse Corcoran's controversial mural at the Crying Room Gallery on 157 E. Cordova Street in Vancouver. Credit: Jules Boykoff.

mural was actually removed because of an anti-graffiti bylaw. Eventually the city relented and the art was reinstalled.[2]

The episode was indicative of a wider dialectic of resistance and restriction in Olympics host cities whereby activists challenge Games-related diktats forced upon the local population while the authorities move to suppress their political dissent. The 2010 Vancouver Winter Olympics galvanized an outburst of sustained protest activity that disputed the purported benefits of the Games and illuminated the deleterious effects that the mega-event can have on marginalized populations. While the *Vancouver Sun* described protesters as a collection of "whiner and grumble-bunnies" who couldn't "hold their tongues even on a special occasion" so Canadians could "relax and cheer on the home team," the reality was a great deal more complicated.[3] A wide array of activist groups and individuals—from grassroots anarchists to civil-liberties organizations to avant-garde poets to tenured professors in local universities—teamed up to express their dissent and to mobilize public opinion against the Vancouver Olympics. Indigenous activists—First Nations, Inuit, and Métis—played an integral role in challenging the Vancouver Games, with "No Olympics on Stolen Native

Land" a central rallying call. Activists organized around three main issues: overspending, Indigenous rights, and the suppression of civil liberties.

This chapter lays out the wider political context for Canada's relationship to the Olympic Games, describes the major activist actions that occurred before and during the Vancouver Olympics, and charts the central strategies and tactics that activists adopted to challenge the Games. Because activists deliberately adopted spatial strategies and tactics, this chapter analyzes their actions through the lens of geographical theory, examining how the production of space, scale bending, and the calculated construction of discursive space helped anti-Olympics activists build camaraderie and challenge the Games. Along the way, I discuss the importance of the media—both mainstream and alternative—to activist efforts.

Activism confronting the 2010 Vancouver Winter Games marked an important historical pivot toward amplified anti-Olympics dissent across the globe. There is no question that the twenty-first century has witnessed a significant uptick in anti-Olympics activism. Rather than a "movement of movements" that subsists through time, Vancouver highlights how anti-Olympics activism tends to take a "moment of movements" formation whereby a collection of activist groups, many of which had not previously worked together in coalition, converged in an effort to challenge the five-ring juggernaut that rolled into their city and then dissolved in the aftermath of the Games. In assembling a temporary coalition of political groups to vigorously contest the Olympics, activists in Vancouver provided a positive demonstration effect for protesters in other cities bidding on or selected to host the Games. In writing this chapter, I contacted activists involved in anti-Games fightback ten years after the mega-event to get their retrospective assessments of their struggle against the Olympic machine.

Canada and the Olympics

Vancouver 2010 marked the third time a Canadian city hosted the Olympics, following the 1988 Calgary Winter Olympics and the 1976 Montreal Summer Games. Christine O'Bonsawin of the Abenaki Nation at Odanak (see chapter 3) has chronicled elsewhere how all three Olympics were met with dissent, much of it emerging from Indigenous communities.[4] David Whitson notes the tendency of these three Olympics' boosters to misleadingly flatten class interests. "Even though the invitation to identify with the civic triumphs that hosting Expositions and Olympics are said to represent is extended rhetorically to the collective 'we,' the reality is that some groups are much better positioned to experience the benefits than others," he writes. "More pointedly, some sectors of the population may actually be hurt when public spending is reallocated to Olympic infrastructure, while lower-profile community facilities and public services have their funding cut."[5]

Activists in Canada have long been willing to challenge the Olympics and their endemic downsides. For example, in Toronto, where local elites formed Olympic bids for the 1996 and 2008 Games, a group of antipoverty activists, union members, and grassroots feminists called Bread Not Circuses coalesced to offer counternarratives. Scholar Helen Jefferson Lenskyj, who was active with the group beginning in 1998, noted that the Bread Not Circuses "focused primarily on poverty and democratic decision making" vis-à-vis the Olympics.[6] It engaged in creative activism, crafting "The *Anti*-Olympic People's Bid Book" to disseminate their message about the opportunity costs that the Olympics ineluctably bring: money spent on the Games is money not spent on social programs, education, and public health. They argued three central points in their alternative "bid book":

> 1) The real needs of the people of Toronto must come first: housing, good jobs, daycare, a safe and clean city, community-based sport . . .
>
> 2) Valuable and scarce public and private resources should not be pumped into megaprojects with only crumbs spilling over for the people of our city.
>
> 3) The people of Toronto must be involved directly with the decision-making in the city. The voice of the people must be heard. Corporations have controlled the agenda designed by and for their own needs for too long.[7]

At the time, Toronto was revving up its bid for the 1996 Summer Games, with Paul Henderson in charge, a former athlete on Canada's national sailing team whose Olympic dream was shattered by Canada's decision to boycott the 1980 Games in Moscow. Henderson was the President of the Toronto Ontario Olympic Council, and he vociferously disagreed with Olympic detractors. In one Christmas card that Henderson wrote to prominent anti-Games critic Michael Shapcott, he asserted, "As you are fully aware, I do not agree with your political stance that you must destroy so as to create what is proported [sic] to be a 'just' society." Henderson also enclosed a donation to the Toronto Christian Resource Centre for $1,000; Shapcott was a community development worker with the organization.[8] Shapcott responded, "I have no doubt that certain people feel uncomfortable when Bread Not Circuses denounces the allocation of billions of dollars in public and private resources towards super-expensive spectaculars at a time when people are literally freezing to death on the streets of

Toronto. The political priorities of this city are wrong." He added, "The real needs of the people of Toronto may interfere with your plan to bring the '96 Games to this city, but we put those needs ahead of megaprojects."[9]

To the satisfaction of activists and the bitter chagrin of Henderson, Toronto lost to Atlanta in the race for the 1996 Games. Henderson asserted that the pushback from Bread Not Circuses "certainly didn't help" the cause. Toronto City Council member Tony O'Donohue noted that because of activist pushback, "We sent out mixed signals internationally that we weren't really with the Games and that really did us a lot of damage," even concluding, "I think we lost the Games because of it."[10] Activists from Bread Not Circuses aimed to inflict additional "damage" on the Olympic machine. The group sent two members to Tokyo in 1990 to protest a meeting of the International Olympic Committee (IOC) alongside anti-Games groups in Japan. Activists from Bread Not Circuses also shared knowledge and tactics with anti-Games groups in Vancouver.[11]

Activists in Toronto demonstrated the effectiveness of fending off bids *before* the IOC has named a host. Once the Games have been allocated to a city, they are much more difficult to rebuff, with modern history offering only one instance, the 1976 Denver Winter Olympics, where an ideologically diverse coalition of activists used a public referendum to jettison the Games (see chapter 2).[12] In February 2003, Vancouver voters were presented with a plebiscite to gauge public support for hosting the Games. The pro-Olympics "Yes" side won out with 64 percent of the vote, although only 40 percent of eligible voters opted to weigh in and boosters spent $700,000 to persuade the public, around 140 times more than the "No" side, and in an atmosphere thrumming with mass-media boosterism.[13] After the vote, the IOC eventually chose Vancouver over Salzburg, Austria, and Pyeongchang, South Korea.

But the selection of Vancouver to host the Games did not stunt dissent. An uncommon blend of activists joined forces—Indigenous dissidents, antipoverty groups, environmentalists, anarchists, socialists, and civil-liberties attorneys—to push back. Despite differences both ideological and tactical, the coalition fomented remarkable, crosscutting solidarity. O'Bonsawin told me that "Although the interests and concerns of the groups and individuals were broad in scope, the No Games 2010 coalition was efficient in that it brought together a large number of activists under one umbrella who then effectively supported the interests of one another."[14] Anti-Games activism consisted of a two-track fightback, working inside the institutional corridors of power and applying pressure from the outside through innovative direct action. Activists adopted a "diversity of tactics" approach by which protesters with diverging styles and preferred methods made a pact to support each other—or at least not publicly denigrate each other—during the extended anti-Games moment.[15]

Drivers of Dissent

As preparations for the Vancouver Olympics unfolded, activist attention united around three central issues: overspending, Indigenous rights, and the suppression of civil liberties. The Vancouver Olympics were a budget-buster. The five-ring price tag was originally estimated at a little over $1 billion.[16] The month before the Games, however, costs had ballooned to $6 billion, and post-Olympics estimates soared into the $7.6 billion to $8 billion range.[17] Knowing the exact cost is complicated by the fact that Olympic organizers refused to share their books. Summing it up, Micheal Vonn, at the time of the Games the Policy Director at the British Columbia Civil Liberties Association (BCCLA), remarked, "the Olympics were an anti-transparency device."[18] The economic collapse of 2008 couldn't have come at a worse time for Olympic organizers, but they had already made a habit of incessantly lowballing costs. Overspending is ingrained into the Olympics, with one study finding that every Games between 1960 and 2016 for which reliable data exist went over budget. In real terms, the average cost overrun was 156 percent, a significantly higher rate than other megaprojects.[19]

Days before the Games began, activist Am Johal told me, "The Olympics are a corporate franchise that you buy with public money."[20] The most egregious instance of the Canadian public being forced to backstop private ineptitude was the construction of the athletes' Olympic Village. The Olympic Village was supposed to be the crown jewel of Olympic development. However, the project became a fiscal debacle that hemorrhaged public funds. Millennium, the private developer that had won the bid to build the Olympic Village, absconded from its fiscal responsibilities while the Village was only half built. *Globe and Mail* columnist Gary Mason called it "one of the biggest financial losses in the City of Vancouver's history." Olympic organizers had initially promised that 20 percent of all units would be converted into nonmarket housing for low-income people. But once taxpayers took on responsibility for construction costs, which ballooned to $875 million a full year before the Games began, the city opted to recoup what it could from condominium sales, thereby injecting an incentive to ditch the social housing promises in the name of fiscal responsibility.[21] In addition, Vancouver used its limited loan guarantees to rescue the developers' epic fail. Moreover, to many, the opportunity costs were flabbergasting: taxpayer money was spent on a weekslong sports party rather than indispensable social services for local residents.

A second front for dissent involved Indigenous rights and the battle against settler colonialism. The Vancouver Olympics were staged on unceded aboriginal (Coast Salish) land. Thus, the spectre of dispossession haunted the Olympics and "No Olympics on Stolen Native Land" became a principal anti-Olympics slogan. Activist Dawn Paley pointed out the importance of brocading economic and Indigenous analysis: "To me the most important thing about the anti-Olympics movement was that our organizing was against capitalism and colonialism."[22] Harsha Walia added, "We forefronted the issue of Indigenous sovereignty as the grounding and the foundation of our resistance. That was significant because it ensured and highlighted the possibility of coming together in coalition, but not in a way that was the lowest common denominator, as often happens in coalition politics, but rather the inverse."[23]

In British Columbia, First Nations have a unique relationship with the Canadian state. In other parts of Canada, the British Crown signed treaties with aboriginal groups in alignment with the Royal Proclamation of 1763, which declared that only the Crown could obtain Indigenous lands. In 1867, when British colonies became confederated as Canadian provinces, aboriginal-settler treaties had already been established. However, in British Columbia, which joined the Confederation in 1871, only fifteen treaties had been forged (the Vancouver Island Treaties, also known as the Douglas Treaties), while aboriginal title to the remainder of the region was left unresolved. With the exception of Treaty 8, negotiated in 1899, and the Nisga'a Treaty, which was completed in 2000, treatymaking stopped, although a 1973 Supreme Court decision—*Calder v. British Columbia*—jumpstarted the possibility of negotiations, with the Court ruling that aboriginal title had actually not been extinguished in BC.[24] According to Indigenous intellectual Taiaiake Alfred, lacking treaty relations British Columbia "remains in a perpetual colonialism-resistance dynamic."[25] This was vital to anti-Games activists in Vancouver who highlighted that Olympic athletes were skiing the slopes and hitting the halfpipes on aboriginal land.

All that said, aboriginal people played a more prominent role in the 2010 Winter Games than in any previous Olympics. In November 2004, four First Nations from British Columbia—the Lil'wat, Musqueam, Squamish, and Tsleil-Waututh peoples—came together to create the Four Host First Nations, agreeing to work together to assist with the Games. For the first time, the IOC recognized aboriginal people as official host partners. The

Olympic mascots were First Nations—inspired: Miga, a mythical sea bear; Quatchi, a sasquatch; and Sumi, an animal spirit. While the Four Host First Nations took center stage at the Olympics—and benefited economically from their willingness to partake—eighty of the 203 Indigenous bands in British Columbia refused to participate, a remarkable statistic in light of ubiquitous pro-Olympic propaganda and the possibility of economic gain.[26] The Vancouver Games, despite their hype, did not bring significant job creation for Indigenous people. In 2006–2007 Aboriginal people comprised 1.2 percent of workers in the Vancouver Organizing Committee. Between 2007 and 2009 this increased slightly—to 3 percent—before unaccountably decreasing to only 1 percent in 2009–2010.[27]

The third driver of anti-Olympics dissent were concerns that civil liberties were being threatened by a massively militarized police force. Policing and security officials tend to leverage the state of exception brought on by the Games as a once-in-a-lifetime opportunity to secure laws and weaponry that might be unavailable during normal political times. This creates a boon for the security industry in the name of squelching potential terrorist activity. But it also translates into a repressive atmosphere for those who may wish to express anti-Olympics dissent. The military-grade fortressification of host cites during mega-events has become commonplace, and the Winter Olympics in Vancouver were no exception. Activist Harsha Walia described the Olympic security apparatus as creating "the overall militarization of Vancouver, an encroaching police and surveillance state."[28]

The security budget was originally estimated at $175 million, but eventually skyrocketed to more than $1 billion, a process Gord Hill, an Indigenous activist from the Kwakwaka'wakw Nation, described to me as "police extortion from the ruling class."[29] Canadian officials used that money to create the Vancouver Integrated Security Unit (VISU)—a fusion of the Royal Canadian Mounted Police and more than twenty policing agencies. VISU patrolled Olympic space, establishing a surveillance-drenched urban terrain while employing 17,000 security agents, including people from the RCMP, the Canadian Security Intelligence Service (CSIS), city police forces, and private security officers. The Canadian Border Services Agency inserted their officers into Vancouver's Downtown Eastside neighborhood—an eight-by-fifteen-block strip of urban space that is Canada's poorest postal code outside of aboriginal reserves—where they demanded residents provide proof of citizenship. Police with semiautomatic weapons attended demonstrations, normalizing militarization. The Office of the Privacy Commissioner of Canada reported the installation of nearly a thousand surveillance cameras in greater Vancouver (see figure 4.2).[30] Helicopters whirred overhead. CF-18 Hornet fighter jets occasionally

FIGURE 4.2. Photograph of surveillance camera attached to a metal post in the Olympic zone. Credit: Jules Boykoff.

zoomed by. Vancouver Integrated Security Unit purchased a Medium Range Acoustic Device (MRAD)—a military-grade weapon battle-tested in places like Afghanistan—although due to negative press and intense pressure from activists and the British Columbia Civil Liberties Association, the MRAD was kept in the box during the Games. Importantly, the high-tech policing equipment acquired during the Olympics-induced state of exception can eventually become the quotidian instruments of the post-Games new normal: military-style weaponry that can be employed in everyday policing.

The "2010 Winter Games Sign Designation and Relaxation Bylaw" mentioned above was supplemented by a slew of extraordinary rules and laws. "Their strategic effect," notes scholar Michael Heine, "sought to censure open dissent."[31] Another function was to make the Olympic space appealing to global tourists and journalists. At the provincial level, British Columbia passed the Assistance to Shelter Act, which criminalized homelessness while sacrificing human rights on the altar of property rights. The law allowed police to forcibly place the homeless into shelters; the timing of the law made it clear it was designed for social cleansing in the name of Olympics spectacle production.[32] In advance of the Olympics, the bland-sounding Project Civil City provided city officials with an opportunity to regulate social classes with an eye on "sanitizing" targeted urban spaces to make them more palatable to the global media.[33]

State surveillance created urban microgeographies of social control. Ahead of the Games, CSIS and other VISU officials refused to rule out the possibility that their infiltrating agents would break the law or try to assume leadership positions within anti-Olympic groups. Victoria Police Chief Jamie Graham even bragged to the audience at the Vancouver International Security Conference that a police infiltrator had wormed his way into the movement, becoming a bus driver who transported activists attending a protest of the Olympic torch relay.[34] Outspoken Olympics critic Christopher Shaw, the author of *Five Ring Circus: Myths and Realities of the Olympic Games*, experienced intense harassment from VISU. Beginning in June 2009, he began getting VISU visits at home, at work, and on the street. Sometimes officials would be holding a copy of his book, alleging they found "disturbing information" they wanted to discuss and that VISU investigator Jeff Francis "says hi." By the time 2010 rolled around these visits were almost daily occurrences, with VISU also questioning his friends, girlfriend, and ex-wife.[35] Activists point out that essentially everyone involved in the Olympic Resistance Network was visited by VISU for questioning.

Activism, Event Coalitions, and the Production of Space

The Olympic Charter forbids the expression of dissent: "No kind of demonstration or political, religious or racial propaganda is permitted in any Olympic sites, venues or other areas."[36] Nevertheless, when the Olympics touch down in a host city, dissent soon follows, with activists springboarding off the event in an attempt to shift politics to their advantage. In Vancouver, the confluence of critiques discussed above roused a groundswell of dissent. Groups like the No Games 2010 Coalition pinpointed the perils of the Olympic industrial complex and began a long-term public education project to demystify the Games. Watchdog groups like Impacts on Community Coalition hosted numerous public panels and seminars. Already existing groups like No One Is Illegal and the Anti-Poverty Committee lent a radical analysis of the Olympic juggernaut rooted in anticolonialism and anticapitalism, with numerous religious, social, environmental, and Indigenous groups also getting involved: Streams of Justice, the Power of Women Group, No 2010 Olympics on Stolen Native Land, Native Youth Movement, and Van.Act!. Many individuals from these groups worked with the Olympic Resistance Network, a highly effective, decentralized, nonhierarchical, antiauthoritarian alliance rooted in consensus-style democracy and mutual aid that was formed in Spring 2008. The paroxysm of activism benefited from the decision of local universities to cancel classes during the Games, creating a fresh infusion of students with newfound free time.

Event coalitions are temporary convergences of activist organizations that coalesce around common goals, tactics, and strategies during a particular episode of contention.[37] Groups rising up to challenge the Olympics have forged contingent alliances with shared interests that build affinities—and sometimes even solidarity—in the extended moment induced by a mega-event. Compared to a social movement that engages in sustained, consistent interactional dissent over time, event coalitions emerge in response to a single event where there is relatively shallow, temporary cooperation between organizations that largely evaporates after the event transpires, when demonstrators return to "normal activism" related to the primary issues that animate them.[38] Anti-Olympics activism in Vancouver was a vibrant *moment* that laid key groundwork for the construction of a transnational anti-Games *movement* whereby site-to-site activist ties between anti-Olympics activists are becoming stronger.

Activists put forth a potent blend of direct-action interventions alongside more traditional protest marches. One prominent example of direct-action protests leading up to the Olympics was the Eagleridge Bluffs blockade. Environmental and First Nations activists combined to oppose the expansion of the Sea-to-Sky Highway connecting Vancouver to Olympic venues in Whistler through environmentally sensitive wetlands.[39] The expansion jeopardized plant and animal life in this unique forest ecosystem, which included an old Douglas fir stand and endangered red-legged frogs. Biologists noted the area was home to twenty-two plants that were rare to the region. The old-growth dry arbutus forest was a nesting space for bald eagles and an array of other protected migratory birds. Environmentalists urged Games organizers to take a different path but were met with bureaucratic inflexibility.[40] The government thwarted activism through the use of questionable legal injunctions. Activists engaging in civil disobedience were tossed in jail. David Whitson asserts the British Columbian government "rode roughshod over citizen opposition" so Olympic construction could meet its deadlines.[41]

One high-profile jailing of activists occurred in late May 2006 when Pacheedaht First Nation elder and activist Harriet Nahanee of the Nuu-chah-nulth peoples was arrested along with environmentalist Betty Krawczyk. Despite their age they were both unceremoniously tossed in jail. In February 2007, while they languished behind bars, the official Vancouver Organizing Committee held an "Olympic Countdown Ceremony" to conjure excitement for the Games. Activists attended the event, and two of them—Indigenous dissident Gord Hill and Anti-Poverty Committee activist David Cunningham—spontaneously hopped onto the stage, seized the microphone, and disrupted the event with the chants "homes not Games" and "fuck 2010." When Nahanee was released from jail she had contracted pneumonia, which ultimately led to her death in 2007. She lived on, however, as a powerful reminder of the stakes involved and part of the symbolic architecture that animated the resistance. The following month, activists caused a stir when they made off with the gargantuan Olympic flag that had been hoisted at City Hall. Shortly thereafter, a photograph of three masked activists posing in front of the flag and carrying a photograph of Nahanee was released by the Native Warrior Society. Hill later commented that the pair of direct actions "set the tone for the resistance with a very strong anticolonial, anti-capitalist analysis."[42]

Another outburst of activism in the years leading up to the Vancouver Games was a series of annual events—in 2008, 2009, and 2010—called the Poverty Olympics that were spearheaded by organizers based at the Carnegie Community Action Project (see figure 4.3). The Poverty Olympics shined a spotlight on the twin crises of homelessness and poverty that beset the city. In 2010, the biggest installation of the alternative games transpired at the Japanese Language School in the Downtown Eastside neighborhood and, under the slogan "End Poverty—It's Not a Game," activists choreographed anti-Olympics skits and played games like "the housing hurdles," the "poverty line high jump" and the broad jump across a bedbug-infested mattress. Activists also rewrote "O Canada," the national anthem, into a critique of the Olympics and created three mascots: Creepy the Cockroach, Itchy the Bedbug, and Chewy the Rat. Organizer Jean

FIGURE 4.3. Poster for the Poverty Olympics. Credit: Jules Boykoff.

Swanson, who today is a Vancouver city councillor, explained, "We had a history of trying to do fun things because that involves people." When the global media arrived, Swanson said the idea was to tell them that "if the money that was spent on the Olympics had been spent on ending poverty, we could have done it."[43]

Poverty Olympics activists hired an artist to construct a huge Olympic torch replete with a plywood flame that activists transported on a hospital gurney. They also created a smaller Olympic Poverty torch made from a plunger and festooned it with ribbons bearing anti-Games slogans. Swanson described buying ribbon from the dollar store and taping it on the side.[44] Little did she know at the time that the torch would make its way around the world. Vancouver activists passed the torch to London (2012)—based anti-Games organizer Julian Cheyne who, in turn, gave it to a New Jersey—based group of Circassian activists protesting the 2014 Sochi Olympics. (See chapter 5 for a consideration of domestic objections to the Games in Sochi.) The alternative torch eventually made its way to Rio (2016) and Pyeongchang (2018) before arriving in Tokyo (2020), where it was prominently featured at the first-ever transnational anti-Olympics summit.[45]

Anti-Olympics resistance built upon these episodes of contention to forge a place-based spatial analysis, and, according to activist Aaron Vidaver, within that analysis "the seizure of space was crucial, central."[46] A high-profile instance of spatial strategies of resistance emerged on February 15, 2010, a few days after the Games' opening ceremonies. Following a rally at Pigeon Park challenging the twin processes of gentrification and homelessness criminalization, campaigners descended on 58 West Hastings Street, where they took control of the space owned by bête-noire developer Concord Pacific and leased to Olympic organizers for use as a parking lot during the Games. The site was strategic: the lot was a highly visible location where spatial injustice is indelibly inscribed in the social landscape; Concord Pacific had a permit in hand to develop a nest of high-priced condominiums on the plot; it was capacious enough to fit the more than one hundred tents that were eventually pitched there.

In what became known as the Olympic Tent Village, activists didn't just seize space, they produced it. Upon entering the tent village, one encountered a sacred fire tended to by aboriginal elders. Another community fire burned in the back of the lot, with music, workshops, and skill-share sessions filling the area. Food Not Bombs provided victuals. Activists from Streams of Justice (a Christian social justice group) and Van.Act! (an outgrowth of the University of British Columbia's Students for a Democratic Society) assisted with logistics. A security crew prevented unwanted outsiders—like the camera-wielding media—from entering camp and helped assuage tensions that arose inside the village, at one point ejecting two suspected police infiltrators from the encampment. Leadership emerged organically from the vital organizing efforts of the Power of Women Group, a collection of Downtown Eastside residents—many of them aboriginal elders—with deep roots in the neighborhood and widespread respect within activist circles. People from this group, along with Dave Diewert of Streams of Justice and Harsha Walia of No One Is Illegal, served as media spokespeople. Every day or so community meetings helped set and enforce camp protocols and create work schedules.[47] Walia noted a tactical shift: "There's an increasing willingness to engage in more creative tactics . . . that break the ritual of protest."[48]

Creating safe spaces for dissent is important in that they provide non-competitive contact points where a diversity of individuals and organizations can work together. The Olympic Tent Village led to rare social interactions, with university students intermingling with unhoused residents, the professoriat with the subproletariat, rich exchanges that wouldn't have happened with more traditional forms of protest. The action helped crystallize relationships between groups that hadn't worked together before, bridging what Henri Lefebvre dubbed the "double morphology" of the city—"practico-sensible or material on the one hand, social on the other."[49] All these horizontal, space-producing processes sliced backward against what scholar Mustafa Dikeç describes as "the spatialization of the Other" by which he means "depriving the inhabitants of certain areas of their rights to the city in the political sense of the term."[50] Those who moved into and volunteered at the Olympic Tent Village lived politics through the everyday interactions of self-management. In the age of breakneck globalization people found ways to slow down and relate to each other. Originally, the plan was to run the tent village for five days, but because of the energy and political considerations, the space seizure was extended beyond the end of the Olympics. Numerous activists stressed that the Olympic Tent Village was not merely a symbolic act, but a material victory, too. Because of the action, approximately eighty-five people secured housing through the City of Vancouver and the state agency BC Housing.[51]

The Olympic Tent Village created what Lefebvre called "counterspace," or "counterplans and counterprojects designed to thwart strategies, plans, and programmes imposed from above."[52] Activists forged another vital "counterspace" at the VIVO Media Arts Centre, an artist-run site whose "Safe Assembly Project" featured programming like "Afternoon School" workshops, screening, and art productions; a pirate radio poetry project;

and "Evening News" events organized by Am Johal, Cecily Nicholson, and Nicholas Perrin that occurred every other night for the duration of the Games. The events at VIVO demanded that art play a pivotal role in reformatting anti-Olympics resistance, rather than be relegated as colorful window dressing. The forum convened video activists and their raw protest footage, practicing artists responding to negative Olympic externalities, and panels of activists and academics around particular themes. According to Nicholson, whose day job at the time was Coordinator of the Downtown Eastside Women's Centre, the two aims of the Evening News events were to construct semiautonomous cultural space conducive to dialogue and to create an archive of community response and critique, goals that "coalesced in the construction of the space."[53] The Evening News forums constructed space in an inclusive way that fostered participation and lateral learning, performing the intermediary function of political-cultural brokerage: connecting previously isolated actors and social sites and putting them in conversation through the explosion of spatial barriers that preclude such relations. It wasn't always silky smooth. On February 17, the BCCLA's David Eby, who was slated to participate on a civil liberties panel, was pied by a disgruntled activist who felt Eby had spoken negatively about the actions of window-smashing protesters, thereby violating the spirit of solidarity that undergirds the diversity-of-tactics approach.

The anti-Olympics push (see figure 4.4) also included militant street protests. On February 13, the Heart Attack March—designed to "clog the arteries of capitalism"—involved militants who broke off from a planned march and used newspaper boxes and metal chairs to break plate-glass windows at corporations like the Hudson's Bay Company. Activists used black-bloc tactics, wearing bandana masks and all black clothing in order to maintain anonymity. Critics maintained such tactics would only alienate the general public and invite the wrath of the cops, while supporters argued that the company's historical ties to British colonialism justified property damage; after all, the Hudson's Bay Company was an integral actor in the Canadian state's effort to extinguish aboriginal title in British Columbia during the nineteenth century.[54] Eby was quoted in the media as saying he was "sickened" by the action, labeling it "thuggery."[55] This diversity-of-tactics breach led to the aforementioned pieing at VIVO and his condemnation by militants. It also sparked a lively debate at VIVO where the conversational temperature was high, but calming yet forceful interventions by Nicholson kept the event constructive. Months after the pie incident Eby dryly noted, "It began a conversation with groups that are concerned about how we make a better world. It began a conversation about tactics . . . and about the black-bloc tactic in particular and whether

FIGURE 4.4. Anti-Olympics poster in Vancouver. Credit: Jules Boykoff.

or not it's actually helping move towards, from a civil-liberties perspective, a more democratic, equal, and participatory kind of culture in Canada, or otherwise." Demonstrating reflexivity, he said he learned a lesson on behalf of the BCCLA: not to act as legal observers and be perceived as movement lawyers during the same episode of contention.[56]

The Evening News helped surface—in a productive way—the ever-present tension between direct-action activists who want immediate change and extant, formalized NGOs that trend toward incremental

change. Activists in Vancouver made it clear this tension is not reduc-
ible to dichotomous camps, with "the traditional parties and centralized
campaigns" on one side and "the new movements organized in horizontal
networks" on the other.[57]

Space is not an empty, apolitical parcel waiting to be trod by bodies and
ideas. Nor is it a passive receptacle, wooden-stiff in its physicality. Rather,
space is dynamic, ever-unfolding, and socially produced through material
and discursive practices playing out on the uneven geography of power
relations. This production of space highlights multiplicity, heterogeneity,
and conflict—three concepts that are key to understanding anti-Olympics
resistance. Space conceived in this way points toward what Edward Soja
calls a "socio-spatial dialectic" whereby the social and the spatial are indis-
solubly linked, mutually constituting one another.[58] So, space produces and
reinforces social relations but also helps challenge them. This coheres with
Lefebvre's critical insight that "Sociopolitical contradictions are realized
spatially. The contradictions of space thus make the contradictions of
social relations operative. In other words, spatial contradictions 'express'
conflicts between sociopolitical interests and forces; it is only *in* space
that such conflicts come effectively into play, and in so doing they become
contradictions of space."[59]

Media play a key role in the proliferation of protester viewpoints and
the production of activist repertoires. In Vancouver, the prospect of using
mainstream media was not especially promising. Both Canwest—which
owned the *Vancouver Sun* and the *Vancouver Province* newspapers—and
the *Globe and Mail* were official sponsors, or "print media suppliers," of
the Games.[60] On top of this, the Olympics International Media Centre
actively squelched dissent when it refused to distribute the BCCLA's press
releases during the Games. The group applied to have its work sent out
through the Centre months in advance but were informed they would not
be allowed to participate a mere three days before the Games began, thus
precluding the possibility of appeal.[61]

True to the US press's parochialism, major newspapers virtually ignored
anti-Olympics dissent. The coverage that did emerge was superficial and
monolithic, embracing a sports-only frame of the Games that reflected an
ostensible apoliticism that is in fact deeply political. When the US media
did cover politics, they parachuted journalists into Vancouver to peddle
poverty porn, capturing images of the intense destitution in the Downtown Eastside without sufficiently explaining *why* such poverty exists. If
demonstrators were mentioned, they were often disparaged as "small"
groups bent on disrupting the lives of everyday Vancouverites and sports-
lovers or as "emotional" troublemakers who seemed hardwired to whine

about police. Canadian press coverage was more complex, breaking things down into three sequential phases: pre-Olympic articles that made space for dissent, articles appearing once the Games commenced where media slipped into the well-established ruts of activist deprecation, and articles appearing toward the end of the Olympics that extolled the police and hailed the mega-event as a "unifying force" for Canada.[62]

The mediascape also featured the noteworthy emergence of the Vancouver Media Co-op (VMC). Led by Franklin López and Dawn Paley and comprised of numerous citizen journalists, the VMC, which was born from the Olympic Resistance Network's Media and Communications Committee, had the radical media machine firing on all cylinders, providing the public with up-to-date information, politically driven art, and all the news that's unfit to print in the corporate media. The VMC consistently mobilized alternative versions of the Olympics and shifted the scale of anti-Olympics dissent by producing two segments for *Democracy Now!*, the leading community media outlet in the United States. López, who worked for *Democracy Now!* as a television producer, helped put anti-Olympics resistance on the program's radar.[63] The VMC's roots go back a half-decade to a publication called the *Dominion*. Once the magazine incorporated as a federal cooperative, Paley set up a co-op local in Halifax in January 2009 and then in Vancouver the following summer. The VMC advanced a revenue model based on sustainers who chipped in between $5 and $20 per month. The co-op put out a broadsheet called *Balaclava* during the Olympics and continued in their wake. According to activist Gord Hill, "the VMC reenergized and raised the standard of the radical alternative media structures that we have in this country."[64] Activists across the anti-Olympics spectrum pointed to the VMC as a chief legacy of the Winter Olympics.

Journalists from the VMC did not totally write off the mainstream media. Paley, who calls the mainstream media "SQUM," or status-quo media, noted that even if we don't admire the mass media, they're not obsolete: "Mainstream media are very relevant because they set the agenda." When it comes to proliferating messages and images to the wider public, the mainstream media still matter. Activists in Vancouver were aware of this, writing op-eds for newspapers like the *Vancouver Sun* and appearing as sources in numerous outlets, offering quotes that helped educate the public about why they were protesting. As with many dichotomies that were exploded in Vancouver, the mainstream media—alternative media quandary was not an either-or but a both-both.

Vancouver Media Co-op journalists were aware of keyboard activism's pitfalls, as captured by Jodi Dean's conception of "communicative capitalism," which deftly reframes the proliferation of social media as ersatz political participation: "Communicative capitalism captures our political interventions, formatting them as contributions to its circuits of affect and entertainment—*we feel political, involved, like contributors who really matter.*" She adds, "the intense circulation of content in communicative capitalism occludes the antagonism necessary for politics, multiplying antagonism into myriad minor issues and events."[65] At the same time that personalized, networked social media intensify capitalism, they also open up possibilities to circulate politically advantageous, if generic, political markers that can advance causes through "the power of many, of number."[66] Although many anti-Olympics activists employed social media to get the word out about events (e.g., using Facebook's "events" function), it was striking how many activists reported being offline and in the streets for most of the Olympics. They emphasized that keyboard activism may supplement boots-to-pavement protest, but it cannot—and should not—supplant it.

Conclusion

More and more, everyday people are troubling the notion that the Olympics are a force of pure good. Activism in Vancouver spurred this trend, setting the stage for amplified political dissent against the Olympic Games across the globe. Paradoxically, in host city after host city in the twenty-first century, the Games have sparked on-the-ground, democratically organized, intersectional coalitions made up of already-existing movements in the host city. Vancouver was an important foretaste of this dissident feast to come. Often, anti-Olympics organizers do not necessarily believe they will stop the Games from transpiring—especially once they have already been allocated to their city, as in Vancouver—but they realize that the Olympics provide a once-in-a-generation opportunity to coalesce activist coalitions that might otherwise not surface. Therefore, as Vancouver demonstrates, the Olympics can unintentionally strengthen activist communities in their battles for social justice.

Olympic powerbrokers often like to use the word "legacy" as they make promises about the benefits of hosting the Games. All too often, however, these legacy claims, packed into bid documents, fail to come to fruition. To take just one example, promises that the Vancouver Games would stoke increased physical activity among young people did not eventuate.[67] Jeff Derksen, a poet and professor at Simon Fraser University who was involved in the activist pushback, asked, "Was the legacy of the Olympics in Vancouver to show really that there is no positive legacy for a city when they host the Olympics?" He added, "Any positive legacy of the Olympics was carved out and imagined by activists, not by the original planning of the Olympics."[68]

Walia emphasized that anti-Olympics activists were "Forefronting an anticolonial and anti-capitalist analysis as the framework through which we understood all other resistance."[69] Paley added, "Our actions were about more than protesting the Olympics; rather, they challenged the interlocking systems of white supremacy and land and resource theft upon which the Canadian state is organized."[70] Franklin López said, "Radicals from Vancouver and beyond were able to elevate anticolonial politics to an international stage, and to educate a new generation of activists in the importance of working in solidarity with Native folks."[71] This anticolonial framework informed specific activist asks on the local policy front; Nicholas Perrin stated, "The anti-Olympic movement in Vancouver attempted to function discursively on two levels: integrating anticolonial critiques and Indigenous perspectives into local historical consciousness while at the same time demanding social housing for Vancouver's disproportionately Indigenous homeless population."[72]

People in the early stages of their activist path gained brass-tacks skills. Mercedes Eng noted that she "learned about what to wear to protect yourself from the police at protests; how to treat people who'd been maced or teargassed; writing on your arm in Sharpie the phone number for legal help in the case of arrest; how to make a chapbook; fancy words like neoliberalism; how to blockade; how fucking fierce the matriarchs and women and Two-Spirit peoples of the Downtown Eastside are; and the history of the Women's Memorial March."[73]

Tactics honed in Vancouver's extended Olympic moment were used again in subsequent struggles. Perrin pointed to the importance of tent cities, which popped up across the city with subsequent activist interventions and were grounded in alliances built during the Games.[74] Walia agreed, adding, "It's not just that there were more tent cities. It's that the politics of those tent cities and the relations of those tent cities are more strongly rooted in an anticolonial analysis and also a decolonial practice. So, for example, sacred fires at tent cities take on a more central role. It wasn't just a matter of there being tent cities as a tactic but also the ways in which they were configured and the social relations that centered Indigenous practices."[75] Hill highlighted the dialectic of resistance and restriction, noting how "the level of militancy that was reached in the three years leading up to the Winter Olympics was unprecedented. We had numerous militant street actions as well as a fairly high level of clandestine direct actions including the arson of several vehicles belonging to companies involved in the Olympics. The street actions were very successful in disrupting the 'countdown' events leading up to 2010, and the Olympic organizers were forced to adopt smaller, less publicized events with large numbers of police protecting them."[76]

Ten years after the Vancouver Games, activists reflecting on the importance of the fightback asserted key "legacies" that emerged from the surge in anti-Olympics dissent. Cecily Nicholson noted how the bonds forged in anti-Olympics struggle emerged in subsequent activist horizons: "New and old relations and alliances have formed in interim years to respond with Occupy, Idle No More, Black Lives Matter, and movement-based calls. Relations formed in anticipation of the 2010 [Olympic] resistance also were groundwork for strengthening land-based struggle and particular relations and support for the Wet'suwet'en at Unist'ot'en."[77] O'Bonsawin also highlighted the vitality of land-based claims. She stated, "A principal 'legacy' of anti-Olympics activism associated with the 2010 Vancouver Games, particularly within Canada, remains the 'No Olympic on Stolen Native Land' mantra. In the lead up to the 2010 Games, the vast majority of Canadians were unaware that Vancouver—and the majority of British Columbia—was, and remains, non-surrendered Indigenous territories." O'Bonsawin added, "Consequently, throughout the Olympic planning and hosting phases, a significant number of Canadians learned, many for the first time, that in this region of the country, Canadian sovereignty was, and remains, in a legally precarious position, and that Indigenous peoples maintain significant legal rights over their unceded territories. In the post-2010 Olympic era, the 'No Olympics on Stolen Native Land' mantra, rooted in anti-Olympic activism, continues to provide educators and activists with an important point of reference for discussing Indigenous rights in settler colonial Canada."[78] Eng concurred with the centrality of Indigeneity in activist struggles as an anti-Olympic legacy, noting that the Olympics "provided us with intersectional models for future organizing and actions that are grounded in solidarity with Indigenous peoples struggles for sovereignty."[79]

The activist outburst against the Vancouver Olympics was a huge step on the road to building transnational momentum against the Games. Today there are vibrant anti-Games campaigns in Tokyo, Paris, and Los Angeles. Shaw noted that Vancouver "served as a very powerful demonstration to other cities and people that the Olympics could be fought." In turn, "the notion that people can fight back and at least make the IOC and local developers work harder to foist this circus on cities. And, increasingly, people in various cities targeted by the Olympics see that they can not only fight, but also win."[80] Hill added, "I think it's important to try and keep this history alive so newer generations will be aware of the campaign that was carried out against the Olympics, and to inform and inspire other regions that are faced with similar megaevents."[81] This activist history may well be the most lasting and important legacy of the Vancouver 2010 Winter Olympics.

Notes

1. City of Vancouver, British Columbia, "2010 Winter Games Sign Designation and Relaxation By-Law No. 9697," July 8, 2008, 4, 6.

2. Marsha Lederman, "Protest Mural Comes Full Circle, Now Back on Gallery Wall," *Globe and Mail*, December 16, 2009.

3. Barbara Yaffe, "PM's Strategy of Controlling Message Fails to Silence Opponents," *Vancouver Sun*, February 12, 2010, B2.

4. Christine M. O'Bonsawin, "'The Olympics Do Not Understand Canada': Canada and the Rise of Olympic Protests," in *Sport, Protest, and Globalisation: Stopping Play*, edited by Jon Dart and Stephen Wagg (London: Palgrave Macmillan, 2016), 227–55.

5. David Whitson, "Olympic Hosting in Canada: Promotional Ambitions, Political Challenges," *Olympika: The International Journal of Olympic Studies* 14 (2005): 29–46. Quote at 40.

6. Helen Jefferson Lenskyj, *Olympic Industry Resistance: Challenging Olympics Power and Propaganda* (Albany: State University of New York Press, 2008), 53.

7. Bread Not Circuses, "The *Anti*-Olympic People's Bid Book," Paul Henderson Collection (hereafter cited as PHC), January 1990, International Centre for Olympic Studies, London, Ontario (hereafter cited as ICOS).

8. Paul Henderson, "Letter to Michael Shapcott," PHC, 26 November 1989, ICOS.

9. Michael Shapcott, "Letter to Paul Henderson," PHC, 15 December 1989.

10. "The Bid for the 1996 Olympics: Not This Time, Toronto," *CBC*, 18 September 1990.

11. Helen Jefferson Lenskyj, *The Olympic Games: A Critical Approach* (Bingley, UK: Emerald Publishing, 2020), 21. Lenskyj points to "The International Network against Olympic Games and Commercial Sports," which emerged in 1998, that brought together activists from Turin, Helsinki, and elsewhere to share resources via email and phone.

12. Adam Berg, "Protecting the Olympic Movement and Trying to Bury the Winter Games: The IOC, Avery Brundage, and the 1976 Denver Olympics," in *The Olympics that Never Happened: Denver '76 and the Politics of Growth* (Austin: University of Texas Press, 2023).

13. Russell Field, "Who Invited You? Party Crashers or Unwelcome Guests: The Legacy of Social Protest at the 2010 Winter Olympics," *Rethinking Matters Olympic: Investigations into the Socio-Cultural Study of the Modern Olympic*

Movement (2010): 192–202, cited information at 195; Helen Jefferson Lenskyj, *Olympic Industry Resistance: Challenging Olympic Power and Propaganda* (Albany: State University of New York Press, 2008), 65.

14. Christine O'Bonsawin interview with author, June 1, 2020.

15. Jules Boykoff, "The Anti-Olympics," *New Left Review* 67 (January-February 2011): 41–59.

16. Christopher Shaw, *Five Ring Circus: Myths and Realities of the Olympic Games* (Gabriola Island, BC: New Society Publishers, 2008), 10.

17. Robert A. Baade and Victor Matheson, "Going for the Gold: The Economics of the Olympics," *Journal of Economic Perspectives* 30 (Spring 2016): 201–18, cited information at 206; Bob Mackin, *Red Mittens & Red Ink: The Vancouver Olympics* (Vancouver: Smashwords, 2012), 204.

18. Micheal Vonn interview with author, August 18, 2010.

19. Bent Flyvbjerg, Allison Stewart, and Alexander Budzier, "The Oxford Olympics Study 2016: Cost and Cost Overrun at the Games," University of Oxford Säid Business School Research Papers (July 2016): 1–27.

20. Am Johal interview with author, February 5, 2010.

21. Gary Mason, "Vancouver's Big Games Turning into a Big Owe," *Globe and Mail*, January 10, 2009, A7; Gary Mason, "Athletes Village to Get $100-Million Loan," *Globe and Mail*, November 6, 2008, A15; Jules Boykoff, *Celebration Capitalism and the Olympic Games* (London: Routledge, 2013), 71–72.

22. Dawn Paley interview with author, May 28, 2020.

23. Harsha Walia interview with author, May 28, 2020.

24. Hamar Foster and Alan Grove, "'Trespassers on the Soil': United States v. Tom and a New Perspective on the Short History of Treaty Making in Nineteenth-Century British Columbia," *BC Studies* 138/139 (Summer/Autumn 2003): 51–84; Cole Harris, *Making Native Space: Colonialism, Resistance, and Reserves in British Columbia* (Vancouver: UBC Press, 2002).

25. Taiaiake Alfred, "Deconstructing the British Columbia Treaty Process," *Balayi: Culture, Law and Colonialism* 3 (2001): 37–65, Q at p. 42.

26. Kim Pemberton, "Aboriginal Groups Divided on Whether to Support Olympics" *Vancouver Sun*, 6 February 2010.

27. Vancouver Organizing Committee for the 2010 Olympic and Paralympic Winter Games (VANOC), "Vancouver 2010 Sustainability Report, 2009–2010," 18.

28. Harsha Walia interview with author, February 6, 2010.

29. Gord Hill interview with author, August 18, 2010.

30. Office of the Privacy Commissioner of Canada, "Privacy and Security at the Vancouver 2010 Winter Games," (August 2009): Available at: http://www.priv.gc.ca/fs-fi/02_05_d_42_ol_e.cfm#004

31. Michael Heine, "Olympic Commodification and Civic Spaces at the 2010 Winter Olympic Games: A Political Topology of Contestation," *The International Journal of the History of Sport* 35 (2018): 898–910, quote at 905.

32. Sophy Chan, "Unveiling the 'Olympic Kidnapping Act': Homelessness

and Public Policy in the 2010 Vancouver Olympic Games," *Intersections and Intersectionalities in Olympic and Paralympic Studies* (2014): 43–47.

33. Philip Boyle and Kevin D. Haggerty, "Civil Cities and Urban Governance: Regulating Disorder for the Vancouver Olympics," *Urban Studies* 48 (2011): 3185–201. Project Civil Society was aborted around a year before the Olympics commenced.

34. Darah Hansen, "Victoria Cop Infiltrated Anti-Games Group, Jamie Graham Says," *Vancouver Sun*, December 2, 2009.

35. Christopher Shaw interview with author, August 17, 2010. VISU paid yet another visit to Shaw just before the G8/G20 summit in Toronto, attempting to flip him into becoming an informant, an offer he flatly denied.

36. International Olympic Committee, "Olympic Charter," June 26, 2019, 90.

37. Suzanne Staggenborg, "Event Coalitions in the Pittsburgh G20 Protests," *The Sociological Quarterly* 56 (2015): 386–411; Nella Van Dyke and Bryan Amos, "Social Movement Coalitions: Formation, Longevity, and Success," *Sociology Compass* 11 (2017): 1–17.

38. Sidney Tarrow, *The New Transnational Activism* (New York: Cambridge University Press, 2005), 170–72.

39. O'Bonsawin, "'The Olympics Do Not Understand Canada,'" 227–55.

40. Annie Casselman, "Highway of Good Intentions? Vancouver Olympic Plans Bulldoze Rare Forests," *Scientific American*, August 4, 2008, https://www.scientificamerican.com/article/highway-of-good-intentions.

41. David Whitson, "Vancouver 2010: The Saga of Eagleridge Bluffs," in *Olympic Games, Mega-Events and Civil Societies: Globalization, Environment, Resistance*, Graeme Hayes and John Karamichas (eds.) (New York: Palgrave Macmillan, 2012), 219–35, quote at 220.

42. Hill interview, August 18, 2010.

43. Jean Swanson interview with author, May 20, 2020. For more details, see: http://povertyolympics.ca/.

44. Swanson interview.

45. Jules Boykoff, *NOlympians: Inside the Fight Against Capitalist Mega-Sports in Los Angeles, Tokyo, and Beyond* (Winnipeg: Fernwood Publishing, 2020), 115.

46. Aaron Vidaver interview with author, August 11, 2010. In 2002 Vidaver participated in the Woodwards squat, a crucial precedent to the Olympics space seizures.

47. Dave Diewert interview with author, August 17, 2010; Harsha Walia interview with author, August 18, 2010.

48. Walia interview, August 18, 2010.

49. Henri Lefebvre, *Writings on Cities*, translated by Eleonore Kofman and Elizabeth Lebas (Oxford: Blackwell, 1996), 112.

50. Mustafa Dikeç, "Police, Politics, and the Right to the City," *GeoJournal* 58 (2003): 91–98, quote at 93.

51. Diewert interview; Walia interview, August 18, 2010. Around forty-five individuals gained housing in the first round, and about forty more subsequently.

52. Henri Lefebvre, *The Production of Space*, translated by Donald Nicholson-Smith (Oxford: Blackwell, 1991), 383.

53. Cecily Nicholson interview with author, August 6, 2010.

54. Foster and Grove, "Trespassers on the Soil," 53.

55. Robert Matas, "Olympics Protest's Vandalism Denounced," *Globe and Mail*, February 15, 2010.

56. David Eby interview with author, August 6, 2010.

57. Michael Hardt, "Today's Bandung?" *New Left Review* 14, March-April 2001, 115–16.

58. Edward W. Soja, *Seeking Spatial Justice* (Minneapolis: University of Minnesota Press, 2010), 89.

59. Lefebvre, *The Production of Space*, 365.

60. International Olympic Committee, "IOC Marketing Media Guide: Vancouver 2010," 35.

61. Vonn interview. See British Columbia Civil Liberties Association, "Provincial Government Shuts BCCLA Out of International Media Centre," February 10, 2010, https://bccla.org/2010/02/provincial-government-shuts-bccla-out-of-international-media-centre.

62. Jules Boykoff, *Activism and the Olympics: Dissent at the Games in Vancouver and London* (New Brunswick: Rutgers University Press, 2014), 129–58.

63. After *Democracy Now!* host Amy Goodman and two of her colleagues were detained and questioned at the US-Canada border in November 2009 on their way to Vancouver where Goodman was scheduled to speak at the public library, the show's producers were definitely aware something unique was going on. Suspicious she intended to speak out against the Olympics, border guards rifled through her personal effects and questioned her about the topics she intended to cover in her talk and whether one of them was the Winter Olympics.

64. Hill interview, August 18, 2010.

65. Jodi Dean, *Democracy and Other Neoliberal Fantasies: Communicative Capitalism and Left Politics* (Durham, NC: Duke University Press, 2009), 49, 24, italics in original.

66. Jodi Dean, *Comrade: An Essay on Political Belonging* (New York: Verso, 2019), 13.

67. Luke R. Potwarka and Scott T. Leatherdale, "The Vancouver 2010 Olympics and Leisure-Time Physical Activity Rates Among Youth in Canada: Any Evidence of a Trickle-Down Effect?" *Leisure Studies* 35, no. 2 (2016): 241–57; Cora L. Craig and Adrian E. Bauman, "The Impact of the Vancouver Winter Olympics on Population Level Physical Activity and Sport Participation Among Canadian Children and Adolescents: Population Based Study," *International Journal of Behavioral Nutrition and Physical Activity* 11 (2014): 1–9.

68. Jeff Derksen interview with author, June 3, 2020.

69. Walia interview, May 28, 2020.

70. Paley interview.

71. Franklin López interview with author, May 25, 2020.

72. Nicholas Perrin interview with author, May 26, 2020.

73. Mercedes Eng interview with author, May 31, 2020.

74. Perrin interview.

75. Walia interview, May 28, 2020.

76. Gord Hill interview with author, May 20, 2020.

77. Cecily Nicholson interview with author, June 4, 2020.

78. O'Bonsawin interview.

79. Eng interview.

80. Christopher Shaw interviews with author, May 21, 2020 and August 17, 2020.

81. Hill interview, May 20, 2020.

CHAPTER 5

Sochi 2014

The Quarry Outside My Window and Other Geographies of Protest

SVEN DANIEL WOLFE

"This was supposed to be my little hotel," Petros[1] explained, indicating a guest house by the orchard on the edge of his property. "I planned it for four rooms and was going to have it open before the Olympics. And I wanted to keep running it after, for the skiers and vacationers who will come later . . . but none of that was possible" (May 2014, Akhshtyr). The guest house was simple but spacious, built by Petros and his sons two years before the 2014 Winter Olympic Games in Sochi, Russia. It had electricity from a dedicated gasoline generator, running water from their own well, and a view overlooking the valley and the river Mzymta. This was in Akhshtyr, one of a string of small villages between the two clusters of Olympic venues in the mountains and on the coast, part of greater Sochi. In theory, the location was ideal for catching the anticipated flows of tourists: only fifteen kilometers to Sochi-Adler, the beach, and the main stadiums and, in the other direction, thirty kilometers to the slopes, the lifts, and an entirely new city being built in the mountains. The trouble was that there was no simple way to get there from Akhshtyr. The highway between Adler and the mountains ran on the opposite side of the river, and residents had to drive many kilometers on an old, rutted road until they could cross over to the more functional transport links. As part of the Olympic urban development agenda, authorities constructed a new elevated highway and, separately, a highspeed commuter train line, both running between the mountains and the coast. The fact that these new linkages were on the Akhshtyr side of the river gave Petros the inspiration to build his small pension hotel. After all, with a planned and promised on-ramp to the new highway (and perhaps someday even a station for the train), his fortunes would be sure to improve. But the fact that these new constructions ultimately bypassed and ignored his village meant that he was left with an unusable investment. This is the origin of Petros's local protest against the Olympics, its exclusionary urban development, and an unresponsive government at municipal, regional, and national scales.

This vignette illustrates some of the dynamics of local contestation against the 2014 Winter Olympic Games in Sochi. From abroad, this mega-event was often framed as a personal project of the Russian president,[2] a soft-power strategy on the geopolitical stage,[3] but Petros's story presents a more nuanced interpretation of these global ambitions. Soft power is not a stable construct, nor is it directed only to an international audience at geopolitical scales.[4] In Sochi, the Olympic soft power project took the shape of a concerted attempt to introduce a "new Russia," tied to a new sense of Russianness, to both international and domestic audiences.[5] This attempt met with partial success domestically but failed at the international level due to the hard power context of the Russo-Ukrainian war and the increased tensions in international relations that followed. These maneuverings at global and national scales were tied to a regional urban development project in Sochi of breathtaking size and cost, reinserting the Russian national government into regional spatial planning practices, and fundamentally restructuring Sochi's economic base and built environment.[6]

What is missing in many analyses, however, is the micro-level effects of these ambitious projects. How did Sochi locals themselves react to hosting the Olympics, with the symbolic politics at play alongside the unprecedented construction activity involved in the redevelopment of their region? This chapter endeavors to shed light on this question through an ethnographic portrait of some of the villagers living between the two major sites of Olympic construction. In so doing it uncovers nuanced dimensions of micropolitical protest on the ground in Sochi. Further, when focusing on protest activity at this level, the chapter is contextualized with, but differentiates itself from, protests that were more visible from abroad, such as the infamous whipping of the Pussy Riot activists outside of the Olympic venues,[7] the international furor over the passage of the controversial so-called "homosexual propaganda law,"[8] or the Circassian activist diaspora who tried to bring attention to the massacres and expulsions that occurred 150 years ago.[9] Instead, this chapter follows the relatively invisible actions of residents who tried—and ultimately failed—to make their voices heard against the roar of Olympic development dictated from above and from afar. From this micropolitical perspective, the chapter details the uneven outcomes of the Sochi regional development project and concludes that, while some areas have indeed been transformed into popular year-round tourist destinations, this definition of successful development excludes many residents, and that the project has in fact taken place at huge environmental and social cost.

This chapter is based on extensive fieldwork, official documentation and reports, and media analysis before, during, and after the 2014 Sochi Olympics, as part of a separate project that did not involve the dynamics of protest. Texts and transcripts were entered into qualitative data analysis software and coded iteratively over time, in dynamic conversation between the field and desk research,[10] from which the themes of micropolitical protest rose inductively. This thematic coding process ultimately revealed a disconnect between the narratives surrounding the Olympic urban development preparations and the actual outcomes on the ground. Occasionally, this disconnection sprouted as small, localized expressions of protest, some of which serve as the empirical basis for this chapter. In the years after the event, periodic efforts were made to remain in contact with several of the participants in order to understand the aftermath once the Olympics left town.

The chapter approaches these small-scale moments using micropolitical thinking. Following Deleuze and Guattari,[11] who acknowledge that "everything is political, but every politics is simultaneously a *macropolitics* and a *micropolitics*," the chapter endeavors to make sense of larger scales through an attention to the "micro," rooted in the notion that neither macro- nor micropolitics can be understood without the other. This is an omnivorous approach that valorizes the relatively invisible actions of small-scale protest, predicated on the understanding that local scales and individual actions have an inherent political immediacy that exists apart from, but saturated with, dominant orders.[12] In this way, the chapter uses local Sochi protest as a means of understanding dynamics within Russia at larger scales and, conversely, using larger political developments to make sense of resident actions within Sochi.

Sochi as Material and Symbolic Project

Hosting mega-events has long been associated with wide-ranging urban development and placemaking agendas.[13] Most famous of these was the creation and propagation of the so-called "Barcelona Model," based on the 1992 Summer Olympics, wherein a city hosts a mega-event and transforms its built environment and tourist attractiveness, ultimately setting itself on a more prosperous trajectory with worldwide renown.[14] This model has spread around the globe, regardless of the fact that the Barcelona games went over budget and displaced local populations.[15] Indeed, the flipside of the potential economic, infrastructural, and (geo)political benefits of hosting mega-events is an array of negative outcomes for host cities and populations.[16] These range from gentrification and other socioeconomic marginalization[17] to ecological devastation.[18] As the promised benefits of mega-events spread to attract potential host cities outside of the traditional heartlands of the global north, so too do the attendant risks and damages.[19]

Russia's recent history of hosting mega-events fits into this picture, and includes the 2013 Summer Universiade in Kazan, the 2014 Winter Olympics in Sochi, and the 2018 FIFA men's World Cup, among many other smaller-scale events. These are part of a multifaceted state strategy to reassert Russia's presence on the global stage,[20] and, at the same time, to reinsert the Russian federal state into spatial planning.[21] The latter is based on the idea of developing chosen territories through specific government attention, in a strategy of so-called extraverted urbanism.[22] Sochi was selected as one of these chosen territories and given unprecedented state attention and funding, to the tune of over $50 billion USD,[23] making it the most expensive Olympics in history. However, Golubchikov notes that approximately 80 percent of this investment went not to sporting facilities but to infrastructure.[24] Thus, the Sochi Olympic preparations are better understood as a massive regional development program, rather than merely hosting a sporting event, however prestigious. The goal here, as stated in government policy and expressed by leaders from the Sochi mayor up to the Russian president, was the wholesale regeneration of Sochi, transforming it from a somewhat dilapidated summer resort into a world-class, year-round tourist destination.

Alongside this far-reaching regional development agenda, there was also a goal of introducing a new sense of Russia and Russianness to the domestic population and the world at large.[25] In the tumultuous years since these Olympics, it is clear that this attempt was a spectacular failure on the international level, but it is important to remember that at the time of the bid and the preparations, there was a concerted effort to present Russia to the world as a growing democracy and an eager partner in global affairs. This is the reason behind the message "Russia—Great, New, Open!" displayed in huge letters in English and Russian at the entrance to the Olympic Park in Sochi. In this light, Russian organizers aspired to use the 2014 Olympics to create and display a nation fully recovered from the fall of the USSR in much the same way that Japanese organizers used the Tokyo 1964 Games to introduce to the world a peaceful, postwar country.[26] Thus, the Sochi Olympics held great significance for the Russian state, in both material and symbolic dimensions, and in domestic and international contexts.

Domestically, this identity project took the shape of a yearslong public relations campaign, aided by the state's increasing control of the media environment. Billboards in cities nationwide featured patriotic imagery linked to hosting, a national sportswear brand launched a fashionable clothing line tied into the patriotic nature of the Games, and numerous television channels broadcast in-depth interviews with famous Russian Olympic champions under the title "One Nation—One Team." This state-led drive for national unity through sport reached its climax during the opening ceremonies on February 7, 2014, a dramatic spectacle that attempted to consolidate Russia's pre-Soviet, Soviet, and post-Soviet history.[27] Imperial narratives of a great nation were delivered not just through reference to Russian cultural and civilizational triumphs, but also through a deliberately edgy, postmodern aesthetic, intended to appeal to broad swaths of the population.[28] The opening ceremony was broadly appreciated in the Russian population, but it nevertheless acted as a polarizing force between those who favored the state's increasingly conservative push and those who resisted, with both groups taking inspiration from the narratives on display.[29]

Protest in Russia and abroad

Missing from most of these economic, infrastructural, and political discussions was the human scale, particularly regarding those individuals who resisted the imposition of the state's ideas of material and symbolic progress. The Sochi regional development and symbolic political programs were inherently top-down, created in Moscow and articulated on the ground by actors with close connections to the federal state.[30] So, what were some of the reactions of the Russian population, both in the rest of the nation and in Sochi itself, to this top-down agenda? This is a particularly salient question because the Sochi Olympics occurred in the aftermath of the 2011 Bolotnaya protests, which saw unprecedented citizen and political mobilization against the authoritarian turn in Russia,[31] but before the further consolidation of power and subsequent crackdown on dissent that followed the Russo-Ukrainian war.[32]

Any mega-event host is subject to the potential for increased protest activity due to the concentrated attention of the global spotlight,[33] and Russia in the preparations for Sochi 2014 was no exception. Internationally, people knew or cared less about Russian domestic politics and instead focused on the passage of a law that effectively criminalized public homosexuality.[34] This was broadly framed as a human rights issue, and in light of the Olympic Charter's emphasis on nondiscrimination, international activists seized on this contradiction to urge international boycotts of both Russian vodka and the Games.[35] Unfortunately for LGBT activists, the majority of the Russian population remained uncomfortable or outright opposed to gay rights, and as such, they supported the government's new conservative laws.[36] The Circassian genocide was another issue that attracted more attention internationally than domestically, as activists in the diaspora organized protests at Russian embassies and consulates, but generated little steam inside Russian borders.[37]

Within Russia, but outside of Sochi, a handful of activists were arrested for an anti-Olympic/pro-LGBT demonstration in St. Petersburg on the eve of the Games.[38] They were arrested even though they adhered to the law that specifically allows solitary individuals to protest without permission. More dramatically, and away from the capital cities, the Museum of Contemporary Art in Perm hosted a radically political and anti-Olympic exhibition by the modern artist Vasily Slonov. This exhibition targeted the Olympics as a vehicle of exploitation, expropriation, militarism, nationalism, and even the rehabilitation of Stalin.[39] In short order, and with no sense of irony in proving the artist's point, the exhibition was shut down, the artist questioned and put under surveillance, and the curator lost his job before later fleeing the country.[40]

Because of the Russian state's draconian responses to physical expressions of protest or dissent, many citizens took to digital spaces to express their opposition through protest hashtags, critical blogs and vlogs, and anti-Olympic or antigovernment articles, cartoons, videos, and songs. Alexey Navalny's Anti-Corruption Foundation—now labeled an extremist group and liquidated from Russia[41]—produced what they called the "Sochi 2014 Encyclopedia of Spending," a detailed accounting of the costs and corruption for each of Sochi's Olympic development projects, linking dirty money to numerous highly placed businessmen and government officials by name.[42] The report was released in Russian and English, in both PDF format and an interactive online site based on a map of Sochi, so users could see at a glance where the projects were sited, how much was spent, and who benefited. The release of this report made waves on the Russian internet, but there was no mention in the rest of the traditional media.

Protest in Sochi

In a sign of how seriously he valued the creation and maintenance of a unified and unquestioned national narrative, President Putin issued a decree that outlawed any protest in or around Sochi. Under pressure from the International Olympic Committee to support free expression, he later softened this restriction to allow the creation of a designated "free speech zone" far from the Olympic venues,[43] but this was little more than a tacit gesture to placate the international set and was not taken seriously by residents. Because of terrorist threats, the entire region was placed under special military and security status, with a reported 100,000 Federal Security Service agents on duty.[44] This represented nearly a quarter of Sochi's pre-Games population and did not even take into account the soldiers deployed in newly-created temporary bases around the region. Aside from all this, the state instituted a wide-ranging package of digital surveillance technologies, allowing the Federal Security Service to monitor all telecommunications traffic in the region.[45] Because of these technologies, some activists received visits by the security services before even organizing any activities.

The most internationally visible protests in Sochi occurred during the Games, when Pussy Riot—the political punk art collective that grew famous for their protest song in the Moscow Cathedral of Christ the Savior[46]—performed a spontaneous protest song at the Olympic venues. Before they could finish singing, they were accosted by the police and even whipped, on camera, by Cossacks.[47] True to form, they rapidly released a video of themselves being whipped and arrested in Sochi, accompanying a song called "Putin Will Teach You to Love The Motherland."[48] Aside from this, not many protest actions were discernible outside of Russian territory. This does not mean that they did not exist, however. Rather, within Sochi, there were a few different flavors of activism and protest, but these actions were largely locally oriented, small scale, spatially dispersed, and quickly repressed by authorities. This local protest can be grouped roughly into two categories: environmental destruction and local disruption, both tied to the overwhelming scale of Olympic construction projects; and the negative reactions they inspired among the population.

Sochi's natural environment is rare and protected by a variety of laws at both the national and international levels. On the coast, the Olympic venues were built on the Black Sea shore, where cleanliness (in terms of both visual aesthetics and pollution) is necessary for the continued attractiveness of the region to tourists. Construction here was risky and threatened the local Black Sea shores with pollution, both visual and chemical. In the mountains, however, the situation was further complicated by environmental law. There, the Olympic venues were sited within Sochi National Park, the only untouched mountain forest remaining in Europe, bordering the Caucasus Nature Reserve, and listed as a UNESCO natural world heritage site. In this protected environment, eleven new sports venues were built, and an entirely new city was founded in order to support these venues and the accompanying flow of tourists. These material interventions were linked with extensive transport connections of road and rail in order to provide seamless flow from the airport and train station transport hubs down on the coast. The construction activity caused colossal damage to the protected natural environment, complicating organizers' promises to "minimize, and when possible eliminate negative environmental impacts in Sochi during the construction and operation of Olympic venues and infrastructure."[49] This was a guiding principle of what Russian organizers claimed would be the "Games in Harmony with Nature," in alignment with the International Olympic Committee's stated environmental concerns.[50] To some extent, environmental considerations forced a change in plans, such as when the United Nations Environment Program complained that the luge and bobsled venues were sited within protected spaces, and local organizers relocated the developments, to international acclaim.[51]

In many other cases, however, organizers' promises to use the Games to protect and increase the size of Sochi's environmental preserves proved little more than greenwashing.[52] In violation of national and international law, construction took place in protected areas and produced spectacular and irreversible environmental damage (see figure 5.1).[53] Unnecessary and extravagant projects were planned and executed, at great cost and in violation of the law, and affecting native populations of yew and boxwood forests, Atlantic salmon, red deer, and wild boar.[54] Speaking off the record, a former director at a local construction company explained how this was accomplished: "They built where they needed to build, for the championship . . . and it was our job to go back, after they were done, and amend the codex so that no laws were violated" (June 2016, Sochi). This legal flexibility speaks to the political priority of the Sochi project, which also explains why environmental protests were so quickly repressed.

Local environmentalists discovered that, under cover of the bustle of Olympic construction, a private villa was being built illegally in the national forest. One prominent activist went to protest the construction site and was promptly arrested by the security services. This did not make the news but was widely discussed in opposition circles. In response, another environmentalist group modulated their activities and decided not to protest actively against the construction. Instead, they dedicated themselves to cataloging the environmental destruction, starting with endangered species featured in the International Union for Conservation of Nature's Red List.[55] The Olympic construction was so vast and swift that this group did not have time to publish their warnings before an endangered species of chamomile flower was destroyed and made extinct. They tried again with

FIGURE 5.1. Hotels under construction before the Winter Olympics in Sochi, taking place in protected national forest, 2013. Credit: Sven Daniel Wolfe.

more endangered species but had the same result. This continued through-out the years of preparations, as the pace of construction and destruction only increased. What is more, one activist shared rather nonchalantly that she and her group had weekly meetings with the federal security services: "Our agent comes by, and we offer him tea. He asks what we're doing, and we tell him what we're working on . . . He always asks if we're planning an action, and we always say no" (August 2013, Sochi). This cool response to state surveillance reveals, all at once, the commonplace nature of government interference in individual lives, the difficulties of protest and opposition, and the personal strength and flexibility of activists. At the same time, these environmentalists were stymied in their attempts to prevent or even mitigate ecological destruction, and had to be content with publishing their list of species made extinct. When even this publica-tion was repressed, Grisha, an environmentalist involved with the project, found himself under intolerable state pressure. Arrested and interrogated on a thin pretext of accepting bribes, he later fled the country.

Similar to the story of Petros that opened this chapter, Grisha had originally been enthusiastic about the Olympics coming to Sochi. Environmental activist is not a well-paid job, so Grisha supported himself by leading
ecotours to distant, untouched areas in Sochi's wild spaces. Shortly after
the Olympic bid had been won, he explained his reasoning:

> It's going to be good, I think ... Currently I have maybe two or three big
> tours in a summer ... Of course, most people coming to Sochi are not
> interested in going far into the mountains with me, but I'm certain that
> some will be. And if more and more tourists come, then there's more
> chance. I don't need much, but some more would be nice (December
> 2009, Sochi).

This optimism contrasts starkly with Grisha's attitudes many years later,
from exile:

> There was no chance for any business. None at all. The gangsters control
> everything anyway, and you can't make any money if you're a simple
> person ... More important than that, they ruined Sochi. They killed it
> (April 2017, Hamburg).

Grisha's story parallels Petros's in several ways. At the outset, both
hoped that the coming influx of tourists would help improve their personal fortunes. For one it was guiding people into the wilderness and
teaching them about nature; for the other it was giving people a place to
sleep. Both were investing their futures into a promised increase in the
tourist economy, and it would be easy to imagine a situation where the
two—although they were not acquainted—could have forged a symbiotic
business relationship: Petros would recommend Grisha's services to guests
who were looking for something to do, while Grisha would recommend
Petros's pension hotel to visitors coming to Sochi for an ecotour. None of
these plans came close to fruition, however, and the spoils of increased
tourist activity went instead to well-connected firms and individuals. As
a businesswoman put it, "Who wants to deal with local people when you
have all these international chains?" (July 2015, Roza Khutor). Ultimately,
both Petros and Grisha reflect stories of local hopes dashed by the political-
economic realities of contemporary Russia. Neither of them expressed
particularly anti-Olympic sentiments, particularly not at the start; rather,
they both wanted to be part of the imagined rising tide that was promised
to lift all boats, and they resented the fact that they were left out.

For his part, Petros took a more explicit oppositional and protest pos-
ture. In contrast to Grisha, who was concerned primarily with environmental destruction, Petros was affected by issues of local disruption. This

affected him, and indeed his entire village, in three ways. The first of these was the exclusion from transit connectivity. Petros was overjoyed when he saw the original Olympic plans for the new highway, and incensed when local authorities canceled the promised on-ramp to Akhshtyr. This did not lead him to protest immediately, but rather to engage with activism. A former Hero of the Soviet Union, Petros was unafraid of the authorities and lost no time in writing to the Sochi mayor. When he was ignored, he wrote to regional and then national politicians, all the while collecting local signatures for a petition and contacting legal representation for a court case.

While this played out, two other disruptions took place in Akhshtyr, centered around the need for raw material for the Olympic construction projects. Petros lived at the outside of the village, and his property opened onto a meadow ringed with sparse boxwood forest and a gradual slope to the river. This was not his property, but it may as well have been: his children grew up playing in the meadow and the forest, and the family would often walk through the forest to the river rather than take the road, which was a more circuitous route. This meadow and forest were chosen by local authorities as the site of a new quarry to provide rock for the masses of new construction in the mountains. They dug this quarry not four hundred meters from Petros's house, and work continued nonstop, around the clock, for years before the Games (see figure 5.2). That is a daily punishment of three eight-hour shifts of continuous rock drilling and loading, punctuated by the roar of oversized KAMAZ construction trucks arriving and departing every hour of every day without cease. "I dust the window sills in the morning," Petros's daughter Anja explained, "and by the afternoon I already have to dust again. There is so much powdered rock in the air. It is an outrage, but what can we do? They don't listen, and they won't listen" (August 2013, Akhshtyr). It did not matter to authorities that the quarry was sited illegally in protected forest, and they were also unconcerned about the nearby villagers. They steadfastly continued to ignore Petros's letters.

Aside from this noise and air pollution, the endless string of KAMAZ trucks also presented a separate disruption to the residents of Akhshtyr. At all hours of day and night, they tore up and down the mountain, hauling rock or heading back for more. They raced along the unmaintained village road, endangering drivers and pedestrians alike, and the roar of their engines and their powerful bright lights woke residents throughout the night. One day, when Anja was driving home, she found herself stopped by a man in uniform, who told her the road was closed and she could not pass. Apparently, the KAMAZ trucks had eroded the road so much that

FIGURE 5.2. Illegal quarry dug in preparation for the Winter Olympics in Sochi. Petros's house and failed pension hotel, part of the village of Akhshtyr, is visible behind the quarry ridge. Credit: Sven Daniel Wolfe.

it was now dangerous. Construction workers dug a chasm to refill and repair, but had left it open for the time being. All residents were required to park their cars several kilometers away from their homes until repairs were complete. Anja took her groceries, crossed the chasm by means of a makeshift bridge, and dialed her father, who came down in a separate car to fetch her. This became their routine for the following weeks, and was repeated at regular intervals whenever the road needed to be shut.

On top of this, the KAMAZ trucks were so heavy that they destroyed local wells. Petros's family, long accustomed to being able to drink from their tap, suddenly found themselves without potable water, as did the other families in the village. After a series of increasingly vocal complaints, local authorities provided a water delivery truck once a week, but there was no hint that this would continue after Olympic construction ceased. Petros explained the situation: "We were living fine before. Yes, maybe we were poor but at least we had water and we had peace. Now we have neither one nor the other . . . I don't believe they will provide water later. What are we supposed to do?" (August 2013, Akhshtyr). Thus, far from providing increased economic opportunities for residents, the arrival of the Olympics substantially damaged local lives and livelihoods. Because his complaints about these injustices were ignored, Petros turned his attention to the possibilities of physical protest.

Since there was only one road that connected the village to the rest of Sochi, and this road was vital for the regional construction projects, Petros reasoned that this would be a good target for disruption. He elaborated: "I didn't want to destroy anything, of course. I simply wanted the authorities to listen to us" (December 2013, Sochi). Over the course of a week, Petros visited every family in Akhshtyr, trying to muster support for his plan to block the road. The initial plan was to build barricades, but he soon realized that KAMAZ trucks could drive over anything the villagers could muster. Instead, the plan was to block the road with their bodies, preventing the trucks from passing until local needs were met. "A lot of people supported the idea, but didn't want to go out," he said, "and some people didn't support the idea at all. And some people said they did, but I think they were lying" (December 2013, Sochi). It is unclear whether anyone in the village informed the security services, or whether they learned about Petros's plans thanks to the institution of new surveillance technologies, but either way, the village earned a visit from a pair of FSB (Federal Security Service) agents. They went door to door and calmly stopped the protest before it could start. Petros explained:

> They told me that someone in government would address my concerns, and they advised me not to block the road. Then they told me I was free to ignore their advice, but that they couldn't tell what would happen if I did . . . I'm not a fool. I didn't go out. How could I? What would it accomplish? (December 2013, Akhshtyr).

In this way, security authorities put an end to the potential protests in Akhshtyr. Local grumbling was permitted but direct action was not. The drilling work continued and when the quarry was too deep and wide, they dug a second quarry further up the mountain.

Conclusion

These micropolitical snapshots of the geographies of protest in Sochi highlight the need for a fuller, more inclusive understanding of mega-events and global affairs. A fair examination of the 2014 Winter Olympics is incomplete if it focuses only on regional urban development and geopolitical image management, without considering the lives of the host city residents. It is insufficient to discuss the narratives of a "new Russia," for instance, without taking into account the intended audiences of those narratives. Likewise, it is an oversight to assume that the only audiences for this mega-event soft power project are located abroad. In this light, Sochi residents can be forgiven for taking officials at their word when they promised a new Russia. Far from the great nation narratives on display during the Olympic opening ceremonies—to say nothing of the full-throated nationalism after the annexation of Crimea in 2014—the new Russia that these residents believed in and desired was far more material. They were promised improvements to their daily lives, such as decent transit connections to the metropolitan centers, gas and water hookups for their rural homes, and expanded opportunities for earning a living. Put another way, they cared less about the Olympics than they did about what the presence of the Olympics might mean for their lives. When it became clear that the Olympic tide did not benefit everyone, they grew disenchanted. Some fled, some tried to protest, and many more remained silent. To some degree, all were caught up in the spectacle of the Games once they began, and a clear majority of Russians thought the Olympics were successful, worth the expense, and a source of patriotism and pride.[56] This is true despite the fact that they also continued to suffer unnecessary exclusions and deprivations.

In the end, the new Russia that developed after the Olympics was not a flourishing democracy, equitably integrated into international systems, and with meaningful material improvements for the lives of host city residents. Instead, what transpired was a nation locked into an increasingly authoritarian spiral, at war with its neighbor, aggressive toward and isolated from the west, and with drastically curtailed rights and freedoms for citizens. For Sochi residents, the context of increasing political closure has translated into even fewer opportunities for expression or dissent. Inspired by Navalny's exposés, some activists began investigating municipal and regional officials for corruption. They published their findings in local blogs and other media outlets, but one by one these have been shuttered, their owners driven to flee or imprisoned. It is clear that a line has been drawn: criticizing the president or his allies is the same as criticizing the nation, and both are now forbidden. It is a sign of the severity of the authoritarian turn in Russia that the pre-Olympic period—with all its restrictions and repressions—can now be seen as a time of relative political liberty and free expression.

At the same time, Sochi does enjoy some important benefits of Olympic development. With newly built and upgraded infrastructure, the region has indeed become a year-round tourist magnet, and enjoys higher economic activity than most other Russian regions.[57] There are jobs in Sochi, and things to do, and beautiful places to see, and this attracts people from all around the nation—even during the coronavirus pandemic. To some extent, even some of the pre-Olympic promises have been fulfilled. Gas lines were finally extended to the residents of Akhshtyr, for example, though they were made to pay high fees for hookups to make the gas flow. In response to these mixed results, Petros's daughter Anja summed up her feelings:

> Yes, there is some movement and life in Sochi . . . but we lost so much. I moved away from Akhshtyr into the city. I have an apartment and everything is more or less okay. My father still lives back home, but I rarely go and visit him. It's too sad to see how things are now (February 2021, Sochi).

Notes

1. Names and identifying details in this chapter have been changed in the interests of anonymity. Parentheticals following quotations from those I interviewed include the places and years in which we spoke.

2. Robert W. Orttung and Sufian N. Zhemukhov, *Putin's Olympics: The Sochi Games and the Evolution of Twenty-First Century Russia*, 1st edition (London: Routledge, 2017); Fred Weir, "Sochi Olympics: Putin's Moment at World Podium," *Christian Science Monitor*, February 6, 2014, https://www.csmonitor .com/World/2014/0206/Sochi-Olympics-Putin-s-moment-at-world-podium.

3. Jonathan Grix and Nina Kramareva, "The Sochi Winter Olympics and Russia's Unique Soft Power Strategy," *Sport in Society* 20, no. 4 (2017): 461–75, https://doi.org/10.1080/17430437.2015.1100890; Emil Persson and Bo Petersson, "Political Mythmaking and the 2014 Winter Olympics in Sochi: Olympism and the Russian Great Power Myth," *East European Politics* 30, no. 2 (2014): 192–209, https://doi.org/10.1080/21599165.2013.877712.

4. Sven Daniel Wolfe, "'For the Benefit of Our Nation': Unstable Soft Power in the 2018 Men's World Cup in Russia," *International Journal of Sport Policy and Politics* 12, no. 4 (2020): 545–61, https://doi.org/10.1080/19406940.2020 .1839532.

5. Sven Daniel Wolfe, "A Silver Medal Project: The Partial Success of Russia's Soft Power in Sochi 2014," *Annals of Leisure Research* 19, no. 4 (2016): 481–96, https://doi.org/10.1080/11745398.2015.1122534.

6. Oleg Golubchikov, "From a Sports Mega-Event to a Regional Mega-Project: The Sochi Winter Olympics and the Return of Geography in State Development Priorities," *International Journal of Sport Policy and Politics* 9, no. 2 (2017): 237–55, https://doi.org/10.1080/19406940.2016.1272620; Martin Müller, "After Sochi 2014: Costs and Impacts of Russia's Olympic Games," *Eurasian Geography and Economics* 55, no. 6 (2014): 628–55, https://doi.org/ 10.1080/15387216.2015.1040432.

7. BBC News, "Pussy Riot Whipped at Sochi Games by Cossacks," February 19, 2014, sec. Europe, https://www.bbc.com/news/world-europe-26265230.

8. Marc Bennetts, "Russia's Anti-Gay Law Is Wrong—but So Is Some of the Criticism from the West," *The Guardian*, February 5, 2014, sec. Opinion, http://www.theguardian.com/commentisfree/2014/feb/05/russia-anti-gay -law-criticism-playing-into-putin-hands; Human Rights Watch, "Russia: Anti-LGBT Law a Tool for Discrimination," June 29, 2014, https://www.hrw.org/ news/2014/06/29/russia-anti-lgbt-law-tool-discrimination.

9. NBC News, "Who Are The Circassians, And Why Are They Outraged At Sochi?," February 7, 2014, updated February 9, 2014, https://www.nbcnews .com/storyline/sochi-olympics/who-are-circassians-why-are-they-outraged -sochi-n23716; Dave Zirin, "The Sochi Games Are Being Held on the Land of Genocide," February 17, 2014, https://www.thenation.com/article/archive/ sochi-land-circassians-they-cant-hide-anymore/.

10. Robert Thornberg and Kathy Charmaz, "Grounded Theory and Theoretical Coding," in *The SAGE Handbook of Qualitative Data Analysis*, edited by Uwe Flick, 1st edition (Los Angeles: SAGE Publications Ltd., 2014), 153–69.

11. Gilles Deleuze and Felix Guattari, *A Thousand Plateaus* (London: Bloomsbury Academic, 2013), 249.

12. Gilles Deleuze and Felix Guattari, *Kafka: Toward a Minor Literature* (Minneapolis: University of Minnesota Press, 1986).

13. Brian Chalkley and Stephen Essex, "Urban Development through Hosting International Events: A History of the Olympic Games," *Planning Perspectives* 14, no. 4 (1999): 369–94, https://doi.org/10.1080/026654399364184; Graeme Evans (ed.), *Mega-Events: Placemaking, Regeneration and City-Regional Development,* 1st edition (London: Routledge, 2020), https://www .routledge.com/Mega-Events-Placemaking-Regeneration-and-City-Regional -Development-1st/Evans/p/book/9781138608283; Hanwen Liao and Adrian Pitts, "A Brief Historical Review of Olympic Urbanization," *The International Journal of the History of Sport* 23, no. 7 (2006): 1232–52, https://doi.org/ 10.1080/09523360600832502; Andrew Smith, *Events and Urban Regeneration: The Strategic Use of Events to Revitalise Cities* (London: Routledge, 2012), https://doi.org/10.4324/9780203136997.

14. Mónica Degen and Marisol García, "The Transformation of the 'Barcelona Model': An Analysis of Culture, Urban Regeneration and Governance," *International Journal of Urban and Regional Research* 36, no. 5 (September 2012): 1022–38, https://doi.org/10.1111/j.1468-2427.2012.01152.x; Maria-Dolors Garcia-Ramon and Abel Albet, "Pre-Olympic and Post-Olympic Barcelona, a 'Model' for Urban Regeneration Today?," *Environment and Planning A: Economy and Space* 32, no. 8 (August 2000): 1331–34, https://doi.org/10.1068/a3331.

15. Robert Baade and Victor Matheson, "Going for the Gold: The Economics of the Olympics," *Journal of Economic Perspectives* 30, no. 2 (Spring 2016): 201–18, https://doi.org/10.1257/jep.30.2.201; Centre on Housing Rights and Evictions (COHRE), *Fair Play for Housing Rights: Mega-Events, Olympic Games and*

Housing Rights—Opportunities for the Olympic Movement and Others (Geneva: Centre on Housing Rights and Evictions (COHRE), 2007), http://www.ruig-gian .org/ressources/Report%20Fair%20Play%20FINAL%20FINAL%20070531 .pdf.

16. Martin Müller, "The Mega-Event Syndrome: Why So Much Goes Wrong in Mega-Event Planning and What to Do About It," *Journal of the American Planning Association* 81, no. 1 (2015): 6–17, https://doi.org/10.1080/01944363 .2015.1038292; Martin Müller and Christopher Gaffney, "Comparing the Urban Impacts of the FIFA World Cup and Olympic Games From 2010 to 2016," *Journal of Sport and Social Issues* 42, no. 4 (May 11, 2018): 247–69, https://doi .org/10.1177/0193723518771830.

17. Christopher Gaffney, "Gentrifications in Pre-Olympic Rio de Janeiro," *Urban Geography* 37, no. 8 (2016): 1132–53, https://doi.org/10.1080/02723638 .2015.1096115; Jacqueline Kennelly, "'You're Making Our City Look Bad': Olympic Security, Neoliberal Urbanization, and Homeless Youth," *Ethnography* 16, no. 1 (March 2015): 3–24, https://doi.org/10.1177/1466138113513526; Paul Watt, "'It's Not for Us,'" *City* 17, no. 1 (February 2013): 99–118, https://doi .org/10.1080/13604813.2012.754190.

18. Carl Death, "'Greening' the 2010 FIFA World Cup: Environmental Sustainability and the Mega-Event in South Africa," *Journal of Environmental Policy & Planning* 13 (2011): 99–117; John Karamichas, *The Olympic Games and the Environment* (Houndmills, Basingstoke, Hampshire, England: Palgrave Macmillan, 2013).

19. Robert Baade and Victor Matheson, "An Analysis of Drivers of Mega-Events in Emerging Economies," *Economics Department Working Papers*, Paper 153, September 1, 2015, http://crossworks.holycross.edu/econ_working_ papers/153; Scarlett Cornelissen, "The Geopolitics of Global Aspiration: Sport Mega-Events and Emerging Powers," *The International Journal of the History of Sport* 27, no. 16–18 (2010): 3008–25, https://doi.org/10.1080/09523367.2010 .508306; Ekain Rojo-Labaien, Álvaro Rodríguez Díaz, and Joel Rookwood (eds.), *Sport, Statehood and Transition in Europe : Comparative Perspectives from Post-Soviet and PostSocialist Societies* (London: Routledge, 2020), https:// doi.org/10.4324/9780429325847.

20. Grix and Kramareva, "The Sochi Winter Olympics and Russia's Unique Soft Power Strategy."

21. Oleg Golubchikov and Sven Daniel Wolfe, "Russia and the Politics of Extraverted Urbanism in the 2014 Winter Olympics and the 2018 FIFA World Cup," in Rojo-Labien, Díaz, and Rookwood, *Sport, Statehood and Transition in Europe: Comparative Perspectives from Post-Soviet and PostSocialist Societies*, 214–32.

22. Nadir Kinossian, "Stuck in Transition: Russian Regional Planning Policy between Spatial Polarization and Equalization," *Eurasian Geography and Economics* 54, no. 5–6 (December 2013): 611–29, https://doi.org/10.1080/153 87216.2014.901176; Golubchikov, "From a Sports Mega-Event to a Regional Mega-Project."

23. Müller, "After Sochi 2014."

24. Golubchikov, "From a Sports Mega-Event to a Regional Mega-Project."

25. Wolfe, "A Silver Medal Project."

26. Paul Droubie, "Phoenix Arisen: Japan as Peaceful Internationalist at the 1964 Tokyo Summer Olympics," *The International Journal of the History of Sport* 28, no. 16 (2011): 2309–22, https://doi.org/10.1080/09523367.2011.62 6683.

27. Sergei Akopov et al., "Is 'E' for 'EMPIRE'?: Re-Imagining New Russian Identity through Symbolic Politics of 'Sochi-2014,'" *Russian Journal of Communication* 9, no. 1 (2016): 1–18, https://doi.org/10.1080/19409419.2017.12622 06.

28. Irina Anisimova, "'E' for Empire: Postmodernism and Imperial Ideology in the Context of the Sochi Olympic Games," *Studies in Russian and Soviet Cinema* 12, no. 2 (2018): 136–52, https://doi.org/10.1080/17503132.2018.14473 51.

29. Susan Tenneriello, "Staging Sochi 2014: The Soft Power of Geocultural Politics in the Olympic Opening Ceremony," *Theatre Research International* 44, no. 1 (2019): 23–39, https://doi.org/10.1017/S0307883318000822.

30. Elena Trubina, "Mega-Events in the Context of Capitalist Modernity: The Case of 2014 Sochi Winter Olympics," *Eurasian Geography and Economics* 55, no. 6 (2015): 610–27, https://doi.org/10.1080/15387216.2015.1037780.

31. Karrie J. Koesel and Valerie J. Bunce, "Putin, Popular Protests, and Political Trajectories in Russia: A Comparative Perspective," *Post-Soviet Affairs* 28, no. 4 (2013): 403–23, https://doi.org/10.2747/1060–586X.28.4.403; David White, "Political Opposition in Russia: The Challenges of Mobilisation and the Political–Civil Society Nexus," *East European Politics* 31, no. 3 (2015): 314–25, https://doi.org/10.1080/21599165.2014.990628.

32. Maria Lipman, "How Putin Silences Dissent: Inside the Kremlin's Crackdown in Putin's Russia," *Foreign Affairs* 95, no. 3 (2016): [i]-46.

33. Jon Dart and Stephen Wagg, *Sport, Protest and Globalisation: Stopping Play* (London: Springer, 2016).

34. Helen Jefferson Lenskyj, *Sexual Diversity and the Sochi 2014 Olympics: No More Rainbows* (Houndmills, Basingstoke, Hampshire, England: Palgrave Macmillan, 2014).

35. Tom Balmforth, "Western Activists Urge Vodka Boycotts, Visa Bans To Protest Russia's Antigay Laws," RadioFreeEurope/RadioLiberty, July 29, 2013, https://www.rferl.org/a/lgbt-russia-vodka-boycott-gay-protest/25060328 .html.

36. Levada Center, "Rossiyanie o novykh konservativnykh zakonakh [Russians on the new conservative laws]," March 7, 2013, https://www.levada.ru/ 2013/07/03/rossiyane-o-novyh-konservativnyh-zakonah/.

37. Lars Funch Hansen, "Local Circassian Reactions to the 2014 Sochi Olympic Winter Games," *Sport in Society* 20, no. 4 (2015): 518–31, https://doi.org/ 10.1080/17430437.2015.1100891; Emil Persson, "Tears in the Patchwork: The Sochi Olympics and the Display of a Multiethnic Nation," *Euxeinos- Online*

Journal of the Center for Governance and Culture in Europe 12/2013 (December 2013): 15–25; Bo Petersson and Karina Vamling, "Fifteen Minutes of Fame Long Gone: Circassian Activism Before and After the Sochi Olympics," *Sport in Society* 20, no. 4 (2015): 505–17, https://doi.org/10.1080/17430437.2015.110 0887.

38. Sunnivie Brydum, "Russian Activists Cited for Protest Linking Sochi Olympics to 1936 Berlin Games," February 6, 2014, http://www.advocate.com/news/world-news/2014/02/06/russian-activists-cited-protest-linking -sochi-olympics-1936-berlin-games.

39. Giulia Mangione, "Accusations of Censorship as More Exhibitions Are Shut down at Perm Festival," New East Digital Archive, June 10, 2013, https://www.calvertjournal.com/articles/show/1048/perm-festival-white -nights-censorship.

40. Marat Guelman, "Why Russia Produces (and Quashes) so Much Radical Art," CNN Style, November 28, 2017, https://www.cnn.com/style/article/ russia-protest-art-saatchi-gallery/index.html.

41. Andrew Roth, "Russian Prosecutors Move to Liquidate Navalny's 'Extremist' Movement," *The Guardian*, April 16, 2021, http://www .theguardian.com/world/2021/apr/16/russian-prosecutors-move-to-liquidate -navalnys-extremist-movement.

42. Anti-Corruption Foundation, "Sochi 2014: Encyclopedia of Spending. The Cost of Olympics Report by the Anti-Corruption Foundation," 2014, https:// www.readkong.com/page/sochi-2014-encyclopedia-of-spending-9323483. This is an alternative link to the original report. The Russian state deleted the original website and report from the internet after declaring the Anti-Corruption Foundation an extremist organization. The skeleton of the original site is still on view at http://sochi.fbk.info/en/.

43. France 24, "Putin Allows Designated Protest Zone at Sochi Olympics," January 4, 2014, https://www.france24.com/en/20140104-russia-putin-allows -protest-zone-2014-sochi-olympic-games.

44. Ariel Cohen and Cassandra Lucaccioni, "Sochi: Security and Counterterrorism at the 2014 Winter Olympics," The Heritage Foundation, January 6, 2014, https://www.heritage.org/terrorism/report/sochi-security-and -counterterrorism-the-2014-winter-olympics.

45. Soldatov, Andrei, and Irina Borogan, *The Red Web: The Struggle Between Russia's Digital Dictators and the New Online Revolutionaries,* 1st edition (New York: Public Affairs, 2015).

46.-Olga G Voronina, "Pussy Riot Steal the Stage in the Moscow Cathedral of Christ the Saviour: Punk Prayer on Trial Online and in Court," *Digital Icons: Studies in Russian, Eurasian and Central European New Media* 9 (2013): 69–85.

47. BBC News, "Pussy Riot Whipped at Sochi Games by Cossacks."

48. Andrey Tolokonnikov, "Putin Fails to Teach Pussy Riot to 'Love the Motherland' at the Sochi Olympics," HuffPost, February 21, 2014, https://www

.huffpost.com/entry/putin-fails-to-teach-pussy-riot-to-love-the-motherland
_b_4831033.

49. Sochi 2014 Organizing Committee, *Official Report: Sochi 2014 Olympic Winter Games* (Sochi: The Organizing Committee of the XXII Olympic Winter Games and XI Paralympic Winter Games of 2014 in Sochi, 2015), 50.

50. International Olympic Committee (IOC), "Olympic Movement's Agenda 21: Sport for Sustainable Development," https://stillmed.olympic.org/media/Document%20Library/OlympicOrg/Documents/Olympism-in-Action/Environment/Olympic-Movement-s-Agenda-21.pdf; Sochi 2014 Organizing Committee, *Sochi 2014 Candidature File: Gateway to the Future* (Moscow: The Organizing Committee of the XXII Olympic Winter Games and XI Paralympic Winter Games of 2014 in Sochi, 2006).

51. United Nations Environment Programme (UNEP), "Russia to Relocate Olympic Sites after UN Expresses Environmental Concerns," UN News, July 7, 2008, https://news.un.org/en/story/2008/07/265442-russia-relocate-olympic-sites-after-un-expresses-environmental-concerns.

52. Environmental Watch on North Caucasus (EWNC), "EWNC Raises International Concern about the Environmental Impact of Sochi 2014 Olympics," accessed March 18, 2024, http://www.governance.bsnn.org/pdf/RU2.pdf; Molly O'Hara, "2014 Winter Olympics in Sochi: An Environmental and Human Rights Disaster," in *The State of Environmental Migration 2015: A Review of 2014*, edited by Francois Gemenne, Caroline Zickgraf, and Dina Ionesco (Geneva: Internation Organization for Migration [IOM], 2015), 203–20, http://labos.ulg.ac.be/hugo/wp-content/uploads/sites/38/2017/11/The-State-of-Environmental-Migration-2015-203-20.pdf.

53. Suren Gazaryan, "Sovmeshennaya Doroga 'Adler-Krasnaya Polyana' Unichtozhila Mzimtinsky Samshitovy Les [The Combined 'Adler-Krasnaya Polyana' Road Destroyed Mzymta's Boxwood Forests]," Environmental Watch on North Caucasus, 2010, http://www.ewnc.org/node/5634 (report no longer available online); Suren Gazaryan and Dmitry Shevchenko, "Sochi-2014: Independent Environmental Report" (n.p., Environmental Watch on North Caucasus, 2014), http://ewnc.org/files/sochi/Doklad-Sochi-2014_EWNC-Eng.pdf.

54. Igor Chestin, "Sochi Olympics Have Left a Trail of Environmental Destruction," The Conversation, February 14, 2014, http://theconversation.com/sochi-olympics-have-left-a-trail-of-environmental-destruction-23112.

55. International Union for Conservation of Nature and Natural Resources (IUCN), "The IUCN Red List of Threatened Species. Version 2021–1," 2021.

56. Levada Center, "Itogi olympiskhikh igr v Sochi [Results of the Sochi Olympic Games]," March 3, 2014, https://www.levada.ru/2014/03/03/itogi-olimpijskih-igr-v-sochi/.

57. Golubchikov and Wolfe, "Russia and the Politics of Extraverted Urbanism in the 2014 Winter Olympics and the 2018 FIFA World Cup."

CHAPTER 6

PyeongChang 2018

Making Sense of "Failed" Resistance

LIV YOON

From grassroots movements to global advocacy networks, the opposition to sport mega-events is no longer a mere fringe sentiment. Activists have come together to raise their voices spanning a spectrum of issues, including the displacement of local communities (human and nonhuman), escalating costs that strain public resources, environmental destruction, and human rights violations. The 2018 PyeongChang Winter Olympic and Paralympic Games in South Korea garnered attention from activists domestic and beyond for the degradation of a protected mountain to build an Alpine ski venue. In this chapter, I explore South Korean activists' discontent and resistance surrounding the controversial Alpine venue development—their efforts to shed light on the paradox between the glossy image projected and the harsh realities created by the Olympic and Paralympic Games. In doing so, I highlight their endeavors to challenge the status quo and usher in a critical reevaluation of the values associated with—as well as those overlooked by—sport mega-events.

Mount Gariwang is located in Jeongseon county of the northeastern province of Gangwon in South Korea, about fifty kilometers from the city of PyeongChang, which has a total population of around 39,000 (about 0.07% of the total South Korean population). Before being chosen as the official Alpine ski venue for the 2018 PyeongChang Winter Olympic and Paralympic Games, Mount Gariwang was a protected area that had been considered sacred for over five hundred years. It was distinguished as class 1 (on a descending scale of 1 to 3) on the South Korean Ministry of Environment's "Ecological Naturalness Scale," warranting the highest degree of protection for endangered species and ecosystem vulnerability.[1]

It was also classified as a degree 9 (on an ascending scale of 0 to 10) on the "Degree of Green Naturality" scale, under which forests with trees over fifty years of age with a degree 9 designation are protected from "any kind of development activities."[2] Mount Gariwang is—although perhaps no longer—home to over a hundred endangered mammal, bird, and plant species. One of these is the Wangsasre tree—the rare hybrid birch unique to the Korean Peninsula.[3] In June 2013, the "protected area" label was lifted from parts of Mount Gariwang in order to allow venue development for Olympic Alpine skiing events under the newly legislated "Special Act:"

> [For] Games-related facilities in a conservation zone . . . the Minister of the Korea Forest Service *may revoke the designation of all, or a part of a conservation zone* . . . in consideration of opinions of relevant specialists after establishing a plan to revoke the conservation zone for forest genetic resources, and to protect, conserve, and reinstate forests.[4]

Despite resistance from many environmental and civic groups, as well as some local residents, construction was undertaken and completed in September 2015. It was not just the forest (and its nonhuman species) that were affected; there was a small community at the base of the mountain, where the finish line for the ski course is now located. This small community of about fourteen households was displaced to pave the way for development, including the main registration building, two hotels (only one of which was built to completion), parking lots, and access roads. Those who owned land registered under their names were compensated to relocate to a new residential area that was built adjacent to the hill, while tenants with no land ownership (including those who had transferred over their land titles to their children's names) were given only nominal moving fees.[5] As a result, many had no choice but to move to cheaper areas, as land value around Mount Gariwang skyrocketed due to the Olympics, or took on additional debt to build their new homes in the new community.[6] Not only homes, but farm-based lifestyles and livelihoods, as well as a longstanding sense of community were also lost.[7]

The goals of this chapter are twofold. Firstly, I aim to add to the growing literature on sport-related environmental activism. This is an important contribution as the environmental impacts of sport and leisure-related events are increasingly hard to ignore. This is also a way to provide examples of responses to sport-related environmental concerns other than those offered by industry leaders—whom Wilson and Millington refer to as "sport management environmentalists" (SMEs).[8] These "managers" could represent a threat to genuine environmental activism surrounding sport, given their status and influence as "leaders" in the industry and the innocuous ways in which their profit-driven policies are articulated through their efforts to do and portray their environmental work. To this end, this chapter is an attempt to learn more about the different responses to environmental issues in sport mega-events beyond those offered by the elite. This is particularly important at a time when the industry seems open to improve its environmental practices, and yet, also seems limited in what is regarded as feasible.[9]

Secondly, I examine activists' emotions *after* a movement has ended to see how they make sense of their experience, particularly following a movement that did not achieve its objectives. This point builds on research by Max Haiven and Alex Khasnabish, who studied the space between "not-success and not-failure" of social movements in Nova Scotia, Canada.[10] They claim that there is immense value in exploring this space, germane to the ability to dream of different worlds, to "live between those worlds and this one, between 'not-success' and 'not-failure.'"[11] In other words, somewhere between the diametrically opposed preconceptions of success and failure exists a possibility for an unexpected outcome—that which represents a departure from the entrenched hegemonic power structure. As Haiven and Khasnabish claim, studying "failures" is important as they are "potential sites of rupture and possibility."[12] In doing so through examining activists' reflections after a movement that did not achieve its objectives, I reassess what "success" and "failure" could mean in (environmental) social movement settings, keeping in mind that most movements dwell in "the gap between success and failure."[13]

The commitment to a movement's cause is an emotional one. Most research to date focuses on emotions leading up to and during, rather than *after*, a movement. There is some research that examines what activists do, say, or feel after the movement's conclusion. Driscoll examines personal biographies of activists to identify what—beyond organizational membership—influences persistent commitment to environmental activism.[14] Among other reasons, he finds that an individual's relationship with nature was a significant factor that supported many activists' steadfast devotion to environmental causes. While his research was not an analysis of emotions per se, Driscoll nonetheless encourages an in-depth examination of how activists give meaning to their previous experiences.[15] With Driscoll's call as a departure point, this chapter considers activists' reflections on their emotions after the resistance to the development of Mount Gariwang by examining how activists attribute resonance to their experiences.

Sport Mega-Events, Development, Activism, and Resistance

The concept of "development" serves as a dominant metanarrative that helps explain the perceived need and yearning to build the Alpine venue on Mount Gariwang. To better understand how sport mega-events and the notion of development have come to be intertwined with one another requires considering sport mega-events through a political economy lens. Richard Gruneau and John Horne detail the relationship between sport mega-events and the neoliberal turn in international economics, the acceleration of the mobility of capital, and the resulting increase in social and ecological destruction.[16] They claim that sport mega-events play a significant role in "expanding the realm of capitalist exchange on a global scale" and act as a logical capital response to the overproduction for satiated markets.[17] David Harvey suggests that the production of immaterial goods (e.g., services, knowledge, experiences, and events) emerged as new forms of commodification to address the relationship identified by Gruneau and Horne.[18] Leveraging events as commodities has facilitated economic growth by universalizing the market and expanding the "sphere of exchange" by introducing a form of capital that can be launched and recuperated quickly, as commodities related to events, for example, are ephemeral and activity-oriented.[19]

Gruneau and Horne observe that while there is a plethora of academic work that identifies the tangible and intangible legacies of mega-events, there remains a need to focus more on the contradictory features of mega-events, particularly with respect to issues of injustice, inequality, social polarization, and domination.[20] These issues transcend nation state boundaries, as sport mega-events are integral to processes of globalization. Scholars have documented different responses to issues associated with sport mega-events and sport-related infrastructure projects, ranging from: responses to stadium development;[21] activist resistance in host cities;[22] journalists' response to (i.e., media coverage of) Olympic-related resistance;[23] and alternatives to urban planning policies.[24] Related research has focused on the experiences of marginalized populations in host cities[25] and responses to mega-event related environmental issues.[26]

Of particular relevance to this chapter are studies that examine responses to specific sport-related infrastructure developments, as they shed light on why sport-related events and projects are often linked with notions of modernity, progress, and an urban cosmopolitanism.[27] Many cities that want to adopt a postindustrial image and reposition themselves as key players on the global stage seek out mega-event hosting rights and transform public spaces into entertainment-oriented centers because there exists a sense of optimism that sport stadiums can stimulate urban development.[28] Scholars note how sport-related infrastructure projects (e.g., stadia, ski hills) align with the neoliberal capitalist hegemony and are believed to contribute to creating the image of a cosmopolitan city booming with entertainment and (sporting) culture, attracting people and capital.[29] As Gary Bridge and Sophie Watson put it, "cities are not simply material or lived spaces, but they are also spaces of representation that, in this case, are deeply aligned with neoliberal discourses of urban development."[30] The desire for reaping these benefits is more prominent in nations and locations considered peripheral, including PyeongChang, South Korea.

As demonstrated elsewhere in this collection, historians and sociologists of sport have examined Olympic-related activism and protests mainly with respect to both athlete-led activism (e.g., Tommie Smith's and John Carlos's Black Power salute in the 1968 Mexico Olympics) and actions by political groups that strategically leveraged the mega-event to amplify their message.[31] However, only a few scholars have examined sport-related activism centered around environmental concerns. Some studies have examined the contested nature of sport's impact on the environment, focusing on the competing stakeholders and the multiple meanings attached to the natural world in sport settings.[32] Others have explored the efforts of activists in these settings. Belinda Wheaton interviewed the UK-based group Surfers Against Sewage (SAS) and concluded that while there are limitations to political significance and impact, sport-related subcultural groups such as SAS provide a platform through which a "politicized trans-local collectivity" can be formed.[33] Wheaton calls for more exploration into the relationship between leisure, consumption, and new social movements, particularly around environmentalism. Another example is provided by John Stolle-McAllister, who examined the conflict over the construction of a golf course in Tepoztlán, Morelos, Mexico, and the resulting movement against the project.[34] Kyle Bunds has examined the relationship between sport and environment-related charity causes.[35] This organizational auto-ethnography provides a rich account of the "messiness of activism from the inside" of a UK-based global water charity that raises funds through the use of sport (e.g., leveraging philanthropic running events).

The Experience of Resisting the Development of Mount Gariwang

In what follows, I center the voices of activists from various South Korean organizations (e.g., related to sport, environment, or civic empowerment)

FIGURE 6.1. Activists at the Mount Gariwang Alpine Venue during the 2018 PyeongChang Olympic Winter Games. Credit: Liv Yoon.

speaking about how they made sense of their resistance work *against* destruction that was already happening *due to* a sport-related event (as opposed to planning and running events to raise money *for* a cause *using* sport). The analysis offered here is based upon open-ended, semi-structured interviews with fourteen individuals involved in various activities of resistance toward the development of Mount Gariwang. They were all part of the coalition "People Against the Deforestation of Mount Gariwang"(가리왕산 벌목을 반대하는사람들의 모임). The four most prominent groups of the coalition were: the environmental NGO (ENGO) "Green Korea" (녹색연합); two sport-related NGOs (SNGO)—"Center for Sport Culture" (스포츠문화연구소) and "Physical Education & Citizens Association" (체육시민연대); and one civil society group, "Cultural Action" (문화연대). All four organizations are nonprofit, independent bodies separate from governmental structures, and geographically based in Seoul. The goal of the interviews was to hear what stories and impressions these individuals were left with from their experience resisting the development of Mount Gariwang for the 2018 Olympics (see figure 6.1). Although activists were not explicitly asked about their emotions (e.g., through questions like "how did this experience make you feel?"), what stood out most in their responses was the affective dimension (i.e., how activists seemed to feel about what they experienced). This emotional dimension of their resistance experience emerged as the most prominent and striking aspect of the interviews. In this way, hearing the activists recount their experiences was an effective way to understand how activists felt about, and made meaning out of, a movement that did not achieve its original goal(s).[36]

The main themes that emerged from the interviews organized themselves around the questions of: (1) what stories do activists tell themselves (and others) after an unsuccessful environmental social movement, and in doing so, what emotions are conveyed?; and (2) what implications do their emotions have with respect to sustaining future activism and social change at large? Through these questions, I hope to understand how activists responded and reacted to a "failed" movement, and how certain experiences may or may not influence an activist's worldview or future capacity for action. The findings as presented here are centered around activists' accounts, with respect to: (1) frustrations about broader structural constraints; (2) regrets about, and questioning of, their own practices; and (3) accepting, overcoming, and utilizing challenges.

Frustrations and Anger Surrounding Political (Mis)affairs

Most stories told by activists revealed their frustrations and anger about the state of social and political affairs in South Korea at the time of their collective actions. Many expressed that they felt as if they were fighting a losing battle when considering the broader political and institutional climate. In particular, they pointed to corruption over private financial interests and a lack of transparency throughout decision-making processes, including public consultations, as most distressing. Members of a civic action group explained:

> A big problem with this controversy was that the political and administrative sides weren't honest. So many things are run based on personal/ private interest and benefit—this controversy made that clear—everyone in power is intricately networked and they're taking the country to ruin.

Specifically, some bemoaned the holes in regulations and special laws that paved the way forward for the development of Mount Gariwang and filled the pockets of construction company owners. Activists conveyed distrust toward procedures that were supposed to serve as "checks and balances":

> The Environmental Impact Assessment (EIA) is the go-to procedure for beginning a development. Rather than actually assessing whether it makes sense for the development to go ahead, it's more of an answer key and a green light, symbolically.

There needs to be mechanisms put in place so that the law can't keep making exceptions for itself—for example, the Ministry of Environment's protection law for Mount Gariwang, and then another law that exempts itself from the former. These cases must be forbidden—we need citizens' democratic voices to create change here.

The mistrust of government extended beyond laws and processes to those working in related public offices. A civil society group member expressed his discontent with them, through which he concluded that the core problem lies in the structural constraints that shape the actions of civil servants:

Public servants? They should be called private servants! There's no system in place for [safe] internal whistleblowing. They have no mechanism through which they can say no to powers above. When you meet them personally, sure they're good people, but in the system, they're agents of [systemic] violence. Say one's had enough, stir shit up and take an exit, are they rewarded or applauded? Never!

On a similar note, an ENGO member expressed his frustration and exasperation upon realizing that what his group was promoting was in fact *not* falling upon deaf ears:

When I meet with people from the provincial government, they'll even say, "I know that this shouldn't happen . . . but it is, and there is no other way." I'll hear this kind of thing often in private interactions like over a meal. It's one thing to feel that what we argued was perhaps uncompromising nonsense, but to know that those on "the other side" also see it as valid and yet, nothing can happen.[. . .] that brings on a whole other level of helplessness. So yeah, we were pretty drained towards the end. [. . .] It felt like we were talking to a wall.

What further contributed to the activists' anger about structural constraints was that there was no way to let those in power know of their grievances. Setting aside this discontent, many activists wanted to have a discussion with the decision-makers first and foremost about the controversy. However, their requests were ignored, as noted by a member of a cultural action group:

We wanted a thorough debate so we contacted the PyeongChang Organizing Committee for the 2018 Olympic and Paralympic Winter Games (POCOG) and the Ministry of Culture, Sports and Tourism often but they ignored us, basically treating us as if we're invisible. If open, productive debates could happen here, it may trigger citizens to think more critically about the Olympics but nope, no chance.

That is not to say that the decision-makers were always shrouded in secrecy—they did, in fact, host press conferences and consultation sessions. But, as one civil society member put it, they often had a foregone conclusion:

> When debates or consultations do happen, this concept of "communication" is already out the door. [POCOG and other decision-makers] invite only those who they know will say things they like, and they call this a debate.

Such repeated negative encounters, however, may have led activists to be more resistant to accepting "solutions" (or compromises) offered by those in power. A case in point is the activists' dismissal of POCOG's self-promoted collection of Certified Emission Reduction (CER) credits (or "carbon offset credits") in order to "offset" greenhouse gas emissions resulting from the Games. CERs allow event organizers to financially contribute to carbon-reducing initiatives, such as renewable energy projects, often based in developing countries where projects are cheaper.[37] However, this idea of "offsetting" has been problematized due to the lack of standardization and accountability in these projects, as well as a failure to guarantee that projects would not have taken place without the CER purchase.[38] In this way, frustration and disappointment at the actions and antics of the elite served as an additional mechanism by which activists were able to critically assess the motivations behind offers of these material solutions—"solutions" that did not actually address deeper issues of power and inequality.

It is possible that the frustration and anger played a role in pushing the activists to see the purpose—rather than the pain—of their actions. Akin to how *apocalypse* means a disclosure of knowledge or revelation, the sense of gloom that frustration and anger elicited could have reminded the activists that what they were resisting was much bigger than Mount Gariwang alone. Another possible interpretation is that there may be a sense of satisfaction in the fact that the resistance was challenging, because there could be a shared belief that "worthy causes are not supposed to be easy."

"Would've, Could've, Should've": Questioning the Strategies Used

While looking back upon their work around the Mount Gariwang controversy, rather than focusing explicitly on how they *felt*, many activists reflected upon, and questioned, strategies they used—from which I gathered a sense of regret and reflexive questioning. For example, many talked

FIGURE 6.2. Activists protesting during the 2018 PyeongChang Olympic Winter Games, dressed as trees that were cut down to make way for the Alpine venue. Credit: Liv Yoon.

about the limits of using "only the environmental frame" (i.e., emphasizing the issue of Mount Gariwang solely, versus other issues related to sport mega-events), as members of Green Korea suggested:

> I've wondered if we should've perhaps hidden our true intentions [to save Mount Gariwang] and started with the [negative issues associated with] PyeongChang Games in general.
>   Sure, people's awareness of climate change and other environmental issues has increased, but the economic development logic still triumphs.

Reflecting upon their strategies—and particularly, feeling regretful about some—also led activists to consider what assumptions they had held. In this case, thinking about the ineffectiveness of their environment-focused framing revealed their (perhaps cynical) assumptions about what the broader public's priorities are, and how the public may perceive the salience of environmental issues (see figure 6.2). In this vein, an activist from the citizen group Cultural Action questioned whether their movement's focus on nonhuman species was conducive to their goal of encouraging people to think more critically about development activities:

> One of the things activists get scolded on the most is putting animals and plant species at the center and not [local] humans. Their response

is often, "so the sheep can live, but we should die?" Basically, what was supposed to be a discussion of a specific environmental issue becomes an endless battle of values and ideologies.

Other activists questioned their focus on affective dimensions (as opposed to "hard facts") in their campaign efforts. As ENGO activists put it:

> I think environmental activists are emotionally more in tune or sensitive to begin with [. . .] but coming up with arguments based on their concern for nature alone is useless for people who think they're getting neglected from [economic] prosperity due to prioritizing nature.

When activists mulled over the "would've, could've, should've" moments in this manner, empathy seemed to surface. Empathy—"the act of imaginatively experiencing the feelings, thoughts and situations of another"[39]—is most commonly linked to self- and social transformation.[40] In this light, activists' questioning of their own practices and the empathy it elicited could lead to a change in their outlook and strategies for future resistance work.

Other activists were less precise when outlining their regrets, expressing instead their tendency to question the broader value system that surrounds "nature." For example, a photographer (who does not identify himself as an activist, but has been involved with the resistance) pointed out that the affective dimensions of nature are undervalued. When explaining why he did not include names of each species in his book of photographs from Mount Gariwang, he said:

> I think our education system has made people always yearn for facts and answers. Like, when you look at a flower, you *need* to know its name. So when people look at my book, their first comment is, "why are these not labeled?" rather than "wow they are beautiful!" This need to satisfy the cerebral is dominant, and that can hinder getting across things like the invaluable worth of nature.

In these ways, activists' reflections seemed to provoke thinking, especially about what constitutes strategic, persuasive communication for a successful movement. These moments seemed to serve as a way for the activists to slow down and practice mindfulness—crystallizing the intention of their actions and reflexively asking what overarching values informed their objectives.

Lastly, many activists attributed the lack of support or interest in their cause to the timing of controversy. In late 2016 and early 2017, public affairs in South Korea were enveloped by the impeachment scandal involving former President Park Geun-hye. Activists acknowledged "bad timing" as a significant factor that hindered their resistance. At the same time, given the sheer impact of the impeachment scandal, particularly in motivating citizens to voluntarily assemble and speak out, an ENGO activist reflected on her group's activities and the desire to have "piggybacked" on the controversy:

> Timing was uncanny. When this scandal was slowly breaking, we had been investigating unrelatedly into real estate investments in PyeongChang and noticed that [Choi Soon-sil, a figure involved in the impeachment scandal] was the owner of a bunch of land designated for development [for the Games], and her name kept coming up in the Games' budget documents. So had everything about the scandal fully been revealed just a year earlier and we connected the dots, things may have turned out differently.

However, while many activists regretted the inopportune timing of their campaign efforts coincident with the impeachment scandal, they acknowledged that some things were "just outside their control" and therefore could not be fussed over. In doing so, they seemed to come to terms with, or find a way to utilize, challenges they faced. Necessary in this process were acceptance and a summoning of empathy and love for those with whom they disagreed.

Accepting, Overcoming, and Utilizing Challenges

A civic activist articulated how the anger resulting from the above challenges sometimes led to a sense of dejection and loss that made it difficult to carry on:

> Whenever this kind of controversy happens, those who actively oppose and speak up are just a handful of environmental and civic groups. Almost every time, winners and losers are already decided from the get-go. We know that too, so sometimes when we encounter an issue, we feel a sense of rage and despair at the same time . . . We lose our self-regard a little bit and often feel lonely.

What further added to this sense of loneliness was that there was not much support from local residents. In fact, a prevailing sentiment across the activists was that the resistance against the development of Mount Gariwang was a movement only of and by activist groups as opposed to collectively led by various members of the public who do not necessarily identify themselves as "activists." Most activists expressed dismay at the locals' hostility, apathy, or both, identifying this as the main reason behind why the movement did not grow past organizational boundaries. Green Korea (ENGO) activists explained that garnering local support was nearly impossible as the sentiment of the locals—at least that promoted by the local representatives—was pro-development. They added that the lack of local support resulted not only from taking an opposite stance, but also from apathy and indifference. Talking about this in particular was usually accompanied by a look of resignation.

At the same time, however, the lack of local support pushed the activists to think about why many locals supported the development—and this process seemed to involve summoning empathy and love for those with whom the activists disagreed, people who had displayed hostility toward them. As a result, it is possible that this challenge presented an opportunity for the activists to think about whether one can be exceptional when it comes to the empathy and love required in activism. In other words, even though activists portrayed exasperation toward the locals who advocated for the development as well as the Games' decision-makers, the feelings of frustration they felt toward the locals seemed to have a different feel, color, or temperature to them than the feelings they felt toward the decision-makers in power. This complicated set of both similar and contradictory emotions directed at different groups seemed to present a tricky emotional space for the activists to navigate.

Further, the lack of local support led to activists joining forces with other organizations. Many mentioned that they were happy about the coalitions that formed, specifically the banding together of groups unlikely to have interacted with one another otherwise. Even though the protests and rallies they held together were never massive in scale, the synergy resulting from the banding of "unlikely" partners was claimed by many interviewees as a valuable asset to carry forward into future social movements. Reflecting on the activities of the coalition provided in turn an opportunity for each organization to reflect on their own practices as well. An ENGO activist stated:

> My perspective has changed. Environmental activist groups have a particular identity that they approach issues with. But this Mount Gariwang case has shown us the limits of that identity and perspective [. . .]. Our intents and claims wouldn't have any clout without those also from sport and civic groups. Our senior members have told us that "social movements are all [about] coalitions and partnerships" and we really felt that this time.

This reflection reveals the need for activists to have critically reviewed their strategies to date. Other ENGO activists reconsidered concepts they had previously dismissed, such as the idea of quantifying environmental value:

> There's a lot of taboo about quantifying and putting financial figures to nature among environmental activists. Yet, if [nature] isn't quantified, its value can't be measured, rendering it impossible to decide whether to conserve or destroy something. So, I think activists may benefit from being more open to [quantifying environmental value]—especially when trying to convince citizens—to boil it down to "would you rather take this much now from developing" versus "you can get a lot more later by conserving."

In this manner, reflections and regrets seemed to open up avenues activists had not previously considered, paving new possible ways for future campaigns. For some of the activists interviewed, this reckoning seemed to reveal a humble parting with some of the ideas they long held as right and true.

The stories the activists I interviewed told themselves after this movement had not only to do with themselves and their organizations, but also with the public. For example, many activists indicated that there was no platform through which people could speak up about injustices—both personal and otherwise—and in this way, some activists seemed to express empathy for the locals who were often unsupportive of the activists' work. As a critical sport action group member said:

> [Controversies like this] would turn out differently if civil society's responses included regular people . . . more so, the space for people to say what they need—[this creation of space] is probably what we as an organization should be after. That may lead to people realizing that this is supposed to be a participatory democracy, and that if we don't act it out, current and future lives will be more desolate.

In this manner, undergoing challenges fueled activists to ask bigger questions. Specifically, through their reflections, activists pondered the ways they could contribute to enabling a more emancipatory and participatory public sphere for those powerless and most directly affected.

"Moral Battery": Anger, Frustration, and Humility

In light of activists' stories, it is important to consider the emotional dimensions of their reflections. Jonathan Turner notes that it is difficult to define "emotion" because it operates at many different levels (e.g., biological and neurological, behavioral, cultural, structural, and situational).[41] Laura Pulido refers to "emotions, psychological development, souls and passions" as constituting the "interior" dimensions of social movements, while Hyojoung Kim argues that overlooking the emotional dynamics when researching social movements "risks a fundamental misunderstanding of the dynamics of collective action."[42] Here, I adopt the broad sociological view that emotions are "converging forces that activate . . . states of conscious and unconscious affect that shape thought, behavior, interaction and patterns of social organization."[43]

Scholars like Deborah Gould and James Jasper have highlighted the dynamism of emotions in movements—in other words, emotions in movements, while patterned, are also mobile, and thus can be transformed into a force for social change.[44] Others have, more specifically, detailed the utility of anger in particular, claiming that as the dominant response to perceptions of injustice, anger can motivate action more than other emotions can.[45] Gould's analysis of the movements against the US government's neglect of HIV-AIDS victims in the 1980s, illustrates how emotions such as loss and shame were transformed and mobilized into pride and anger. She highlights three characteristics of emotions that influence their dynamism in social movements: (1) emotions are non-static (i.e., they are subject to change due to events, relationships, and experiences both personal and collective); (2) emotions are combinatory (e.g., despair can come bundled with grief and sadness, but also activate anger); and (3) how emotions work is indeterminate and unpredictable.[46]

Jasper introduced the term "moral battery" to refer to the synergy that arises from a combination of "a positive and a negative emotion, and the tension or contrast between them [that] motivates action or demands attention."[47] Eduardo Romanos's longitudinal analysis of emotional practices of Spanish anarchists under Franco's dictatorship found that the use of hope allowed the anarchists to positively assess the effectiveness of their strategies in challenging the authorities, while invoking indignation in onlookers helped gather support.[48] Romanos suggests that the movement's political power came precisely from the combination of hope and anger.

Another example of a moral battery is the combination of anger and joy. Helen Ransan-Cooper, Selen Ercan, and Sonya Duus examined the emotional fabric of the anti-coal seam gas (CSG) movement in rural Australia, and found that while anger was central in mobilizing various people as anti-CSG protesters, it was the combination of anger and joy—specifically through "doing community"—that helped sustain the movement.[49] They found that values held in high regard such as civility, hospitality, loyalty, and inclusivity led movement participants to hold back from confrontation, which helped to build solidarity across difference. This also led to the development of new activist skills and strategies around maintaining relationships with others who held different views within that particular setting.

Although Ransan-Cooper, Ercan, and Duus focus on the role of emotions in mobilizing and sustaining the anti-CSG movement (i.e., rather than analyzing emotions in the aftermath of a "failed" movement), their use of the "affective practices approach" is particularly instructive. According to Margaret Wetherell, the affective practices approach recognizes that although emotions may be considered typical and familiar, they are also context specific and may not be immediately apparent or communicable.[50] Considering emotions as relational and embodied, this approach focuses on making sense of emotions (e.g., how they are expressed and interpreted), as well as how they are physically manifested. Using this approach means examining physical, symbolic, and relational elements of emotions altogether, as well as being sensitive to how contextualized individual and collective experiences shape emotions and vice-versa.[51] The affective practices approach puts a spotlight on the everyday experience of emotions and aims to capture how expressions of emotions both influence and are influenced by particularity of context.

In the opposition to the development of Mount Gariwang, frustration, anger, as well as reflexive humility (e.g., empathy with pro-development locals, acknowledgment of shortcomings, and questioning of strategies used) were the predominant emotions portrayed by the activists. At the same time, the humility with which they reflected upon their strategies and relatively privileged status seemed to give rise to a sense of empathy with the pro-development locals. In this way, the combination of anger, frustration, and humility seemed to remind activists that a better strategy would be one that also resonated with pro-development locals. For instance, rather than dismiss the pro-development locals' desires for economic growth as greedy or shortsighted, they acknowledged that it would be better to introduce the question of whether Olympic-related developments are the only way to obtain growth. In this way, the juxtaposition of dissimilar emotions encountered in activism created space to accentuate the broader raison d'être of their activism—that is, to hold those in power accountable, and to address the broader, deeply entrenched issues of inequality underlying sociopolitical-environmental issues.

Echoed here is the claim that emotions often appear in combinations, and that it is the interaction of these emotions that influence action.[52] Similar to the anti-Francoist activists in Romanos's study, frustration and anger provided direction for seeking who should be held accountable for the destruction of Mount Gariwang and the subsequent social and ecological consequences.[53] In this way, "negative" emotions like anger may actually be useful for motivating punitive and preventative demands against injustice.[54] Moreover, looking back upon the movement led to a critical and reflexive assessment by activists of their tendency to blame locals (i.e., for making them feel isolated and unsupported throughout the movement), and to reconsider who should be held accountable for the injustices, and what root causes need to be redressed.

Another example illustrative of the synergy incongruent emotions can bring was found in how activists felt toward the local residents. On one hand, activists voiced their resignation and resentment about the lack of local support that rendered their efforts fruitless. On the other hand, however, they also understood why the locals may not have wanted to stand behind them—considering the historical sociopolitical currents that led them to yearn for economic development over environmental protection. Thus, the activists simultaneously felt lonely and helpless in their efforts while they also empathized with the locals. Perhaps for this reason, for many activists, the lack of local support often resulted in comments about broader structural constraints that led to this situation, and reflections on how they may navigate around similar challenges in the future.

There is research that also indicates a surprising inverse relationship between "positive" emotions (e.g., empathy) and outcomes in social movements.[55] Joseph de Rivera, Elena A. Gerstmann, and Lisa Maisels found that while sympathy for those in unfortunate circumstances may motivate action in a direct personal relationship, it does not seem to fuel political action in movement contexts.[56] Instead, what was more effective in motivating action was anger and moral outrage at injustice. Nonetheless, in PyeongChang, the fissure between the emotions of anger and empathy served to create an outcome the activists did not explicitly have in mind, which was to think about and challenge the larger structural factors that led the (pro-development) locals to adopt the position they did. In this way, rather than breaking down with a sense of isolation and despair from the lack of local support, activists found direction and purpose in competing emotions.

As such, perhaps defining "success" differently is the key to sustaining activism. The wide range of at times conflicting emotions portrayed by activists when telling their stories invites a reconsideration of what "success" and "failure" in a movement means. Even though the goal of protecting Mount Gariwang from development was not achieved, the stories told and emotions embedded within activists' accounts did not necessarily convey pure "failure." There is generative capacity in falling short of a goal in activism by encouraging activists to interrogate their own understandings of structures and relationships that constitute successful movements, so as to create a space in which new approaches can emerge.

Conclusion

The stories told by activists—and the emotions revealed through them—convey the "dissonance and noise, the confusion and the contradiction, the joys and sorrows of the mess" that Haiven and Khasnabish claim are important to assess and capture social movements' true potential.[57] Attending to the emotions embedded in the stories told by activists sheds light on what supports their persistent commitment despite not achieving their goal, the lived realities that make up the fabric of resistance work, as well as fissures created for imaginaries of alternative societies and ways of life. While the movement against the development of Mount Gariwang could be deemed unsuccessful with respect to achieving its goal, it was considered neither a success nor a failure by activists. It is this space between "not-success and not-failure" that Haiven and Khasnabish argue is fertile for recognizing "unrealized expectations, and unexpected openings and possibilities."[58]

The activists who resisted the development of Mount Gariwang transformed a lack of "success" into an opening for continued interference with the broader structural issues that informed the Mount Gariwang controversy. In this, they found an opportunity to reflect and reassess their resistance strategies carrying forward. Even as the 2018 Winter Olympic and Paralympic Games have concluded, they continue to voice concerns about the residues of the development, stating that problems will only get more dire especially as the media spotlight has come and gone after the spectacle of the Games has concluded. In this sense, the activists' endeavors are far from over.

Notes

1. Dae Uk Jeon and Jinhyung Chon, "System Thinking in the Resilience of the Ecosystem and Ecotourism of Mount Gariwang Based on the Controversy around the Venue Construction for PyeongChang 2018 Olympics," *Korean System Dynamics Research* 15, no. 13 (2014): 61–79; Rebecca Kim, "They Went and Did It! 500-Year-Old Primeval Forest at Mount Gariwang Unlawfully Destroyed for 2018 PyeongChang Winter Olympics," Games Monitor, (November 22, 2014), http://www.gamesmonitor.org.uk/node/2228; Ministry of Environment,

"Defining 'Ecological Naturalness,' Ministry of Environment, 2009, accessed April 29, 2024, https://www.data.go.kr/data/15124210/fileData.do.

2. Kim, "They Went and Did It!"

3. Julian Cheyne, "The Giant 'Wangsasre,' a Hybrid Birch Unique to Korea in Mt. Gariwang-san," Games Monitor (January 19, 2013), http://www.games monitor.org.uk/node/1942; Jeon and Chon, "System Thinking."

4. Special Act on Support for the 2018 Pyeongchang Olympic and Paralympic Winter Games, "Article 34 (Special Exceptions to the Forest Protection Act)," Korea Legislation Research Institute and the Korean Law Translation Center, https://elaw.klri.re.kr/kor_service/lawView.do?hseq=49678&lang=ENG. Italics added for emphasis.

5. JungMin Park, "PyeongChang Winter Olympics Just Means 'Pain' to Us," NoCut News, May 1, 2014, http://www.nocutnews.co.kr/news/4017216; Liv Yoon, "Understanding Local Residents' Responses to the Development of Mount Gariwang for the 2018 PyeongChang Winter Olympic and Paralympic Games," Leisure Studies 39, no. 5 (2020): 673–87.

6. Hanju Kim, "That Alpine Venue—That Used to Be My Home': Local Residents Kicked Out by the PyeongChang Olympics," Workers, November 14, 2017, http://workers-zine.net/27760.

7. Yoon, "Understanding Local Residents' Responses."

8. Brian Wilson and Brad Millington, "Sport and Environmentalism" in Routledge Handbook of the Sociology of Sport, edited by Richard Giulianotti (New York: Routledge, 2015), 366–76.

9. Ibid., 367.

10. Max Haiven and Alex Khasnabish, The Radical Imagination (Halifax, NS: Fernwood Publishing, 2014).

11. Ibid., 130.

12. Ibid., 123.

13. Ibid., 86.

14. Daniel Driscoll, "Beyond Organizational Ties: Foundations of Persistent Commitment in Environmental Activism," Social Movement Studies 17, no. 6 (2018): 697–715.

15. Ibid., 715.

16. Richard Gruneau and John Horne, "Mega-Events and Globalization: A Critical Introduction," in Mega-Events and Globalization: Capital and Spectacle in a Changing World Order, edited by Richard Gruneau and John Horne (London: Routledge, 2016), 1–28.

17. Ibid., 9.

18. David Harvey, The Condition of Postmodernity: An Enquiry into the Origins of Cultural Change (New York: Blackwell, 1989).

19. Gruneau and Horne, "Mega-Events and Globalization," 9.

20. Ibid.

21. Anouk Bélanger, "Sport Venues and the Spectacularization of Urban Spaces in North America," International Review for the Sociology of Sport 35,

no. 3 (2000): 378–97; Kimberly S. Schimmel, "Deep Play: Sports Mega-Events and Urban Social Conditions in the USA," *The Sociological Review* 54, no. 2 (2006): 160–74; Jay Scherer and Michael P. Sam, "Public Consultation and Stadium Developments: Coercion and the Polarization of Debate," *Sociology of Sport Journal* 25 (2008): 443–61; Michael P. Sam and Jay Scherer, "Fitting a Square Stadium into a Round Hole: A Case of Deliberation and Procrastination Politics" *Sport in Society* 13, no. 1 (2010): 1458–68.

22. Helen J. Lenskyj, *Inside the Olympic Industry: Power, Politics, and Activism* (Albany: State University of New York Press, 2000); Helen J. Lenskyj, *Olympic Industry Resistance: Challenging Olympic Power and Propaganda* (Albany: State University of New York Press, 2008); Jules Boykoff, "Space Matters: The 2010 Winter Olympics and Its Discontents," *Human Geography* 4, no. 2 (2011): 48–60; Jules Boykoff, *Celebration Capitalism and the Olympic Games* (New York: Routledge, 2014); Jules Boykoff, "Sochi 2014: Politics, Activism, and Repression," in Gruneau and Horne, *Mega-Events and Globalization*, 131–48.

23. Brian Wilson and Nicolien VanLuijk, "Covering Protest at the Vancouver 2010 Olympics: A 'Peace Journalism' Inspired Analysis," *Sociology of Sport Journal* 36, no. 1 (2019): 32–47.

24. Anne-Marie Broudehoux, "Seeds of Dissent: The Politics of Resistance to Beijing's Olympic Redevelopment," in *Dissent and Cultural Resistance in Asian Cities*, edited by Melissa Butcher and Selvaraj Velayutham (London: Routledge, 2009), 14–32; Christopher Gaffney, "A World Cup for Whom? The Impact of the 2014 World Cup on Brazilian Football Stadiums and Cultures," in *The Country of Football: Politics, Popular Culture, and the Beautiful Game in Brazil*, edited by Paulo Fontes and Bernardo Buarque de Hollanda, (London: Hurst & Co. Ltd, 2014), 189–208; Christopher Gaffney, "The Urban Impacts of the 2014 World Cup in Brazil," in Gruneau and Horne, *Mega-Events and Globalization*, 167–85; Caitlin Pentifallo and Robert VanWynsberghe, "Mega-Event Impact Assessment and Policy Attribution: Embedded Case Study, Social Housing, and the 2010 Winter Olympic Games," *Journal of Policy Research in Tourism, Leisure and Events* 7, no. 3 (2015): 266–81.

25. Anne-Marie Broudehoux, "Mega-Events, Urban Image Construction, and the Politics of Exclusion," in Gruneau and Horne, *Mega-Events and Globalization*, 113–30; Jacqueline Kennelly, "'You're Making Our City Look Bad': Olympic Security, Neoliberal Urbanization, and Homeless Youth," *Ethnography* 16, no. 1 (2015): 3–24; Jacqueline Kennelly, *Olympic Exclusions: Youth, Poverty, and Social Legacies* (New York: Routledge, 2016); Jacqueline Kennelly and Paul Watt, "Sanitizing Public Space in Olympic Host Cities: The Spatial Experiences of Marginalized Youth in 2010 Vancouver and 2012 London," *Sociology* 45, no. 5 (2011): 765–81; Jacqueline Kennelly and Paul Watt, "Seeing Olympic Effects through the Eyes of Marginally Housed Youth: Changing Places and the Gentrification of East London," *Visual Studies* 27, no. 2 (2012): 151–60; Jacqueline Kennelly and Paul Watt, "Restricting the Public in

Public Space: The London 2012 Olympic Games, Hyper-Securitization and Marginalized Youth," *Sociological Research Online* 18, no. 2 (2013), https://doi.org/10.5153/sr0.3038; Christine M. O'Bonsawin, "No Olympics on Stolen Native Land': Contesting Olympic Narratives and Asserting Indigenous Rights within the Discourse of the 2010 Vancouver Games," *Sport in Society* 13, no. 1 (2010): 143–56.

26. Helen J. Lenskyj, "Sport and Corporate Environmentalism," *International Review for the Sociology of Sport* 33, no. 4 (1998): 341–54; Jules Boykoff and Gilmar Mascarenhas, "The Olympics, Sustainability, and Greenwashing: The Rio 2016 Summer Games," *Capitalism Nature Socialism* 27, no. 2 (2016): 1–11; John Karamichas, *The Olympic Games and the Environment* (Houndsmill, Basingstoke, Hampshire, England: Palgrave Macmillan, 2013); Graeme Hayes and John Horne, "Sustainable Development, Shock and Awe? London 2012 and Civil Society," *Sociology* 45, no. 4 (2011): 749–64; Graeme Hayes and John Karamichas, *Olympic Games, Mega-Events and Civil Societies: Globalization, Environment, Resistance* (New York: Palgrave Macmillan, 2012); Kyoungyim Kim and Heejun Chung, "Eco-Modernist Environmental Politics and Counter-Activism around the 2018 PyeongChang Winter Games," *Sociology of Sport Journal* 35, no. 1 (2018): 17–28; Brad Millington and Brian Wilson, *The Greening of Golf: Sport, Globalization and the Environment* (Manchester, England: Manchester University Press, 2016); Simon Darnell and Brad Millington, "Modernization, Neoliberalism, and Sports Mega-Events," in Gruneau and Horne, *Mega-Events and Globalization*, 65–80.

27. Maurice Roche, *Mega-Events & Modernity: Olympics and Expos in the Growth of Global Culture* (London: Routledge, 2000).

28. Bélanger, "Sport Venues," 390; Sam and Scherer, "Fitting a Square Stadium," 1458–68.

29. Michael Silk, "A Tale of Two Cities: The Social Production of Sterile Sporting Space," *Journal of Sport and Social Issues* 28, no. 4 (2004): 349–78; Michael Silk and David Andrews, "The Fittest City in America," *Journal of Sport and Social Issues* 30, no. 3 (2006): 315–27; Schimmel, "Deep Play," 160–74; David Whitson, "Bringing the World to Canada: 'The Periphery of the Centre,'" *Third World Quarterly* 25, no. 7 (2004): 1215–32.

30. Gary Bridge and Sophie Watson, *City Imaginaries: A Companion to the City* (Oxford: Blackwell Publishing, 2000): 452.

31. Jules Boykoff, "Protest, Activism, and the Olympic Games: An Overview of Key Issues and Iconic Moments," *The International Journal of the History of Sport* 34, no. 3–4 (2017): 175.

32. Millington and Wilson, *The Greening of Golf*; Brad Millington and Brian Wilson, "Contested Terrain and Terrain that Contests: Donald Trump, Golf's Environmental Politics, and a Challenge to Anthropocentrism in Physical Cultural Studies," *International Review for the Sociology of Sport* 52, no. 8 (2017): 910–23; Mark C. J. Stoddart, "Making Meaning Out of Mountains: Skiing, the Environment and Ecopolitics," PhD thesis, University of British Columbia,

Vancouver, Canada, June 2008, https://dx.doi.org/10.14288/1.0066436, especially page 194.

33. Belinda Wheaton, "Identity, Politics, and the Beach: Environmental Activism in Surfers Against Sewage," *Leisure Studies* 26, no. 3 (2007): 279–302; Belinda Wheaton, "From the Pavement to the Beach: Politics and Identity in Surfers Against Sewage," in *Tribal Play: Subcultural Journeys through Sport*, edited by Michael Atkinson and Kevin Young (Bingley, UK: JAI Press, 2008), 113–34.

34. John Stolle-McAllister, "Contingent Hybridity: The Cultural Politics of Tepoztl‡ n's Anti-Golf Movement," *Identities: Global Studies in Culture and Power* 11, no. 2 (2004): 195–213.

35. Kyle Bunds, "On the Messiness of Activism from the Inside: Global Water Charities, Organizational Ethnography, and the Politics of Change," *Review of Education, Pedagogy, and Cultural Studies* 38, no. 3 (2016): 236–59; Kyle Bunds, *Sport, Politics, and the Charity Industry: Running for Water* (New York: Routledge, 2017); Kyle Bunds, Simon Brandon-Lai, and Cole Armstrong, "An Inductive Investigation of Participants' Attachment to Charity Sports Events: The Case of Team Water Charity," *European Sport Management Quarterly* 16, no. 3 (2016): 364–83.

36. For a more detailed discussion of the methods used in this study, see Liv Yoon, "Mount Gariwang: An Olympic Casualty," PhD dissertation, University of British Columbia, 2019, https://dx.doi.org/10.14288/1.0378394, especially chapters 2 and 4

37. Brian Wilson, "Sport, the Environment, and Peace: Debates and Myths about Carbon-Neutral Sport," in *Sport & Peace: A Sociological Perspective* (Don Mills, Canada: Oxford University Press, 2012), 156–77.

38. Ibid., 170.

39. Kimberly C. Davis, "Oprah's Book Club and the Politics of Cross-Racial Empathy," *International Journal of Cultural Studies* 7, no. 4 (2004): 403.

40. Carolyn Pedwell, "Transforming Habit: Revolution, Routine and Social Change," *Cultural Studies* 31, no. 1 (2017): 93–120.

41. Jonathan H. Turner, "The Sociology of Emotions: Basic Theoretical Arguments," *Emotion Review* 1, no. 4 (2009): 340–54.

42. Laura Pulido, "The Interior Life of Politics," *Ethics, Place and Environment* 6, no. 1 (2003): 46–52; Hyojoung Kim, "Shame, Anger, and Love in Collective Action: Emotional Consequences of Suicide Protest in South Korea, 1991," *Mobilization: An International Quarterly* 7, no. 2 (2002): 159–76.

43. Turner, "The Sociology of Emotions," 342.

44. Deborah B. Gould, "Political Despair," in *Politics and the Emotions: The Affective Turn in Contemporary Political Studies*, edited by Simon Thompson and Paul Hogget (New York: Continuum, 2012), 95–114; James M. Jasper, "Constructing Indignation: Anger Dynamics in Protest Movements," *Emotion Review* 6, no. 3 (2014): 208–13.

45. Victoria L. Henderson, "Is There Hope for Anger? The Politics of

Spatializing and (Re) Producing an Emotion," *Emotion, Space and Society* 1, no. 1 (2008): 28–37; Hedda Ransan-Cooper, Selen A. Ercan, and Sonya Duus, "When Anger Meets Joy: How Emotions Mobilise and Sustain the Anti-Coal Seam Gas Movement in Regional Australia," *Social Movement Studies* 17, no. 6 (2018): 635–57.

46. Gould, "Political Despair," 107–8.

47. James M. Jasper, "Emotions and Social Movements: Twenty Years of Theory and Research," *Annual Review of Sociology* 37 (2011): 298.

48. Eduardo Romanos, "Emotions, Moral Batteries and High-Risk Activism: Understanding the Emotional Practices of the Spanish Anarchists under Franco's Dictatorship," *Contemporary European History* (2014): 545–64.

49. Ransan-Cooper, Ercan, and Duus, "When Anger Meets Joy."

50. Margaret Wetherell, *Affect and Emotion: A New Social Science Understanding* (Los Angeles: SAGE, 2012).

51. Margaret Wetherell, "Trends in the Turn to Affect: A Social Psychological Critique," *Body & Society* 21, no. 2 (2015): 139–66.

52. James M. Jasper, "Choice Points, Emotional Batteries, and Other Ways to Find Strategic Agency at the Microlevel," *Strategies for Social Change* 37 (2012); Romanos, "Emotions, Moral Batteries and High-Risk Activism," 545–64; Ransan-Cooper, Ercan, and Duus, "When Anger Meets Joy," 635–57.

53. Romanos, "Emotions, Moral Batteries and High-Risk Activism," 545–64.

54. Henderson, "Is There Hope for Anger?," 32.

55. See, for example, Sonia Kruks, "Simone de Beauvoir and the Politics of Privilege," *Hypatia* 20, no. 1 (2005): 178–205.

56. Joseph de Rivera, Elena A. Gerstmann, and Lisa Maisels, "The Emotional Motivation of Righteous Behavior," *Social Justice Research* 7, no. 1 (1994): 91–106.

57. Haiven and Khasnabish, *The Radical Imagination*, 239.

58. Ibid., 131.

CHAPTER 7

Oslo 2022

The Ethics of the Norwegian People and the Spirit of the Olympic Movement

JAN OVE TANGEN AND BIEKE GILS

In the summer of 2011, the City of Oslo and the Norwegian Confederation of Sport started the application process to host the 2022 Olympic Winter Games (OWG). While some of the major stakeholders in this process motivated the Oslo bid as Norway's responsibility to help modernize the International Olympic Committee (IOC) and strengthen the organization's claimed human rights values, among other aspects, the bidding campaign ended about three years later, on the first of October 2014. That morning the most widely read Norwegian newspaper, *VG*, reported that the IOC had demanded free liquor, a party with the Norwegian king and queen, private traffic lanes on the road to sports facilities, and fifty luxury cars at its disposal during the hosting of the 2022 OWG, among several other things (see figure 7.1). That same evening, the Conservative Party's parliamentary caucus voted against the bid, making it impossible to establish a parliamentary majority supporting a governmental guarantee and funding. The bid was now canceled.[1]

A press release shortly after revealed the primary reason for the bid's cancelation: "Without sufficient enthusiasm [in the Norwegian population], hosting the 2022 Olympic Winter Games in Oslo could not be justified."[2] Eli Grimsby, CEO for the Oslo 2022 provisional municipal agency that planned and organized the bid, explained: "The gap between the Norwegian national character and the Olympic movement is too large."[3] *Inside the Games* ran the headline: "'Pompous' IOC demands led to withdrawal of the Oslo 2022 Olympic bid."[4] These and other explanations suggest that the bid was abandoned primarily due to a moral-based emotional response on the part of the Norwegian general public ("the people"). It is

FIGURE 7.1. Breaking the News on *VG*'s front page: "These are the OL-bosses' conditions: DEMANDS FREE DRINKS FROM THE KING. Invite themselves to the Royal Castle. Lanes on the road for IOC only. 50 luxury cars with chauffeurs. Used with permission from *VG*.

the abovementioned "gap" we aim to explain in this chapter, by examining and juxtaposing Norwegian moral values repertoires and the operating values characteristic of the Olympic movement.

As this book has demonstrated, Olympic bids have been canceled and abandoned for a variety of reasons. According to Harry Hiller, "there clearly is no single explanation for why bids that apply to all potential host cities are canceled, [but] what has received much less attention is the way in which local residents encounter the bid and, above all, how their assessments of the bid evolve when a plebiscite/referendum is held as a critical step to continuing the bid."[5] Hiller refers to the "urban affect," i.e., how emotional responses among local inhabitants in a city have the potential to impact the political decision of hosting Olympic Games. He emphasizes that "public moods" can impact political decisions and vice versa.[6]

As Hiller indicates, very few studies have focused their analyses specifically on public morality as a reason for opposing the hosting of Olympic Games. In an earlier study of the Oslo 2022 bidding campaign this chapter's first author pointed to how, despite significant efforts on the part of various stakeholders to convince inhabitants of Oslo and Norwegians in general to support the bid, people used their democratic power to counter it. He found that this legitimate democratic resistance had obvious economic and moral groundings.[7] It is these moral groundings we elaborate on further. In this chapter, Hiller's "public moods" can be compared to the general public's emotional responses to the Oslo 2022 bid, extending from national moral repertoires and heavily mediated by nationwide polls and other media.

We draw on Max Weber's famous study *The Protestant Ethic and the Spirit of Capitalism,* supported by other theoretical concepts and perspectives, to explain the gap in moral values repertoires between Norway and the IOC. Aware that Weber's thesis is controversial and heavily debated,[8] we argue that the close connection between the protestant ethic and the spirit of capitalism from the Reformation and onwards somehow dissolved, differentiated, and developed further in other parts of Western societies. We claim that the protestant ethic became the ethical but secular bedrock of the social-democratic welfare-state of Norway. At the same time, a more cynical capitalist spirit took a foothold in international organizations like the IOC, aiming at producing spectacular and limitless sporting performances. In the Oslo 2022 bidding process, tensions between morals and money were mediated by the mass media and elicited much disagreement and resistance. We argue that the mass media mediated and shaped the political and moral discourses in this bidding process. This mediation was a necessary but not a sufficient condition for canceling the bid.

To describe the resistance against the hosting of the OWG in Oslo in 2022, we rely on existing research addressing this particular bidding process, a large number of nationwide polls carried out by both national and local newspapers from October 26, 2011 to October 30, 2014, and public opinions expressed in the referendum and news media more generally. Our detailed analysis of the poll results provides the foundation for a more elaborate and theoretical explanation of the decision to abandon the bid.

Discourses Surrounding the Oslo 2022 Olympic Winter Games Bid

In November 2011, the Norwegian Olympic and Paralympic Committee and Confederation of Sport (NIF) encouraged the City of Oslo to evaluate the possibilities for hosting the Olympic and Paralympic Winter Games in Oslo. Against the backdrop of earlier Olympic Winter Games bidding processes in the Norwegian context, this suggestion triggered public and political discourses about the location and financing of the Games. These discourses surrounded two crucial political events: the local advisory referendum in Oslo initiated by the City of Oslo (see below for details), and secondly, the final debate and voting in Parliament (*Stortinget*) about whether the Government should partly finance and partly guarantee to balance out potential cost overruns.

The joint application from the City of Oslo and the NIF to the Department of Culture for a governmental guarantee and funding mentions three *stakeholders:*[9] the City of Oslo, the NIF, and the Norwegian Government and Parliament. The sponsors, investors and entrepreneurs, the volunteers, the Norwegian population, and future generations—although mentioned only in passing in the application—can also be viewed as stakeholders. What we know less about is what some of these additional stakeholders' motivations or interests were and how they communicated them. In what follows, we present four forms or levels of communication these stakeholders used to express their support for, or resistance to the application. These include the levels of (1) *political* decision-making; (2) *public* discourse; (3) *organizational* priorities; and (4) opinion *polls*.

On the *political* level, the Progressive Party (liberal) was relatively quick to express its resistance against hosting the OWG, both in Parliament and in the Oslo city council. However, the final decision to vote against state funding and an unlimited state financial guarantee was not taken before May 2014. Around the same time the referendum took place (September 9, 2013), the Socialist Left Party decided not to back the bid, becoming the first political party to adopt a position on a national level. The country's two largest political parties, the Conservatives and the Social Democrats, never took an explicit stand on the issue. However, during this period, Norway was governed by a minority government, consisting of a coalition between the Conservative Party and the Progressive Party. Since the Progressive Party had already signaled its opposition to the OWG in Oslo, it was the Conservative Party's parliamentary caucus that held the key to opening or closing the door to the bid. This party, however, followed the public discourse closely to get a sense of the general public's opinion.

Within the Oslo city council, similar political disagreements erupted over the OWG bid. The city council was at that time ruled by a three-party coalition. The coalition feared a lack of support within the city council. When the City's budget for 2013 was about to be approved, a budget settlement was reached between four of the political parties represented in the city council. One element in the budget settlement was an agreement that an advisory referendum would be held on the same day as the national parliamentary elections to gauge the opinion of voters on the OWG bid. The result of this referendum was not binding.

This decision resulted in a more heated public debate. Elected officials and other representatives of the City of Oslo regularly participated in the public discourse to influence the vote, as did representatives from other stakeholders. Ørnulf Seippel et al. reviewed the national newspaper coverage addressing the bidding process in the year leading up to the referendum (September 9, 2012-September 9, 2013). Their findings were surprising. Forty-three percent of the articles were coded "neutral," and the supportive and critical articles were almost equal in numbers (29% and 28%, respectively). The most critical voices, however, did not have a clear affiliation and could not be identified as representatives for any institution or stakeholder.[10] They were representatives for "the people"— a stakeholder group with seemingly little power in this particular public discourse.

The outcome of the public debate ended positively for those who were in favor of hosting an OWG. In the advisory referendum, 55 percent voted "yes" to the question, "Should Oslo City apply for hosting the Olympic Winter Games and Paralympics in 2022?," while 45 percent voted "no." The voter turnout was 68 percent. These numbers were interpreted as clear signals to start the process of preparing a bid, and so it began.

On the *organizational* level, two organizations were vital: (1) the umbrella sports organization NIF consisting of more than fifty sport federations, such as the Norwegian Football Federation, the Norwegian Ski Federation, and so forth; and (2) the City of Oslo's provisional municipal agency in charge of planning and coordinating the application process. The

City of Oslo appointed Eli Grimsby as CEO of this provisional agency. She became one of the public faces of the bid, commenting regularly on the process and polls in news media, in an attempt to convince Norwegians to support hosting the Games.

The internal processes going on within the NIF were also critical to the bid. Very early on, the NIF board pointed to Oslo as the only potential candidate city for a 2022 bid from Norway. Due to the lack of proper processes within the organization, however, this proclamation caused friction within Norwegian sport. In 2008, the NIF's board had chosen Tromsø, a city in the north, as the most favorable candidate for a 2018 OWG bid. When the NIF found out that Tromsø had no sport facilities that were up to the IOC's standards and that every Olympic facility would have to be newly built, it rejected the Tromsø bid. Much of the financing for these new facilities would have had to be drawn from the state lottery budget, which was otherwise used for the yearly funding of regular sport facilities. According to the NIF, the facilities intended for "all" would suffer too much from reduced funding in the case of an OWG in Tromsø. The NIF's decision to reject the bid left sport representatives in the north embittered. This center-periphery conflict flared up again in 2011 when the NIF and Oslo jointly presented new plans to host an OWG, only three years after the dismissal of Tromsø. This conflict also surfaced in the polls carried out from the end of October 2011 until September 30, 2014.

Polls: The Voice of the People

One significant contribution of polls is letting people's voices be heard.[11] Opinion polls, despite their shortcomings and depending on which and how questions are asked, may reflect people's emotions, beliefs, and thinking around societal issues and events.[12] Polls can be considered indicators of political successes and failures. They can function as social "thermometers," or as the so-called "canary in the coalmine." As journalists, politicians, and other stakeholders interpret, comment on, and use polls and poll results, they can play vital roles in politicians' decisions to support or turn down a motion or application.

We analyzed thirty-four polls administered by regional and nationwide newspapers from October 26, 2011 to October 30, 2014, including the lengthy articles accompanying the results found on newspapers' web pages with comments from experts, high-ranking politicians, and sports leaders, as well as a few laypeople. The polls were based on representative samples from the Norwegian population (Norway has a population of about 5.5 million) with an average sample size of about one thousand

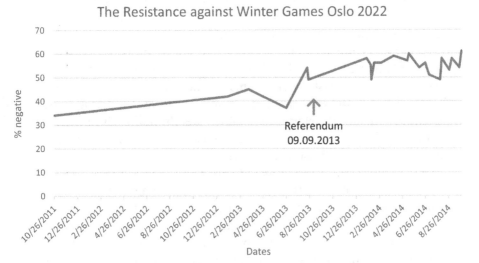

FIGURE 7.2. Opinion poll results detailing public opposition to Oslo 2022 OWG bid. Credit: JA Snoen, OL stemningen, https://www.minervanett.no/ol-stemningen/147567.

respondents per poll, and with a margin of error of about 3 percent. In addition to the poll-specific media reports, we reviewed about five hundred media articles reporting on the Oslo 2022 bidding process retrieved from a database containing all available Norwegian newspaper coverage since 1999.[13] We did not carry out a systematic review of these articles but tried to obtain an impression of the "public mood" expressed in the coverage for the period under investigation, a mood we consider decisive in shaping public resistance against the Oslo 2022 OWG bid. All articles were written in Norwegian. To do justice to their original meaning (and mood), we translated some of the quotes relatively freely in the analysis that follows.

Figure 7.2 is based on a complete overview of polls put together by a Norwegian journalist.[14] On four dates, more than one poll was carried out. Arithmetic means were calculated for the polls executed on the same day. Figure 7.2 indicates, despite the visible fluctuations, an increasing resistance against hosting the OWG in Oslo, before and after the advisory referendum. In almost every poll, the resistance against the Games was larger than the support. The group representing those who were unsure fluctuated considerably, from 6 percent to 21 percent with an average of about 15 percent.

Note that 55 percent of the Oslo population in the referendum was positive towards hosting the games, and 45 percent was against it. The voter turnout was 68 percent. About the same time (August 24, 2013), a nationwide poll showed that 49 percent of the population was against the Games, 33 percent was for them, and 18 percent had not yet decided. These numbers indicate that the political discourse probably had a more successful impact on the citizens of Oslo than on the rest of Norway. The positive result of the Oslo referendum kept the hope of hosting the Games alive locally and nationally. However, the aim of the political discourse now became to convince the Norwegian public, thereby indirectly influencing their political representatives in Parliament and in Government about the values and benefits of hosting an OWG.

Major findings in these polls indicate that older people were more against hosting the OWG than younger, women were more against than men, and the resistance was much more prominent in the Northern part in Norway than in the rest of the country. The reasons for the resistance can be explained by examining the comments accompanying the statistical analyses. What follows is a chronological rundown of numbers and commentaries by various stakeholders on various polls for the period under investigation.

The main stakeholders were not very alarmed by the negative trend in the initial phase. Commenting on the numbers in the first poll (October 26, 2011), for example, NIF's president said that he was not too concerned about the numbers showing only 41 percent in support of the Games. "However, it goes without saying," he said, "that the NIF-board needs support from more than half of the Norwegian population."[15]

More than a year later (January 24, 2013), the numbers in support of the bid among the general public were still low. Only four out of ten indicated support for an application, while four out of ten did not. The former CEO of the Holmenkollen Ski Festival claimed that these were alarmingly low numbers. He did not doubt, however, that the main reason for this OWG skepticism was cost related. "It is very uncertain what the Games will cost, and whether this [the costs] will affect other important social functions."[16] Two months later, another poll confirmed the numbers. "These are positive numbers, but we need to convince more people. The International Olympic Committee is very concerned with gaining the population's support in the host country," Eli Grimsby said.[17] Commenting on the findings that young people are more positive about the Games than older ones, she added: "Not everybody remembers the Winter Olympic Games in Lillehammer in 1994. We should take it seriously that young people also want to experience the Games in their own country." The article, however, was more concerned with the costs than the polls. One politician from the Labour Party said: "I am sure that the costs will be considerably higher than calculated."[18] This poll, in other words, revealed that uncertainty about the Games' associated costs was a primary reason for the lack of public support.

In June 2013, polls indicated that something had happened: 45 percent of the general public was now in favor of the Games, 37 percent was against, and 18 percent had not yet decided. Grimsby responded with excitement, stating that it was "very encouraging to have a plurality that wants to have the Games in Norway."[19] The support for hosting the Games at this point in time was strongest among the younger generations. NIF's president was therefore very adamant about getting this group to vote at the referendum. However, in this poll, respondents were not given any information about the costs of the Games. Bernt Aardal, a psephologist and professor in political science, commented at the time that such information was vital. As a result of its absence, the "main question somehow keeps hanging in the air because it is not clear who is paying the bill. Quite a few members of the general public are unaware of how much this will cost."[20]

A couple of weeks before the referendum in Oslo, the public mood had changed again. In the first nationwide poll (August 21, 2013), the respondents were asked, "Should Norway apply for the OWG in Oslo 2022?"[21] Fifty-four percent answered "no." Surprisingly, this time around, the resistance was more significant in Oslo (57%). In the northern part of Norway, the opposition was 72 percent. The "no" group was also larger than the "yes" group in every political party. The comments accompanying the poll also informed readers that representatives from NIF had been campaigning in the streets, handed out pamphlets, and tried to convince the general public of the benefits of hosting these Games. One person who was approached gave the very engaged response, "I could put this paper up my ass. We cannot afford it! Come down to earth," while he tore the pamphlet to pieces.[22]

The last poll before the referendum (August 24, 2013) indicated that only 41 percent of the Oslo city's population was in support of hosting the Games.[23] Nationwide, 37 percent of the male respondents were positive, while only 29 percent of the female respondents were positive. Norwegian IOC member Gerhard Heiberg commented that these were "high negative numbers. We have to work harder the next couple of weeks."[24] According to Grimsby, they would have to "inform people that there is a referendum,"[25] implying that many were not aware of this vital event. This poll also documented the north-south conflict and the more positive attitude among the younger generations (46% positive).

Entering 2014, the year when the decision had to be made, the polls focused more on the economic aspects of the OWG. The January 24, 2014, poll asked the public explicitly for its opinion about the governmental guarantee.[26] The respondents were also informed about the calculated cost of the Games (about 3.5 billion US dollars). Fifty-eight percent were against the guarantee, and only 26 percent were for it. Outside the eastern part of Norway, where Oslo is located, and where most of the population has reasonably easy access to transportation and opportunities to watch potential OWG events in person, opinion was strongly against the guarantee. Strong resistance was also registered in the northern part of Norway.

Another poll on February 5, 2014, indicated that 56 percent of the Norwegian population was against the Games, while 35 percent was in favor. Even in Oslo, most people now seemed to dislike the idea of hosting the Games. The resistance was overwhelmingly negative in the northern part of Norway. Almost 82 percent of the northern population was against. In the middle of Norway, 65 percent were against, in the western part 64 percent, and in the southern part 53 percent. The mayor of Tromsø, the "capital" of northern Norway, voiced his standpoint very clearly: "the IOC has to change dramatically before I support an application hosting the Games! This is a clique of people who have forgotten the original Olympic values. They have to be replaced with people that can revive these ideals!"[27]

The OWG in Sochi (February 7–23, 2014) was a great success for Norwegian athletes. (See chapter 5 for a discussion of protest at the Sochi Games.) They brought home twenty-six medals: eleven gold, five silver, and ten bronze. These victories, however, did not seem to affect the Norwegian public's attitude towards hosting the OWG. A poll in the following week (February 27, 2014) showed that 56 percent were against hosting the Games, 33 percent were for, and 11 percent had no opinion. Grimsby, again, admitted that she would have wished the results were better. "It is difficult to know [the reason for the low numbers]" she said. "My impression is that people are against the IOC, not the Olympic Games."[28]

Grimsby's comments also need to be seen in light of a 2014 Sochi Winter Olympic controversy that involved Norwegian athletes, the IOC, and a Norwegian IOC member. One of the Norwegian cross-country skiers learned about the passing of her brother while she was competing in Sochi. A few of her teammates decided to show support by wearing mourning bands during the first women's cross-country ski race on the program (women's 15 km). The IOC did not approve of this, as personal and political displays by athletes were banned. This became controversial when Gerhard Heiberg, a Norwegian IOC member and previous CEO of the Lillehammer OWG, commented: "Norway is known to be arrogant. This [the wearing of mourning bands] does not improve that image." Later, he added: "[o]ne would hope that when we apply for the 2022 OWG, the IOC's rules will be respected and that we do not carry on as if we know everything and can do anything!"[29] It might be that his description of the IOC's opinion about Norwegian athletes, leaders, and journalists was expressed in the IOC's meetings, behind closed doors. A few days later (March 3, 2014), a poll was carried out with the question: "Has the incident, involving the Norwegian IOC-member, influenced your opinion about a Norwegian application for the Games, and if so, how?" Thirty-one percent responded that this had made them more negative towards Oslo 2022; 54 percent said that the IOC member's statement had had no impact on their views.[30]

The poll on May 10, 2014, revealed a still-increasing resistance against hosting the Games. Almost six out of ten respondents were against the Games. However, the main topic addressed in newspaper comments was the explicit standpoint from one of the two parties in the coalition government. As mentioned earlier, in their national congress, the Progressive Party decided to say "no" to a governmental guarantee. The Minister of the Treasury, a member of this party, voted against the OWG. This rather unconventional action by a member of the coalition government spurred on reactions among other politicians from other parties. One important politician, from the opposition in Oslo Council, said that "The government has to clarify the confusion created following the resolution from the Progressive Party."[31] The Minister of Culture replied that this resolution was not binding for the Government and that the Government would make a final decision in October. The leader of the parliament's Standing Committee on Finance, Hans Olav Syversen, said that "[t]here is no grassroots support for an application at the moment."[32]

A week later, a new poll showed the second-highest resistance in the population (60%) during the whole period. The parliamentary leader of the Progressive Party commented: "[i]t is very clear that the government needs to start calling a halt to this event, putting it on ice, so to speak."[33] Another parliamentary leader, from the Socialist Left Party, said: "[t]his is a strong reaction to the corrupt ruling of the IOC and the wasteful use of money in megaevents."[34] In short, other politicians' interpretations of the poll results pointed to the costs and IOC culture as the main reasons for the resistance. One of the interviewees argued that the marketing of the Games had not been successful and that something had to be done in the final stage of this process.

In June, the resistance had increased to 62 percent. In this poll, the respondents who were against hosting the Games were asked, "How decisive are the following factors to your wish that Oslo should not apply for the OWG?" The main factor was "the costs" (90%). The second factor was "my impression of the IOC." Heiberg found these to be "surprising numbers."[35] One commentator summed up the answer as "[t]he fear of the costs and the IOC's greediness" and wrote proudly that "no one is as democratic and morally righteous as Norwegians,"[36] indicating four elements in the resistance: costs, greediness, democracy, and moral righteousness.

A poll in August confirmed once again the strong resistance on the part of the general public. No part of the country at this point was still interested in hosting the Games. Eighty percent of the northern population was against, as was 65 percent in the western part of the country. One of the former presidents of the NIF, and former Director-General of the Norwegian Ministry of Culture, criticized the current Minister of Culture for genuflection to the IOC and for handing over the power to host the Games to the IOC. The Minister of Culture admitted and confirmed, indeed, she would respect the Olympic Charter, implying that the IOC would be able to define the economic aspects of the event and thus decide, regardless of Norway's wishes, how money would be used.

As a comment to the persistent resistance documented in a poll on August 28, 2014, just a month before the final parliamentary decision, the CEO of DnB, the largest bank in Norway, said that "[t]his should be the last nail on the coffin! . . . I would love to have World Championships in Bicycling and Winter Sports," he added, "but we should not host the Olympic Winter Games for the third time in seventy years."[37]

At this stage of the process, reducing the costs by reusing former Olympic arenas in Lillehammer was publicly discussed. In a poll on September 4, 2014, the general public was asked if a reduction of costs and spreading of the events more geographically would make them more positive towards hosting the games.[38] Among those against the games, 62 percent replied that these changes would not make them change their minds; 17 percent said that such changes might change their opinion about these matters. The NIF's secretary general was not happy with these results. During a debate on national television, he was asked what he thought about the public's resistance. He emotionally proclaimed: "Since the beginning of this process we have argued that the decision should be made in Parliament, where the people's elected representatives sit!"[39]

The same topic was raised in a poll on September 24, just a week before the Conservative Party's parliamentary caucus was about to decide on how they should vote in Parliament. It appeared that more people were positive to hosting the games if the costs were reduced. This time, 38 percent voted for, compared to 29 percent in June. This increase in positive responses, however, was accounted for by a decrease in those who answered, "Have no opinion." The resistance in the September poll was the same as in June (54%).[40] So, a possible reduction of costs did not seem to have changed the minds of those who were against the Games.

The last polls were presented on September 30, 2014. One poll reported significant changes. When asked if Norway should host the OWG, 64 percent answered "no," while 29 percent answered "yes." When those who responded "no" and "don't know" were asked if they would support hosting the games if the costs could be reduced by reusing the facilities in Lillehammer (OWG 1994), 54 percent answered "yes." These answers indicate once again that costs were a decisive aspect for the general public. In another poll the same day, another newspaper presented results under the headline "New poll: seven out of ten don't believe in a 'low-cost-OWG'!"[41] The day after, the Conservative party's parliamentary caucus voted against supporting a state guarantee. Consequently, a formal vote in Parliament was not necessary.

Mediating the Resistance

Our polls analysis clearly shows that media played a crucial role in mediating public opinion and resistance in the case of the Oslo OWG discussion, a role that was disregarded in the public discussion in Norway[42] and underestimated in the published research after October 1, 2014.[43] We find it important that the "invisible power" embedded in the mediation process of this decision process is acknowledged and analyzed more closely. We want to stress in particular that the mass media tapped into, or used, Norwegian cultural and moral repertoires when they presented arguments for or against hosting the Olympic Games. The mediation by the mass media was necessary, but not a sufficient condition for the political and moral discussion to have an effect on the final decision of canceling the bidding process. We could also argue counterfactually: what could have been the outcome of the bidding if the mass media had not mediated these political and moral discourses? In what follows we elaborate on how mediation happened by pointing to three crucial ways in which mass media operate, and how this influenced public opinion.

First, the mass media always select from a vast range of possible events and incidents, presenting some of these but not others as "news." In their influential study on how news media report foreign affairs, Johan Galtung and Mari Ruge identified twelve selection criteria or *factors* that steer the media's internal "gatekeepers" to evaluate the newsworthiness of different events to then select which event will become news. In the context of this chapter, six of these factors seem particularly applicable: the event's magnitude; cultural proximity; unexpectedness; elite persons, organizations, and nations; personification; and the negative traits and consequences of an event.[44]

Second, according to Niklas Luhmann, "[w]hatever we know about our society, or indeed about the world in which we live, we know through the mass media."[45] The general public in Norway had no direct access to the political discussions that took place in the Oslo city council or those held among political parties. It also did not have the opportunity to meet the delegates of the IOC face to face to speak with them about their thoughts and motivations for hosting the OWG in Oslo. When ordinary citizens are informed that the costs for Oslo 2022 are calculated around NOK 35 billion, they have no way of knowing how this calculation is done or whether it is correct. Also, when news media spread stories about the greed and corruption of IOC members, the general public is inclined to believe it. In other words, Norwegians had to rely on what the mass media presented to them, including journalists' analyses of the polls and the bidding process, and the commentaries by sport leaders and politicians, to gather the necessary information to decide whether to support an Oslo 2022 OWG bid.

Third, the mass media seem to neglect, or at least not admit, the power they have in this process. According to Luhmann, the mass media cannot see the "glasses" they themselves use when they look for "news" in society.[46] For example, in an article in Norway's most widely distributed newspaper a few days before the final parliamentary discussion, journalists described how former elite athletes, members of the social elite, and public relations bureaus worked hard as lobbyists to convince both the Norwegian general public and the elected representatives of Parliament to change their minds about the OWG.[47] According to the journalists, this cost a lot of money, but how much money was spent on lobbying was not documented. So, what about the driving forces behind these mass media themselves? Journalists rarely seem to address themselves as key "players" or "lobbyists" or even "gatekeepers," in this media power nexus. They might instead see themselves as taking on respectable, valued, and legitimate roles or functions in Norwegian society, such as being "watchdogs."

Keeping in mind the influence of the media in shaping public opinion, one journalist who had followed the bidding process closely and had commented often since the beginning in 2011 summed up what he considered to be the five main elements on which the resistance was based:[48] the costs of hosting the Games; the way IOC had acted on different occasions showing an organizational culture Norwegians found objectionable; the center-periphery issue based on tensions between Oslo city and the rest of Norway; the elites in Oslo and IOC against the people; and the impact of news media and social media. Our findings reflect the same issues, but how could this resistance then be explained as moral resistance?

The Moral Repertoires
of the Norwegian People

In 1920 Weber aimed to explain why some cultural phenomena, such as capitalism, emerged only in Western societies.[49] His answer was that Protestantism and its ethic, in particular the Calvin-inspired version of Luther's new view on Christianity, encouraged a universal tendency in individuals to strive for profit and gain in all economic transactions, emphasizing that success based on hard work and modesty was a sign from God that they were among those selected few that were guaranteed salvation. Weber claimed that the emergence of a religious-minded middle class and how its members ran their businesses based on a certain work ethic and modest use of money, combined with the rational organization of free labor, made modern capitalism possible.[50]

In short, Weber established a connection between two different sets of ideas and interests and their reciprocal development, conceptualizing the connection as "elective affinity" to explain why capitalism and other social and cultural phenomena emerged in Europe.[51] This type of explanation is neither causal nor functional.[52] The elective affinity between puritanism and capitalism paved the way for the development of modern welfare states in Europe and elsewhere. However, we posit that the elective affinity between puritanism and capitalism weakened in the last sixty years or so. New elective affinities were established between puritanism and the Nordic welfare states, and between the Olympic movement and modern capitalism,[53] producing a cultural gap between the Norwegian population and the IOC.

Gøsta Esping-Andersen argues that the Scandinavian countries differ from other clusters of welfare states in extending the principle of universalism and de-commodification of social rights to the new middle and working class. This social-democratic regime type "pursued a welfare state that would promote an equality of the highest standards."[54] Some scholars claim that the roots of the welfare states, in particular the Scandinavian variants, are grounded in the Lutheran tradition and its ethic. Two main traits in the Norwegian welfare state clearly show this: everybody has a right to work, and generous social security is provided for those who fall out of the work force.[55] Dag Thorkildsen goes even further and claims that the Nordic model represents secularized Lutheranism.[56]

Compared to many other nations, one could say that the collective identity of Norwegians is rather uniform and strong. Today, the Norwegian social-democratic welfare state operates from a self-image based on values such as "equality," "goodness," "altruism," and "responsibility," which are considered its pillars. Norway often considers itself a "peace loving country," altruistic and morally better than other countries, "a humanitarian superpower."[57]

Studies of Norwegian middle-[58] and working-class[59] cultures have shown that moral values are vital in the culture of both classes. Researchers have described two moral repertoires in the middle class and three in the working class. In both classes, a "Christian-humanist" moral repertoire was operative. Important values in this repertoire were found to be altruism, honesty, and compassion. A second moral repertoire of social responsibility was based on equality and solidarity values. In the working class, researchers also found a third repertoire grounded on values such as work ethic and diligence. From these findings, researchers claim that the three repertoires can be represented by three ideal moral types: the Good Samaritan, the socially responsible citizen, and the hardworking person. This complex of values, particularly the egalitarian tradition, "might be related to a specific secularized Lutheranism."[60] Put otherwise, social actors in Norway more or less rely on national moral repertoires when they observe and judge societal events and processes.[61]

The above research on national moral repertoires also asked respondents what kinds of persons and actions they disliked, revealing what respondents considered reprehensible and immoral. For example, those who do not help others in need and do not show compassion are not "Good Samaritans." It is probable that the Norwegian general public considered the IOC's sanctions against the Norwegian cross country skiers wearing mourning bands as insensitive and not helpful, opposing this type of moral ideal. When it comes to the moral values associated with the idea of Norwegian "goodness," these include equality, solidarity, and responsibility, as well as equal distribution of resources. The massive resistance against hosting the OWG in Oslo can therefore also be seen as a violation of this idea of the good and socially responsible citizen. Spending 35 billion NOK on a fourteen-day *folkefest* (folk festival) is not very responsible given other societal needs in other sectors. In *Nettavisen*, October 10, 2014, one young politician wrote, "The weaker ones shall not suffer, the Eastern part of the city shall not suffer. We have enough of these wasteful OWG . . . Oslo has better causes to use this money for. The city council chose to waste money on a OWG the population didn't want."[62] The Norwegian general public may also have heard about the research by Flyvbjerg and Stewart which documented that almost every Olympic Games since 1964 had experienced cost overruns.[63] Risking cost overruns is not socially responsible.

Other reprehensible actions that violate this ideal-type include evading or exploiting the system and not contributing economically or socially to the community. The general public may have interpreted the IOC list of demands as a huge violation of this type of moral repertoire. Add to this the fact that it is the host city, and eventually the whole country, that has to pay the bill, primarily as a result of the IOC's extravagant demands. Most importantly, the tradition of egalitarianism seems to elicit, particularly in the working class, a distaste for economic and social elites and their culture.[64] Comments in the articles accompanying some of the polls indicate that such morally grounded aversion was foremost directed towards the IOC, but also towards the social and political elite in Oslo. In other words, the public resistance against hosting an OWG in Oslo was grounded in national repertoires of moral values.

Not surprisingly, politicians and sport leaders sensed an increasing aversion in the population against hosting the OWG in general and against the IOC in particular. To dampen this hostility, the mayor of Oslo, Fabian Stang, argued that the city considered itself obligated to host such a costly mega-event to help secure the OWG; otherwise, in the future, only non-democratic regimes would apply. The city also believed it had a moral duty to change the IOC's values and demanded the IOC be more conscious of costs, human rights, equality, recycling of sports facilities, and sustainability.[65] The NIF's secretary-general, Inge Andersen, expressed the same political and moral motivation for bidding for and hosting the Olympic Games. He claimed it was important for Norwegian sport to contribute to the modernization of the IOC.[66] While seemingly noble, these politicians and sport leaders' motivations also attest to Norway's tendency to consider itself as altruistically and morally superior to other countries. The vital question is: why did Norwegians have this negative impression of the IOC, the Olympic movement, and the so called "Olympic family?"[67] Part of the answer is suggested above. But there is a need to also look more closely at the Olympic movement's (the IOC's) organization, ideals, values, and working principles.[68]

The Spirit of The Olympic Movement and Its Affinity to Capitalism

The Olympic movement can be considered another form for collective identity, constructing boundaries between itself and other collective identities such as nations. The IOC's values are excellence, respect, and friendship, and the organization describes its guiding philosophy, Olympism, as "a philosophy of life, which places sport at the services of humankind."[69] The IOC's mission is to ensure the uniqueness and the regular celebration of the Olympic Games, to put athletes at the heart of the Olympic movement, and to promote sport and the Olympic values while focusing on young people. The working principles are universality and solidarity, unity in diversity, autonomy and good governance, and sustainability. The IOC boldly claims that the Olympic Spirit promotes "mutual understanding with a spirit of friendship, solidarity, and fair play."[70]

Several scholars have discussed in detail how the Olympic movement in general and the IOC in particular more often than not fail to live up to their stated values and ambitions. Some of those who dug deep to reveal the ugly Janus face of the IOC include, though are not limited to, Vyv Simson and Andrew Jennings; Helen Lenskyj; Paul Close, David Askew, and Xu Xin; Christine Toohey and Anthony Veal; Christopher Shaw; Monroe Price and Daniel Dayan; Liv Yoon; and Andrew Zimbalist.[71] These and other researchers provide strong indications that there are vital differences between ideals and realities in the operations of the IOC. Looking at its historical and contemporary legacy, there are numerous examples of how the IOC and the Olympic Games have paid and continue to pay large disservices to humankind. Numerous researchers and reporters have repeatedly documented how the Olympic Games have harmful impacts on cities and their inhabitants, particularly the poorest and least powerful of a city's residents. Controversies, scandals, boycotts, and suspensions instead of peaceful cooperation are more rule than exception in the history of the IOC.[72] Such reports were cited in Norwegian newspapers too.

We posit that the Olympic motto "Citius, Altius, Fortius" captures the organization's true ideal and values—its real spirit. This motto symbolizes the distinctiveness and operations of modern sport in general, and Olympic sport in particular, as well as capitalism's urge for incessant growth.[73] In other words, in modern and Olympic sport no stone remains left unturned to win and set new records. The Olympic spirit, vividly expressed in the Olympic motto, is in other words a manifestation of modernity's most striking feature, which Luhmann would have described as *contingency*, i.e., nothing in modernity is natural or necessary, everything could be different.[74] Embedded in every decision and action is the possibility that things could be otherwise. According to Weber, Calvinists also asked themselves "How can I know that I am saved?" Tradesmen and industry owners may have reflected upon "How can we earn more money?" Today, an athlete may ponder "How can I improve my performances and win the next competition?" This contingency makes individuals, organizations, and societies restless. The solution seems clear: improve! But how? Believe harder and live more modestly? Work hard and earn more money? Train more efficiently and use performance-enhancing substances? One must take risks.

No individuals, organizations, or societies can avoid this. Contingency is inevitable in modernity.

To cope with contingency, the IOC, the Olympic movement, and the Olympic family established an elective affinity with modern capitalism over the past sixty years. This is ironically exemplified by the fact that chairs and CEOs of TOP Partners, i.e., sponsors such as Coca-Cola, Kodak, McDonald's, Omega, Panasonic, Samsung, Visa, and so forth, are included in the Olympic family. Close, Askew, and Xin argue that "there is an extraordinary convergence, or elective affinity, between modern Olympism and the ideals and tendencies of modern market capitalism,"[75] noting that:

> the part being played by Olympism in the construction of the globalized world—and thereby of global society—may be primarily dependent upon its elective affinity with modern market capitalism. Olympism's contribution to the construction of global society may hinge mainly upon the way in which the principles, values and ideals it enshrines coincide with, are compatible with, and help consolidate the principles and practices associated with modern market capitalism.[76]

Tying this assessment of the Olympic movement back to Weber, one could say that while the Protestant ethic in its Lutheran version since World War II developed an elective affinity with the Nordic welfare state model, the Olympic movement developed a similar elective affinity with modern capitalism. This led to different societal developments of the two social phenomena: the Norwegian welfare state and the Olympic movement and IOC. This does not mean that capitalism does not play a vital role in Norwegian society. Of course, it does, but in a regulated fashion and in the form of a mixed economy. The State controls a greater part of the industries and services (state-planned economy), while providing opportunities for private enterprises to exist (market economy). And likewise, some welfare values can be observed in the Olympic movement but understood and applied in line with a capitalistic perspective and logic.

Conclusion

This study aimed to explain the Norwegian population's resistance against hosting OWG in Oslo in 2022. Our poll analysis shows how the resistance increased from 30 percent at the end of October 2011 to 60 percent at the beginning of October 2014. Major stakeholders explained this resistance as a discrepancy between the Norwegian national character and the pompous demands made by the IOC. Drawing on Max Weber's work on *The Ethics of Protestantism and the Spirit of Capitalism* as well as other supplementary sociological concepts and perspectives, we examined whether these stakeholders' explanation was plausible.

Our analyses of commentaries accompanying the polls that were carried out between October 2011 and October 2014 provided strong evidence for our theoretical assumptions. Our analysis also revealed how the mass media shaped and strengthened the tensions between the Norwegian population and the IOC. The impact of mass media and social media on the public's opinion in the case of the Oslo OWG 2022 is thus not to be underestimated.

Finally, and most significantly, we found strong indications that the Norwegian resistance was grounded on Protestant moral value repertoires developed in the Norwegian welfare state. Norwegians find it important to be "Good Samaritans," socially responsible citizens, hardworking persons. These moral values stood in stark contrast with Norwegian perceptions of the IOC as pompous, greedy, elitist, and capitalist. Even the costs of the mega-event were criticized on moral grounds as members of the general public expressed that such large sums of money "should be used to alleviate more worthy societal needs."[77] *VG*'s publishing of the IOC's demand list in October 2014 was therefore "the final straw that broke the camel's back."

Notes

1. See Jan Ove Tangen, "Observing the Limits of Steering—Norway's Abortive Bid for the 2022 Olympic Winter Games in Oslo," *International Journal of Sport Policy and Politics* 14, no. 1 (2021): 1–18, https://doi.org/10.1080/1940 6940.2021.1993303.

2. Ibid., 3.

3. Eli Grimsby, *Evalueringsrapport: Oslo2022*, versjon 8.12.2014, http://mm.aftenposten.no/2014/12/10-OSLO2022-evalueringsrapport/rapport_8_12_2014_endelig.pdf.

4. Zjan Shirinian, "'Pompous' IOC Demands 'Led to Withdrawal of Oslo 2022 Olympic Bid,'" *Inside the Games*, October 3, 2014, https://www.insidethegames.biz/articles/1023008/pompous-ioc-demands-led-to-withdrawal-of-oslo-2022-olympic-bid.

5. Harry H. Hiller, "The Calgary 2026 Olympic Bid Plebiscite as Affective Urbanism," *Journal of Sport and Social Issues* 45, no. 6 (2020): 487–508, https://doi.org/10.1177/0193723520964971, 488.

6. Ibid., 492.

7. Tangen, "Observing the Limits of Steering," 15.

8. See John A. Hughes, W. W. Sharrock, and Peter J. Martin, *Understanding Classical Sociology: Marx, Weber, Durkheim* (London: Sage, 2003), 102.

9. Stian Berger Røsland, and Børre Rognlien, *Olympiske og paralympiske leker Oslo 2022—Søknad om statstilskudd og statsgaranti*, Oslo Kommune og Norges idrettsforbund, 2013, accessed April 30, 2024, https://www.idretts forbundet.no/contentassets/1d852ed0fceb4fc792476659885802d9/oslo2022 —soknad-om-statstilskudd-og-statsgaranti.pdf.

10. Ørnulf Seippel, Trygve B. Broch, Elsa Kristiansen, Eivind Skille, Terese Wilhelmsen, Åse Strandbu, and Ingfrid Thorjussen, "Political Framing of Sports: The Mediated Politicisation of Oslo's Interest in Bidding for the 2022 Winter Olympics," *International Journal of Sport Policy and Politics* 8, no. 3 (2016): 439–53, https://doi.org/10.1080/19406940.2016.1182047.

11. Humphrey Taylor, "The Value of Polls in Promoting Good Government and Democracy," in *Navigating Public Opinion: Polls, Policy, and the Future of American Democracy*, edited by Jeff Manza, Fay Lomax Cook, and Benjamin L. Page (Oxford: Oxford University Press, 2002), 316.

12. See Jeff Manza, Fay Lomax Cook, and Benjamin L. Page (eds.), *Navigating Public Opinion: Polls, Policy, and the Future of American Democracy* (Oxford: Oxford University Press, 2002).

13. Our starting point for finding pretinent news coverage was Retriever, https://www.retrievergroup.com.

14. Jan Arild Snoen, "OL stemningen," *Minerva*, July 17, 2014, updated February 1, 2022, https://www.minervanett.no/ol-stemningen/147567.

15. Knut Arne Hansen, "Stor VG-undersøkelse: her er folkets OL-dom," October 26, 2011, https://www.vg.no/sport/i/npWdo/stor-vg-undersoekelse -her-er-folkets-ol-dom.

16. Ingar Johnsrud, "Bare 4 av 10 vil at Oslo skal søke OL," *VG*, January 24, 2013, https://www.vg.no/nyheter/innenriks/i/nd5wd/bare-4-av-10-vil-at -oslo-skal-soeke-ol.

17. Daria Almo and Andrea Kluge, "Halvparten av folket vil ikke ha Oslo-OL 2022," *NRK*, March 20, 2013, https://www.nrk.no/sport/delte-meninger -om-oslo-ol-1.10956353.

18. Ibid.

19. Mette Bugge, Espen Hofoss, Daniel Røed-Johansen, and Andreas Slettholm, "Flertall for OL-søknaden," *Aftenposten*, June 26, 2013, https://www .aftenposten.no/sport/i/4qLr96/flertall-for-ol-soeknaden.

20. Ibid.

21. Eva Hongshagen, Nicolay Andre Ramm, Marius Skjelbæk and Kim Peder Rishmyr, "OL-oppslutningen stuper:—Bedrøvelige tall," *NRK*, August 21, 2013, https://www.nrk.no/sport/flertallet-sier-nei-til-oslo-ol-1.11194254.

22. Ibid.

23. Fredrik Saltbones, and Nils Mangelrød, "Bare 40,8 prosent av Oslo-folket vil ha OL," *VG*, August 24, 2013, https://www.vg.no/sport/i/K0×0y/bare-40 –8-prosent-av-oslo-folket-vil-ha-ol.

24. Ibid.

25. Ibid.

26. Nils August Andresen, "Massivt nei til Oslo-OL," *Minerva*, January 24, 2014, https://www.minervanett.no/massivt-nei-til-oslo-ol/144528.

27. Bjørnar Hjellen and Anne Rognerud, "Fortsatt stor motstand mot Oslo-OL,"*NRK*, February 4, 2014, https://www.nrk.no/sport/fortsatt-stor-motstand -mot-oslo-ol-1.11381809.

28. Øyvind Herrebrøden, "Ny meningsmåling sier klart nei til Oslo-OL," *VG*, https://www.vg.no/sport/i/05xAa/ny-meningsmaaling-sier-klart-nei-til -oslo-ol.

29. Bjørn Skomakerstuen, "Norge er i utgangspunktet kjent for å være arrogante," *Nettavisen Sport*, February 10, 2014, updated February 12, 2014, https://www.nettavisen.no/sport/norge-er-i-utgangspunktet-kjent-for-a-vare -arrogante/s/12-95-3754116.

30. Nicolay Andre Ramm, and Ingrid Kjelland-Mørdre, "Økt OL-motstand etter Heibergs uttalelser," *NRK*, March 3, 2014, https://www.nrk.no/sport/ okt-motstand-mot-oslo-etter-sotsji-1.11581055.

31. Sindre Øgard, "Ny OL-måling: Sterkt nedslående tall," *VG*, May 10, 2014, https://www.vg.no/sport/i/1Ewzq/ny-ol-maaling-sterkt-nedslaaende-tall.

32. Ibid.

33. Hans-Olav Rise, and Kim Peder Rismyhr, "Motstanden aukar: 60 pro-sent seier nei til OL," *NRK*, https://www.nrk.no/sport/motstanden-mot -oslo-ol-aukar-1.11714733.

34. Ibid.

35. John Rasmussen, "62 prosent av befolkningen sier nei til OL i Oslo," *Dagbladet*, June 26, 2014, https://www.dagbladet.no/sport/62-prosent-av -befolkningen-sier-nei-til-ol-i-oslo/61031864.

36. Ibid.

37. Anders K. Christiansen, and Øyvind Jarlsro, "Ny VG-måling: OL-støt-ten synker igjen," *VG*, August 28, 2014, https://www.vg.no/sport/i/0mgwE/ ny-vg-maaling-ol-stoetten-synker-igjen.

38. Jonas Wikborg, "Ny undersøkelse: OL-støtten har aldri vært svakere," *VG*, September 4, 2014, https://www.vg.no/sport/i/w19vn/ny-undersoekelse -ol-stoetten-har-aldri-vaert-svakere.

39. Ibid.

40. Hanne Mellingsæter, and Eirik Windsnes, "OL-støtten øker etter fore-slått milliardkutt," *Aftenposten*, September 23, 2014, https://www.aftenposten .no/sport/i/awGaV4/ol-stoetten-oeker-etter-foreslaatt-milliardkutt.

41. Bjørn S. Kristiansen, "Sjokkmåling: Folket sier JA til billig-OL," *Dag-bladet*, September 30, 2014, https://www.dagbladet.no/nyheter/sjokkmaling -folket-sier-ja-til-billig-ol/60950240.

42. Grimsby, *Evalueringsrapport*.

43. Ørnulf Seippel, Trygve B. Broch, Elsa Kristiansen, Eivind Skille, Terese Wilhelmsen, Åse Strandbu, and Ingrid Thorjussen, "Political Framing of Sports: The Mediated Politicisation of Oslo's Interest in Bidding for the 2022 Winter Olympics," *International Journal of Sport Policy and Politics* 8, no. 3 (2016): 439–53.

44. Johan Galtung, and Mari Holboe Ruge, "The Structure of Foreign News: The Presentation of the Congo, Cuba and Cyprus Crises in Four Norwegian Newspapers," *Journal of Peace Research* 2, no. 1 (March 1965): 64–90, https://doi.org/10.1177/002234336500200104.

45. Niklas Luhmann, *The Reality of the Mass Media* (Stanford: Stanford University Press, 2000).

46. Ibid.

47. Anders K. Christiansen, Ole Kristian Strøm, Lars Joakim Skarvøy, Cato Husabø Fossen, Pål Ertzaas, Eirik Mosveen, and Eirik Linaker Berglund, "Slik har OL-lobbyistene jobbet," *VG*, October 23, 2015, https://www.vg.no/nyheter/innenriks/i/4P556/slik-har-ol-lobbyistene-jobbet.

48. Jan Aril Snoen, "Slutten,"*Minerva*, October 2, 2014, https://www.minerva nett.no/slutten/148650.

49. Max Weber, *Gesammelte Aufsätze zur Religionssoziologie*, (Tübingen: J. C. B. Mohr, 1920–1923).

50. Max Weber, "Weber's Second Reply to Rachfahl, 1910," in *The Protestant Ethic Debate: Max Weber's Replies to his Critics, 1907–1910*, edited by David J. Chalcraft and Austin Harrington, 93–132 (Liverpool: Liverpool University Press, 2001).

51. Ibid.

52. Richard Herbert Howe, "Max Weber's Elective Affinities: Sociology Within the Bounds of Pure Reason," *American Journal of Sociology* 84, no. 2 (1978): 366–85, http://www.jstor.org/stable/2777853.

53. In recent years, Niklas Luhmann (1984, 1997) developed a similar concept, termed "structural coupling." Niklas Luhmann, *Soziale Systeme: Grundriss einer allgemeinen Theorie* (Frankfurt a. M.: Suhrkamp, 1984); Niklas Luhmann, *Die Gesellschaft der Gesellschaft* (Frankfurt am Main: Suhrkamp, 1997).

54. Gøsta Esping-Andersen, *The Three Worlds of Welfare Capitalism* (Cambridge: Polity Press, 1990), 27.

55. Aud V. Tønnesen, "Velferdsstaten og den lutherske toregimentslæren," *Norsk Teologisk Tidsskrift* 112, no. 3–4 (2011): 196–213, https://doi.org/10.18261/ISSN1504-2979-2011-03-04-05.

56. Dag Thorkildsen, "Religious Identity and Nordic Identity," in *The Cultural Construction of Norden*, edited by Øystein Sørensen & Bo Stråth (Oslo: Scandinavian University Press, 1997): 138–60.

57. Halvor Leira, *Norske selvbilder og norsk utenrikspolitikk* (Oslo: Norsk utenrikspolitisk institutt, 2007).

58. Rune Sakslind and Ove Skarpenes, "Morality and the Middle Class: The European Pattern and the Norwegian Singularity," *Journal of Social History* 48, no. 2 (2014): 313–40, http://www.jstor.org/stable/43306016; Ove Skarpenes, Rune Sakslind, and Rober Hestholm, "National Repertoires of Moral Values," *Cultura* 13, no. 1 (2016): 7–27, https://www.ingentaconnect.com/contentone/plg/cultura/2016/00000013/00000001/art00001?crawler=true&mimetype=application/pdf.

59. Anders Vassenden and Merete Jonvik, "Live and Let Live? Morality in Symbolic Boundaries across Different Cultural Areas," *Current Sociology* 71, no. 3 (2021): 450–469, https://doi.org/10.1177/00113921211034892; Ove Skarpenes, "Defending the Nordic Model: Understanding the Moral Universe of the Norwegian Working Class," *European Journal of Cultural and Political Sociology* 8, no. 2 (March 17, 2021): 151–74, https://doi.org/10.1080/23254823 .2021.1895857.

60. Skarpenes, Sakslind, and Hestholm, "National Repertoires of Moral Values," 17.

61. See Vassenden and Jonvik, "Live and Let Live?"

62. Aisha Naz Bhatti, "DEBATT: De svake skal ikke lide, bydelen skal ikke lide. Nå er det nok med OL sløsing!" *Nettavisen Nyheter*, October 13, 2014, https://www.nettavisen.no/nyheter/debatt-de-svake-skal-ikke-lide-bydelen -skal-ikke-lide-na-er-det-nok-med-ol-slosing/s/12-95-3423127273.

63. Bent Flyvbjerg and Allison Stewart, "Olympic Proportions: Cost and Cost Overrun at the Olympics 1960–2012," Saïd Business School Working Papers (Oxford: University of Oxford, 2012, last revised January 21, 2014), 23 pages, https://dx.doi.org/10.2139/ssrn.2238053.

64. Skarpenes, "Defending the Nordic Model."

65. This was stated by the mayor of Oslo in a debate broadcasted by the Norwegian Broadcasting Corporation on February 11, 2014; see "Dagsnytt 18: 11 februar 2014," *NRKTV*, https://tv.nrk.no/serie/dagsnytt-atten-tv/201402/ NNFA56021114.

66. Inge Andersen, "Slik vil vi påvirke IOC," February 15, 2014, https://www .nrk.no/ytring/slik-vil-vi-pavirke-ioc-1.11544709.

67. "What is the Olympic Family?" in "Frequently Asked Questions," International Olympic Committee, accessed March 19, 2024, https://olympics.com/ ioc/faq/olympism-and-the-olympic-movement/what-is-the-olympic-family.

68. International Olympic Committee, "IOC Principles," https://olympics .com/ioc/principles.

69. Ibid.

70. Ibid.

71. Vyv Simson and Andrew Jennings, *The Lords of the Rings: Power, Money and Drugs sin the Modern Olympics* (London: Simon & Schuster, 1992); Vyv Simson and Andrew Jennings, *Dishonored Games: Corruption, Money and Greed at the Olympics* (New York: SPI Books, 1992); Helen Jefferson Lenskyj, *Inside the Olympic Industry: Power, Politics, and Activism* (Albany: State University of New York Press, 2000); Paul Close, David Askew, and Xu Xin, *The Beijing Olympiad: The Political Economy of a Sporting Mega-Event* (London: Taylor & Francis Group, 2006); Christopher A. Shaw, *Five Ring Circus: Myths and Realities of the Olympic Games* (New York: New Society Publishers, 2008); Kristine Toohey and Anthony J. Veal, *The Olympic Games: A Social Science Perspective* (Wallingford, UK: CABI Publishing, 2007); Monroe Price and Daniel Dayan, *Owning the Olympics: Narratives of the New China* (Ann

Arbor: University of Michigan Press, 2008); Liv Yoon, "Understanding Local Residents' Responses to the Development of Mount Gariwang for the 2018 PyeongChang Winter Olympic and Paralympic Games," *Leisure Studies* 39, no. 5 (2019): 673–87; and Andrew Zimbalist, *Circus Maximus: The Economic Gamble behind Hosting the Olympics and the World Cup* (Washington, DC: Brookings Institution Press, 2015).

72. See, for example, Lenskyj, *Inside the Olympic Industry: Power, Politics, and Activism.*

73. Jan Ove Tangen, "Observing the Limits of Steering—Norway's Abortive Bid for the 2022 Olympic Winter Games in Oslo," *International Journal of Sport Policy and Politics* 14, no. 1 (November 11, 2021): 1–18, https://doi.org/10.1080/19406940.2021.1993303; Jan Ove Tangen, "Is Sport Sustainable? It Depends!" *Frontiers in Sports and Active Living* 3, October 28, 2021, https://doi.org/10.3389/fspor.2021.679762.

74. Niklas Luhmann, *Observations on Modernity* (Palo Alto, CA: Stanford University Press, 1998).

75. Close et al., *The Beijing Olympiad,* 41.

76. Ibid., 81.

77. Bhatti, "DEBATT."

CHAPTER 8

Sapporo 2030

A History of Winter Olympic Bids in Terms of the United Nations' Sustainable Development Goals

KEIKO IKEDA AND TYREL ESKELSON

In September 2015, heads of state and senior UN officials gathered for the 70th Session of the UN General Assembly. One of the most prominent outcomes of these meetings was the articulation of and commitment to a series of sustainable development goals (SDGs) intended to address issues of global concern. With the aim of meeting these targets by 2030, "these objectives form a program of sustainable, universal and ambitious development, a program of the people, by the people and for the people conceived with the active participation of UNESCO."[1]

Figure 8.1 represents the SDGs visually, with the seventeen goals divided into three rows and covering various issues. One third of the goals demonstrate a respect for fundamental human rights and the issues imperiling individual life: "No Poverty," "Zero Hunger," "Good Health and Well-being," "Quality Education," "Gender Equality," and "Clean Water and Sanitation." The second third is more concerned with socioeconomic issues: "Affordable and Clean Energy," "Decent Work and Economic Growth," "Industry, Innovation, and Infrastructure," "Reduced Inequalities," "Sustainable Cities and Communities," and "Responsible Consumption and Production." The third row emphasizes more heuristic issues rooted in natural sciences and inclusive social problems.[2] Within the general outline of the SDGs, each goal is accompanied by more specific targets, complete with measurements and indicators; for example, goal 1.1: "End poverty in all its forms everywhere," includes the target to, "By 2030, eradicate extreme poverty for all people everywhere, currently measured as people living on less than $1.25 a day."[3]

FIGURE 8.1. UNESCO Sustainable Development Goals, 2015. Credit: UNESCO, www.un.org/sustainabledevelopment/news/communications -material/.

Following the lead of the UN, the International Olympic Committee (IOC) amended its own governing documents to align with the SDGs. In October 2017, the IOC introduced its "Sustainability Strategy," which has five areas of emphasis: infrastructure and natural sites, sourcing and resource management, mobility, workforce, and climate. Potential host cities, both those bidding for the Olympic Games and those successful in hosting them, must include sustainability issues within their planning processes. This is because "sustainability matters to the IOC," as the organization explains:

The practice of sport highly depends on the availability of key natural resources such as clean air, clean water and undeveloped land, as well as healthy ecosystems such as green urban areas, mountains, forests, lakes, rivers and oceans. It is the availability of these wells of natural capital—and their contribution to the health and wellbeing of athletes and society—that makes sport and other types of human activities possible ... All these activities have an impact on the world's environmental, social and economic resources. At the same time, the enthusiasm for the practice of sport, and the enjoyment of watching sport, provide ideal opportunities to raise public awareness and educate young generations on the global sustainability challenges being faced and, more importantly, on solutions to address these challenges.[4]

Partially in response to the articulation of the SDGs, the IOC has embarked upon a new bidding process, as well as hosting expectations, for the Olympic Games, one that encourages potential host cities to include sustainability plans in their bids. This chapter considers the preparation of such plans—and the messages used to gather support for bids—in the context of an ongoing bid for the Winter Olympic Games advanced by the city of Sapporo, Japan. Despite this, not every SDG is easily achieved, especially, as this chapter argues, in the case of the Olympics where the priorities of hosting a major sporting event can place individual SDGs in competition with one another, making their concrete attainment a challenge. Moreover, as this chapter demonstrates, the ambition of the SDGs has to coexist with the realities of local and national political agendas.

This chapter focuses specifically on two bids for the Winter Olympic and Paralympic Games—for 2026 and subsequently for 2030—by the Japanese city of Sapporo. Understanding the approach to these bids put forward by the local government requires both a consideration of the environmental legacy of the 1972 Sapporo Winter Olympic Games and the underlying conditions of the Tokyo 2020 Summer Olympic Games. The latter reveals the importance of identifying hidden political intentions, a consideration of which is captured in one journalist's phrase, *Hukkō Gorin*, which literally means "hosting the Tokyo 2020 Summer Olympic Games to recover the devastated area" and highlights the ways in which public support and monies were mobilized behind the 2020 Olympics because they were framed as an effort to help the nation rebuild in the aftermath of the March 2011 earthquake, tsunami, and Fukushima nuclear power station disasters. Similar narratives emerged in the two Sapporo bids, as the 2026 bid was postponed to the 2030 bidding cycle following a 2018 earthquake in Hokkaido. Overall, we argue that the intersection of the superficial idealism of the SDGs and the political discourse surrounding the two Sapporo Winter Olympic bids reveals a sociocultural hegemony that dominates the hosting of sports mega-events such as the Olympic Games.

The Impacts and Legacies of the Olympic Games

Sports are believed to contribute both to individual happiness and general social welfare. Nevertheless, the idea of these being "legacies" of an Olympic Games is a relatively recent phenomenon. Legacy was not terminology included in the Olympics' original educational philosophy, Olympism, as articulated by the movement's initiator, Pierre de Coubertin (1863–1937). His original conception of Olympism was rooted in the individual, with sport allowing "a human being to be a good man."[5] He dreamed that the goodness of an individual could ultimately lead to collective social innovation.

The first appearance of the phrase "Olympic Legacy" occurred around 2000–2002. However, there was no clear definition until after the 2012 London Summer Olympic Games, when legacy subcategories were defined by the IOC bid files in 2013.[6] Five legacies (sporting, social, environmental, urban, and economic legacies) were identified after this event.[7] Nevertheless, this conceptual shift from the idealism of Coubertinian Olympism to the pragmatism of Olympic Legacy obscured a logical distinction between the two concepts. Whereas the rhetoric of "Olympic Legacy" suggests that the benefits of hosting sport mega-events can be widely enjoyed, as Vassil Girginov argues, the ontological origins of "legacy" (as an English word) suggests a "contribution of the present to the future," whereas the French definition of the word emphasizes "the importance of the accumulated past cultural capital and its relationship to the present and future."[8] In both cases, the necessity to demonstrate the legacies (i.e., benefits) of hosting Olympics prevents any criticism of the influential power of the IOC. Moreover, the inclusion of social capital as legacy benefits of a bid encourages alliances between political and business elites and privileges these power structures at the local level. The euphemistic nature of "legacy," Helen Lenskyj argues, reduces emphasis on the absolute costs of sport mega-events, even as the moral undertones of Olympism function to obscure the uncertainty of realizing legacy outcomes.[9]

There is ample evidence challenging the legacies and local impacts of hosting Olympic Games, in part because these events impact on the economic, social, and cultural priorities of communities. In the case of the Nagano 1998 Winter Olympic Games, the bobsleigh facility has earned 7 million yen per year by users, but it has cost 120 million yen in operating costs for maintenance each year.[10] Anthony Gunter is skeptical to even estimate the economic gains generated by sports mega-events. His analysis, using 2014 data from the Office for National Statistics, concluded that the 2012 London Olympic Games coincided with "the largest annual fall in unemployment on record," and "there were 538,000 fewer unemployed people than was recorded the previous year during June to August 2013" in the UK.[11] He concludes that "it is highly unlikely that the 2012 Olympic Legacy will filter down and improve things in East London for the better, if anything it will more than likely continue to change things for the worse with regards to the ongoing exclusionary displacement of its poorer residents."[12] In terms of urban spectacle and contributions to city/nation branding, which are often cited as tangible legacies of hosting sport mega-events, G. G. Basurto argues that "even though the Olympics may provide an unparalleled opportunity to revamp ageing infrastructure and transport system in Tokyo, this event-led regeneration in its current form represents a twentieth-century monumentalism, unfit for the socioeconomic and socio-spatial needs of twenty-first-century local population."[13]

Despite such analyses the IOC expanded upon Olympic Legacy (2013) to incorporate a Sustainability Strategy (2017). Further revisions to the IOC bidding process occurred in 2019 as the IOC embarked upon a "7-year journey to Enhance the Olympic and Paralympic Games value propositions by reducing the cost and complexity of the overall delivery model and better managing the risks and responsibilities of key stakeholders to enhance the flexibilities, efficiency and sustainability of hosting Games."[14] This occurred as potential Olympic bids have increasingly become the focus of social movement resistance and public protests from activists supporting the peace, women's rights, and environmental movements. In addition to the examples provided throughout this book, Jean Harvey et al. aptly illustrate that a range of political activist groups and nongovernmental organizations utilize these sporting occasions as a platform to demonstrate their causes to the world audiences.[15] Even at the local level, as Jung Woo Lee notes, in an examination of the 2018 Winter Olympic Games in Pyeongchang in the context of South Korean cultural politics, "while sports mega-events are essentially an athletic contest, this sporting dimension alone cannot fully explain their operating mechanisms."[16] It was in this context, of increasing resistance to Olympic bids that are often embedded in local political-business structures, that sport leaders and the city government in Sapporo embarked upon a bid for the 2026 Winter Olympic Games.

Two Bids for a Sapporo
Winter Olympic Games

Cities that bid to host the Winter Olympic Games have the same high expectations for urban development as cities who pursue the Summer Olympic Games. In *Nagano Olympics Sōdōki*, Toshihide Aikawa revealed the expectations of officials in Nagano in advance of the 1998 Olympic Games. Nagano Economic Research Institute, a local think tank, under the influence of the local top bank, the Hachijuni Bank, which had been involved with the bid campaign and related enterprises to promote the Olympic bid, estimated that the 1998 Winter Olympic Games would create surplus revenue in the local economy of more than 2.324 trillion yen. They also speculated that the Nagano Prefecture would realize infrastructure benefits as a result of financial support from the Japanese Government. However, it was later determined that the local government may have invested 2 trillion yen for public works projects as a consequence of hosting the Olympic Games, although how local tax revenue was used was not revealed.[17] The case of the 2018 Winter Olympic Games held in Pyeongchang, South Korea, offers another example. Lee concludes that "it is somewhat uncertain whether the Pyeongchang Olympic Games will leave genuine and sustainable positive legacies."[18]

In the same year as the 2018 Pyeongchang Winter Olympic Games, on September 6, a magnitude 6.7 earthquake (with an intensity of 7 in Atsuma town) struck the Iburi region in southwestern Hokkaido, which is the northernmost island in Japan. Prior to this event, Sapporo had been planning a bid to host the 2026 Winter Olympics. Due to the serious disruptions in the area, local attitudes towards an Olympic bid changed. The online Olympic news website, *Inside the Games,* noted that "Sapporo is set to become the latest city to withdraw from the race to host the 2026 Winter Olympic and Paralympic Games following reports in Japan that officials will inform the International Olympic Committee (IOC) of their intention to focus on the 2030 event next week." Accompanied by photos of destroyed houses and landslides and rifts caused by the earthquake, the article went on to detail that:

> According to the *Japan Times* and *Kyodo News*, Sapporo Deputy Mayor Takatoshi Machida will confirm their plan to drop their bid in a meeting with IOC President Thomas Bach. Machida will also brief Bach on a recent 6.7 magnitude earthquake which struck Hokkaido, of which Sapporo is the capital, on September 6. It has been suggested the damage caused by the powerful earthquake has prompted Sapporo to announce its withdrawal earlier than anticipated. The city was due to make a final decision prior to next month's IOC Session in Buenos Aires, where the shortlisted candidates will be confirmed. Sapporo's withdrawal would leave Calgary in Canada, Stockholm in Sweden, Erzurum in Turkey and a joint bid from three Italian cities as the remaining candidates for the 2026 Games. Sapporo pulling out of the race does not come as a massive surprise as the city, which hosted the 2017 Asian Winter Games, has been openly considering the possibility of switching their focus to 2030.[19]

On June 24, 2019, Milan and Cortina d'Ampezzo were elected as the host cities at the 134th IOC Session in Lausanne, Switzerland.

Four months after the Hokkaido earthquake, the confusion had subsided and the damage had mostly been repaired. The January 2019 New Year's edition *Sapporo City Bulletin* renewed its cover photo and replaced the image of "the disaster prevention measures" with one that read "Winter

Sports Town, Sapporo." The mayor of Sapporo, Katsuhiro Akimoto, mentioned the urgent need to recover from the Hokkaido Eastern Iburi earthquake for the upcoming Rugby World Cup games, scheduled to be held in the Sapporo Dome in September 2019. With this rhetorical shift, sports mega-events and the recovery from the earthquake became the two major concerns for the new year's policies in local government.[20]

The *City Bulletin* continued to position Sapporo as having a significant history as a winter sport town in history, providing a short chronicle of winter sports.[21] It noted several upcoming winter sports competitions such as the 2019 National Curling Competition, the 2019 National Sports Festival of Japan [*Kokutai*] for skiing, the 2019 Ski Jump World Cup Sapporo, and the 2019 World Para Nordic Skiing World Cup Sapporo.[22] This coverage of winter sport events provided new impetus for the city to restart its bid campaign, this time for the 2030 Winter Olympic Games. In August 2019, the *City Bulletin* made manifest these intentions with a front cover subtitled, "Special Issues of holding the Winter Olympic Games and Paralympic Games together with Sapporo Citizens." Mayor Akimoto, elected to a second four-year term in May 2019, was quoted as supporting this new bid:

> Although we had been pursuing the campaign of the bid for the 2026 Winter Olympic Games, now our city had to give up the bid for 2026 due to the 2018 earthquake and decided to prioritize the recovery and the reconstruction of the devastated areas. Therefore, we changed the goal to the bid for the 2030 Winter Olympic Games. The Olympic Games will bring the hope and dream for the children and the wellbeing in society through which everybody can enjoy sports and live with happiness. Hosting the Games will encourage the town people to be vital and promote urban development to fit with the times. Sapporo city is currently reviewing the budget not to waste money and the policy how to organize the Games. We will reconsider and remake our scheme based on the opinions provided by the Sapporo citizens. To realize hosting the Olympic Games, the people's support is indispensable. Let us listen to your opinion, please.[23]

This special issue of the *Bulletin* included statistics from the Japan Tourism Agency, used to indicate the impact that a successful bid could have on the still-recovering region. A figure titled "Increased Numbers of Skiers from Overseas during 2013 and 2017" shows a threefold increase in the number of foreign skiers visiting Japan between 2013 and 2017 (299,000 in 2013, 403,000 in 2014, 595,000 in 2015, 661,000 in 2016 and 858,000 in 2017), while another figure titled "The negative prospect of economic fall with the decreasing number of population during 2015 and 2060" details the decreasing population in Sapporo (1,950,000 in 2015, 1,930,000 in 2030, 1,770,000 in 2045 and 1,550,000 in 2060).[24] In combination, these statistics asserted that overseas visitors would help to maintain and activate an economic recovery. The *Bulletin* also suggested that buildings constructed fifty years earlier, for the 1972 Sapporo Winter Olympic Games, were in need of repair or replacement. The city, the report continued, is not planning to construct new stadiums except in the case of ones that are dilapidated.[25] The costs for a proposed 2030 Games and such infrastructure renewal could be kept affordable by relying on sponsorships from domestic private enterprises, IOC funds, and the sale of Olympic merchandise.

As the campaign for the bid continued, the January 2020 cover photo of *City Bulletin* promoted the bid with a picture of Mayor Akimoto and the Director of Special Olympics, Yuko Arimori, a celebrity former women's marathon athlete and silver medalist. The caption proclaimed that the bid would be guided by "urban development with a soft heart for all." This column appealed for the bid to respect all people regardless of age or disability, and the need for coexistence, emphasizing that "sports works for the goal." Arimori used the phrase "'to remove both mental and physical barriers" and asserted that the 2030 Winter Olympic Games will bring great opportunities for urban development that will benefit both overseas tourists and disabled people.[26] After Mayor Akimoto's visit to Lausanne and meeting with IOC president Thomas Bach on January 11, 2020, the Japanese Olympic Committee (JOC) selected Sapporo as the official Japanese bid city for the 2030 Winter Olympics.[27]

Thus, the *Sapporo City Bulletin* transformed the dismal atmosphere created by the 2018 earthquake into support for a bid for the 2030 Winter Olympic Games. With the IOC's Sustainability Strategy issued in 2017, all current bids must address how, as host cities, they would contribute to the achievement of the IOC's sustainability priorities, which are informed by the SDGs. So, even as the bid for the 2026 Winter Games was canceled in order to prioritize the restoration from the 2018 earthquake, the *Bulletin* argued in favor of another bid, basing their support on issues consistent with the SDGs, by suggesting that the Olympics could be based on the new idea of "urban development with a soft heart for all." However, if achieving the targets set out in the SDGs is the true goal for the 2030 Sapporo Winter Games bid, it would be worth recalling a little-remembered protest movement that raised environmental issues surrounding the 1972 Sapporo Winter Olympic Games a half century ago.

Environmental Protests at and Legacies
of the 1972 Sapporo Winter Olympic Games

While the 1994 Lillehammer Winter Olympic Games are often pointed to as a moment when environmental issues were prominent on the Olympic agenda, twenty-two years earlier opposition to the construction of the downhill ski facilities on Mount Eniwa, and concern over conservation of the natural world were prominent at the 1972 Sapporo Winter Olympic Games.[28] J. L. Chappelet writes of the Olympic Movement that "environmental issues became increasingly important during the 1970s and 1980s, notably of Sapporo 1972."[29] Sapporo 1972 was undoubtedly the earliest case of environmental issues, in particular concern for reforestation, impacting the hosting of the Winter Olympic Games. However, this early case is not well known today.

The Hokkaido Nature Conservation Society (HNCS) was established in December 1964 by local naturalists and scientists in Sapporo. As Souya Ishizuka notes, members of the HNCS argued against constructing the Winter Olympic downhill ski facilities on Mount Eniwa for environmental reasons.[30] They proposed that the downhill facilities should be removed after the Games and the venue should be restored to its natural conditions. They sent a petition to IOC president Avery Brundage opposing the use of Mount Eniwa, with signatures collected from the International Union for Conservation of Nature (IUCN).

Ishizuka assumes that this petition was related to another environmental protest taking place in Banff, Canada, as the local newspaper, *Hokkaido Shimbun,* took up the topic on April 20, 1966, seven days before the bid was successful.[31] The group in Banff were opposing a local bid for the 1972 Winter Olympics over environmental issues (see chapter 1). The minutes of the 64th IOC Session, held in Rome from April 24–30, 1966, where the hosts for the 1972 Winter and Summer Olympics were selected, note that:

> The IOC President Brundage related many protests given by the Canadian association and citizens from other countries who were concerned with "Conservation of Nature." They asserted that they did not want to create the examples of giving damage to natural resources in their own country . . . The President thought it impossible to ignore all the protests provided by every group, universities, and clubs. Even if the Prime Minister of Canada supports the standing of Banff, the IOC should avoid the risk of raising international protests and protest movements during the event.[32]

In terms of the HNCS protests, the downhill facilities were removed after the 1972 Winter Games and the venue was reforested. In addition, related plans to construct a new road to the downhill ski venue were canceled in favor of the conservation of nature. The area around Lake Okotanpe, close to the downhill ski facilities on Mount Eniwa, was also designated as a special protection area.[33] Nevertheless, the bid itself was not canceled. Moreover, although local objections over the Sapporo bid had been raised by HNCS prior to the IOC decision, the Sapporo Olympic Organizing Committee avoided these issues for fear that any discussions of these issues may have hurt their bid's chances.

There are two possible reasons why this early example of environmental protest is not more widely known. First, it occurred at the same time as the more internationally influential protest movement opposing the Banff bid. Sapporo may have been selected by the IOC to avoid the more prominent protests from the Canadian Wildlife Association and other groups in favor of the lower-profile resistance provided by the HNCS in Sapporo. Secondly, these protests occurred before environmental sustainability was a prominent global issue. The 1972 Winter Olympics took place twenty years before Agenda 21 was introduced in June 1992 and the UN Conference on Environment and Development was held in Rio de Janeiro, where "combating deforestation" was a prominent component of the discussion on the "Conservation and Management of Resources for Development."[34] Thereafter, the IOC began to consider environmental issues in the hosting plans of the Winter Games.

The history of environmental protests in 1972 remains important as the Sapporo 2030 bid committed itself to "urban development with a soft heart for all." Despite the opposition by HNCS, the 1972 Winter Olympics were motivated more by economic development than the preservation of nature. The cost of urban infrastructure, including constructing roads and subways, amounted to 42.6 billion yen, about 58 percent of the entire cost, while the cost for constructing stadiums was about 10 billion yen, less than 5 percent of the total costs.[35] Yoshihiko Onuma asserts that it was easier in 1972 for Sapporo officials to demonstrate the urban benefits of hosting the Winter Olympic because Alpine ski facilities constructed on the mountain were so geographically removed from Sapporo city (see figure 8.2). Moreover, Onuma argues, facilities for the Summer Olympic Games because of their urban nature often require more negotiation with local communities than Winter Olympic facilities in the natural environment, suggesting that the former are more likely to involve issues affecting how a city should be designed for the future and who pays for the necessary arrangements.

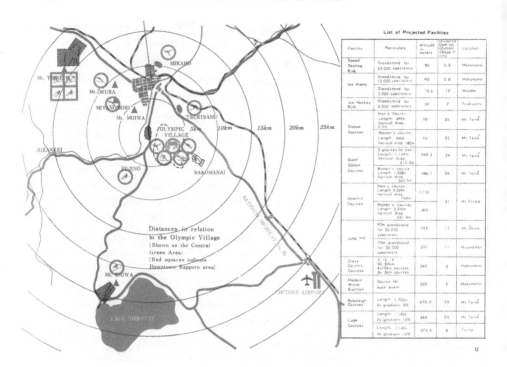

FIGURE 8.2. List of Projected Facilities, XI Olympic Winter Games Sapporo 1972. Credit: Sapporo Olympic Winter Games Preparations Bureau, 1972.

Onuma argues that this difference facilitated the hosting of the 1972 Winter Olympics in Sapporo, contributed to the environmental protests being little remembered in the subsequent fifty years, and resulted in the positive memories that inhabitants of the city associate with the event. These include: (1) the publicity of the Olympic Games led to the name of the city, Sapporo, being diffused internationally. International friendships were struck at both the administrative and community levels; (2) the number of tourists, both domestic and overseas, increased. In particular, the Sapporo Snow Festival and various ski resorts attracted many people after the Olympics; (3) urban development advanced by the equivalent of twenty years, compared with the progress of other urban development projects; (4) The event produced a stable image of Sapporo as a winter sport town with well-supplied facilities that promoted sports to citizens throughout the region.[36] All of these legacies are again being mobilized in support of the 2030 bid.

Hukkō Gorin:
Co-opting support for the Sapporo bid

These memories inherited from a half century ago may influence the support for future Olympic bids. However, Sapporo officials are looking to the more recent past as they position the 2030 bid. The Tokyo 2020 Summer Olympic bid was successful in gaining support from the Japanese public by using the tragedy of the March 2011 earthquake, tsunami, and Fukushima nuclear power station disasters. Olympic officials in Japan argued that the 2020 Olympics would contribute to the rebuilding and recovery from these disasters. A rhetorical strategy that journalist Gentarō Taniguchi has labelled *"Hukkō Gorin."* Taniguchi's 2019 book, *The End of Olympics Has Begun*, and his earlier, "Criminality of *Hukkō Gorin*," rebuked the Tokyo organizing committee for practicing *Hukkō Gorin*, which translates as "hosting the Olympic Games to recover the devastated area."[37] His criticism, and the conceptualization of this term, is based on his belief that suggesting that hosting the Olympics is for the purpose of encouraging the recovery of devasted areas is a criminal act, for the way in which it signifies the political use of people's misfortune and disregards people's life.[38] For Taniguchi, hosting the Tokyo Olympic Games would not accelerate the recovery of the devastated areas and was only an act of political propaganda, using the tragedy of the disaster and people's suffering.

He criticized Prime Minister Shinzō Abe's visit to Fukushima together with IOC President Thomas Bach to inspect the venue for softball for the Tokyo Olympic Games on November 24, 2018. This inspection did not include any sport scientific scrutiny, rather its purpose was to demonstrate the safety of the area after the accident at the Fukushima Nuclear Power Stations in March 2011. Taniguchi also lamented that President Bach did not read the accusatory report written by Hiroaki Koide, former assistant professor at the Institute for Radiation and Nuclear Science at Kyoto University, who led the investigation team that produced the damage report after the Fukushima incident. Taniguchi argues that "if Bach had read Koide's report, he would have been much more shocked by its crucial damage and would never have visited the place for himself." Koide's report denounces the fact that holding the Olympic Games was determined during the period in which "the Declaration of Nuclear Emergency" had not yet been rescinded.[39] Taniguchi excerpted Koide's report as follows:

> Main element which has been contaminating the environment is radioactive substance cesium 137. It takes 30 years to reduce to the half, which means being one tenth in one hundred years. Therefore, Japan

is destined to be bound under "the Declaration of Nuclear Emergency" in the hundred years . . . The Olympics has been always utilized for the purpose of rising nationalism. More recently, the Olympic Games have been targeted by the entrepreneurial purpose of repeating the reconstruction and the construction of sports facilities for the huge gains of construction companies in the dissipative consuming society. What is most significant issue is how we are able to work to dissolve the state of "the Declaration of Nuclear Emergency" with all nation's efforts. The priority must be rescuing the people who have been subjected to suffering from the damage brought by the accident of Fukushima Nuclear Power Stations and sinless children.[40]

There was further evidence of how deceptive the pursuit of *Hukkō Gorin* could be. Taniguchi outlines how the national training center, "J-Village," in Naraha-machi, a local town in Fukushima Prefecture, the epicenter of the nuclear disaster, was to be reopened as part of the Olympic-related recovery. J-Village was initiated as a national facility for soccer training in 1997. It had been mostly used for the campsite for the Japanese national soccer team. The Tokyo Electric Power Company (TEPCO) and Japan Football Association (JFA) partnered financially to build this facility. However, only two months after the bid for the Tokyo 2020 Olympic Games was successful, it was announced that J-Village would be reopened, in the aftermath of the damage caused by the nuclear disaster. Reopening meant that TEPCO withdrew from the restoration work in the J-Village and also closed the nuclear disaster recovery center when 49,554 people evacuated from the Fukushima prefecture were still located elsewhere.[41] Taniguchi interviewed Kazuyoshi Sato, a member of the "Denuclearization Network" before the reopening of J-Village. Sato told him that "TEPCO financially contributed to the initial construction of J-Village in return for the increasing [number of] nuclear power stations. It was their favorite trick of 'carrot and stick.'" In a second interview in November 2013, after the success of the bid for the Tokyo Summer Olympic Games, when J-Village was reopened in order to resume the function of an original training camp for the preparation of international soccer, Sato expressed his resentment: "it is dysfunctional to close TEPCO's restoration work there and reopening the training village to prepare for international matches without confirming the relocation of the alternative headquarters for the restoration work from nuclear disaster."[42]

The deceptiveness inherent in *Hukkō Gorin* is relevant to the bid for the 2030 Winter Olympics because of local officials' use of the September 2018 earthquake to gain support for the bid. In December 2019, Mayor Akimoto asserted in Lausanne that areas damaged by the 2018 earthquake had recovered. He expressed confidence in the preparations that were then underway to move the marathon and racewalking competitions for the 2020 Summer Olympic Games from Tokyo to Sapporo.[43] The infrastructure improvements that accompanied these events occurred despite the fact that it usually takes many years to repair roads in Sapporo, in part because the winter snowfall limits the time available for construction. The hosting of the 2020 Summer Olympic marathon and racewalking events in Sapporo was used to suggest that awarding the 2030 Winter Olympics to the city would result in a similar recovery from the September 2018 earthquake.

Conclusion

Despite the criticism inherent in the concept of *Hukkō Gorin* and the legacy of the environmental protests at the 1972 Winter Olympic Games, the bid for hosting the 2030 Sapporo Winter Olympics is moving forward. The commitment of the 2026 and 2030 bid committees to the preservation of the natural environment is difficult to accept when the memory of the protests from the 1972 Olympics seems to have faded. Forty-four years after the event, *Hokkaido Shimbun*, a local newspaper, reported traces of reforested downhill courses are still discernible on the snow-covered Mount Eniwa: the men's downhill course ran 2,636 meters, the women's downhill course ran 2,108 meters, and a total of 20 hectares were unable to be recovered.[44] Some sport facilities constructed for the 1972 Sapporo Winter Olympics look no more sustainable: the finish-line house for the bobsleigh course was closed in 2000 due to the costs of ongoing maintenance. The half-destroyed facility left in Teine-ward in Sapporo was demolished and removed in March 2017.[45] How much tax revenue Sapporo citizens contributed to this facility since its construction has yet to be publicized.

In the half century since Sapporo first hosted the Winter Olympic Games, the emphasis has shifted from the preservation of nature to economic legacy, which is consistent with the current concept of the SDGs. Even if the Olympics may provide an opportunity to revamp an aging transport system and other infrastructure, they may be unfit for the socioeconomic needs of the local population in the twenty-first century. Nevertheless, Sapporo city continues to prioritize economic legacy. This is not new to local Olympic bids. What is unique to the Sapporo case, as demonstrated by the 2026 and 2030 bids and the 2020 Summer Tokyo Olympic Games, is the way in which the recovery from natural disasters can be easily absorbed and subsumed into the idea of Olympism. The "Criminality of *Hukkō Gorin*," the use of devasted area for holding the

Olympic Games, reflects this discourse as the memory of the earthquake was transitioned in the media and political circles from the recovery from this natural disaster to positioning Sapporo as a winter sport town.

It is important to acknowledge, we argue, that the practice of sport is neutral in such contexts and it is the actions of civic leaders that have embedded sport, in this case, an Olympic bid, in a political context. Taniguchi identifies the logic through which sport and even the SDGs were used to satisfy another political scheme, one that employed the recovery from a natural disaster and people's pain. Although positive experiences of sporting events may sweep aside people's sad memory of the disaster, it should be questioned if this emotional response should be used politically by the mayor. While he set aside the 2026 bid in light of the earthquake and the need for recovery, he never gave up on the idea of bidding for the Winter Olympics, which remains an absolute priority for him connected to his own ideas of development for Sapporo.[46]

Even as local officials prioritize economic development over environmental protection as their form of a commitment to the SDGs, a larger question remains. Is it realistic to expect sport mega-events such as the Olympics, with complicated logistical demands, to achieve multiple sustainable development targets? In such circumstances, different goals are likely to interfere with one another. While many of the SDGs, as noted, have specific targets, these operate largely independent of one another. Achieving these at an Olympic Games is not a simple sum of achieving each goal because the event intersects with multiple goals. Trying to achieve economic development targets, for example, may impact the pursuit of clean energy or damage the environment. The question of which goal should take priority is a difficult one to answer, even as the IOC offers ambiguous support for sustainability: "the enthusiasm for the practice of sport ... and the enjoyment of watching sport provide ideal opportunities to raise public awareness and educate young generations on the global sustainability challenges being faced and, more importantly, on solutions to address these challenges."[47]

Thus, the ambiguity inherent in the holistic concept of the SDGs obscures any frictions between goals. As the case of the 1972 Sapporo Winter Olympic Games demonstrates, the bid itself provided evidence of the struggle between environmental legacy and socioeconomic legacy. As a result, less attention was paid to the environmental protest movement in Hokkaido when the Olympics benefitted a local community where people were anxious to prioritize economic gains and the IOC was absolved from confronting the more influential international environmental protest movement taking place in Banff.

In the age of sustainable development goals, which have a strong focus on improving societal environmental well-being around the planet, new considerations about the Olympic Games are required. Recent headlines such as "IOC and Tokyo 2020 Agree on Measures to Deliver Games Fit for a Post-Corona World"[48] reflect the same political use of nuclear disasters, earthquakes, and the tsunami to support a bid for the Olympic Games. Sapporo will follow in the footsteps of the 2020 (2021) Tokyo Summer Olympic Games with the 2030 Winter Games bid unless a compelling bridge between the original idealism of Olympism for an individual to be a good citizen and new goals for social gains interwoven with Olympic Legacy within the IOC Sustainability Strategy are discerned.

Notes

1. UNESCO, "UNESCO and Sustainable Development Goals," accessed March 19, 2024, https://en.unesco.org/sustainabledevelopmentgoals.

2. Ibid.

3. United Nations (UN), "Targets and Indicators," in "End Poverty in All Its Forms Everywhere," accessed March 19, 2024, https://sdgs.un.org/goals/goal1.

4. IOC, *IOC Sustainability Strategy: Executive Summary* (Lausanne: International Olympic Committee, 2017), 3–8. See also IOC, *IOC Sustainability Report: Sharing Progress on Our 2020 Objectives*, October 2018, IOC-Sustainability-Report-2018.pdf.

5. Shigeo Shimizu, the first Japanese leading scholar of the study of original Coubertin's Olympism, had summarized Pierre de Coubertin's work from 1906–1932 to interpretate his philosophy of Olympism and distinguish it from the concept of Olympism which was later spread by the IOC. According to Shimizu's study, early works on Coubertin's Philosophy of Olympism was based on beliefs about how to make a man a good person, not by a system but by "a way of mind," as an educational goal fostered inside an individual's mind (Coubertin, 1918); a ritual to make a young man into a peaceful and confident human being, conquering the mind of fear (Coubertin, 1919); a school of novelty and moralistic purity (Coubertin, 1932). See Shigeo Shimizu, "Olympism for the Twenty-First Century: Asking Coubertin for the Original Idea" in Tokuro Yamamoto, *Fundamental Studies for Reconstruction of Olympism in the Twenty-First Century*, vol. 22 in the Annual Reports of Health, Physical Education and Sport Science of Kokushikan University (Tokyo, 2003), 98–99.

6. IOC, *Olympic Legacy* (Lausanne: International Olympic Committee, 2013), https://stillmed.olympic.org/Documents/Olympism_in_action/Legacy/2013_Booklet_Legacy.pdf.

7. Ibid.

8. Vassil Girginov, *Rethinking Olympic Legacy* (London: Routledge, 2018), 198.

9. Helen Jefferson Lenskyj, *Society Now: The Olympic Games: A Critical Approach* (Bingley, Bradford, UK; Emerald Publishing Limited, 2020), 93.

10. *Nikkei Shimbun*, "Olympic Legacy Is Now a Burden: Nagano Bobsled Stadium's Survival Is in Jeopardy," November 26, 2016, https://www.nikkei.com/article/DGXLASDG15HE6_V21C16A1CC1000/.

11. Anthony Gunter, "Youth Transitions and Legacies in an East London Olympic Host Borough," in *London 2012 and the Post-Olympics City: A Hollow Legacy?*, edited by Phil Cohen and Paul Watt (London: Palgrave Macmillan, 2017), 287.

12. Ibid., 304.

13. Grace Gonzalez Basurto, "From London 2012 to Tokyo 2020: Urban Spectacle, Nation Branding and Socio-Spatial Targeting in the Olympic City," in Cohen and Watt, *London 2012 and the Post-Olympics City*, 436.

14. The IOC, *Olympic Games Candidature Process*, accessed April 18, 2019, https://www.olympic.org/all-about-the-candidature-process, relocated to a new page, "2026 Host City Election," at a new site, olympics.com, accessed April 29, 2024, https://olympics.com/ioc/2026-host-city-election; Lenskyj, *Society Now*, 93.

15. Jean Harvey, John Horne, Parissa Safai, Simon C. Darnell, and Sebastien Courchesne-O'Neill, *Sport and Social Movements: From the Local to the Global* (London: Bloomsbury, 2013).

16. Jung Woo Lee, "A Game for the Global North: The 2018 Winter Olympic Games in Pyeongchang and South Korean Cultural Politics," in *Olympic Conflict: from the Games of the New Emerging Forces to the Rio Olympics*, edited by Lu Zhouxiang and Fan Hong (London: Routledge, 2018), 109–10.

17. Toshihide Aikawa, *The Disturbance of the 1998 Nagano Winter Olympic Games [Nagano Olympics Sōdōki]* (Tokyo: Soshisha, 1998), 221–26.

18. Lee, "A Game for the Global North," 111–21.

19. Liam Morgan, "Sapporo Set to Withdraw Bid for 2026 Winter Olympic and Paralympic Games," *Inside the Games*, September 13th, 2018, https://www.insidethegames.biz/articles/1069900/sapporo-set-to-withdraw-bid-for-2026-winter-olympic-and-paralympic-games.

20. The mayor of Sapporo, Katsuhiro Akimoto, "A Preface: For a City Where Everybody Can Live, Feeling at Ease with a Smile," *Kohō Sapporo [The Sapporo City Bulletin]*, vol. 706, January 2019, 1.

21. Ibid., 3–4.

22. Ibid., 6–7.

23. The mayor of Sapporo, Katsuhiro Akimoto, in "Winter Olympic and Paralympic Games—We Do It Together," *Kohō Sapporo [The Sapporo City Bulletin]*, vol. 713, August 2019, 6.

24. Figures titled "Increased Numbers of Skiers from Overseas during 2013 and 2017" and "'The Negative Prospect of Economic Fall with the Decreasing

Number of Population During 2015 and 2060," in "Winter Olympic and Paralympic Games—We Do It Together," 8–9.

25. Ibid.

26. *Kohō Sapporo (The Sapporo City Bulletin)*, vol. 718, January 2020, 2–5.

27. T. Morimoto, "Sapporo Has 'Advantages' as Domestic Candidate Site for 2030 Winter Olympics, but Bid Efforts Are Still Fumbling," *The Sankei Shimbun*, January 29, 2020, https://www.sankei.com/sports/news/200129/sp02001290031-n1.html.

28. 1972 Sapporo Olympic Winter Games Preparations Bureau, *XI Olympic Winter Games Sapporo 1972* (Sapporo: 1972 Sapporo Olympic Winter Games Preparations Bureau, 1972).

29. J. L. Chappelet, "Olympic Environmental Concerns as a Legacy of the Winter Games," *The International Journal of the History of Sport*, 25, no. 14, (2008): 1884–1902.

30. Souya Ishizuka, "The Negotiations between the Organizing Committee for the Olympic Games and the Nature Conservation Society of Hokkaido about Construction of the Ski Downhill Site on Mt. Eniwa and Nature Conservation for the Preparation for XI Olympic Winter Games in Sapporo 1972: Analysis of Minutes of the Organizing Committee for the Olympic Games and Bulletins of the Nature Conservation Society of Hokkaido," *Japanese Journal of the History of Physical Education* 31 (March 2014), 21–35; Hokkaido Nature Conservation Society, home page, accessed March 19, 2024, https://nc-hokkaido.or.jp/english.html.

31. Ishizuka, "Negotiations," 23.

32. Souya Ishizuka, "The Controversy Concerning the Change of Ski Downhill Facilities during the Preparation Period for XI Olympic Winter Games in Sapporo," *Japanese Journal of the History of Physical Education* 32 (March 2015): 18.

33. Ishizuka, "Negotiations," 26–27.

34. United Nations Division for Sustainable Development, "United Nations Conference on Environment & Development: Rio de Janeiro, Brazil, 3 to 14 June 1992, AGENDA 21," accessed March 19, 2024, https://sustainabledevelopment.un.org/content/documents/Agenda21.pdf.

35. Yoshihiko Onuma, "Naze mega-sports event ka? [Why Do We Evaluate Mega-Sports Event?]" in *Mega-Sports Event no Shakaigaku [Sociology of Sports Mega-Events]*, edited by Kazunori Matsumura (Tokyo: Nansosha, 2006 [2007]), 240.

36. Ibid., 242–43.

37. Gentarō Taniguchi, *Olympic no Owari no Hajimari [The End of Olympics Has Begun]* (Tokyo: Commons), 2019.

38. Gentarō Taniguchi, "Supōtsu to Masukomi [Sports and Mass Communication: Criminality of 'Hukkō Gorin' which Disregards Human Life]" in *Broadcasting Report [Hōsō Report]* 276, edited by the Media Research Institute (Jan. 2019): 36–37.

39. Ibid., 36.

40. Ibid., 37.

41. Taniguchi, *Olympic no Owari no Hajimari*, 128–29.

42. Ibid., 130–31.

43. *Hokkaido Shimbun*, December 27, 2019.

44. Hokkaido Shimbun Dosh, "Sapporo Olympic Downhill Course Ruins," YouTube video, March 6, 2016, https://www.youtube.com/watch?v=a9smuUZtw6Y.

45. *The Mainichi Newspapers*, March 15, 2017.

46. *Kohō Sapporo* (*The Sapporo City Bulletin*), vol. 713, 6.

47. IOC, *IOC Sustainability Strategy*, 3–8.

48. IOC, "IOC and Tokyo 2020 Agree on Measures to Deliver Games Fit for a Post-Corona World," September 25, 2020, https://www.olympic.org/news/ioc-and-tokyo-2020-agree-on-measures-to-deliver-games-fit-for-a-post-corona-world.

Epilogue

The Evolution of
Winter Olympic Resistance

RUSSELL FIELD

For nearly a century, sport as an institution has been the focal point for protesters and resistance movements of varying scale advocating for a variety of causes. Struggles for social and economic justice and equality have benefited from the visibility of sport. This is increasingly so as athletes—both in the 1960s as well as half a century later—(re)claimed the power of their positions within sport. This has been especially true, although not exclusively so, of professional athletes in North America. Beyond sport as a platform for advancing social change, many activist athletes (and non-athletes) have sought to alter the conditions within which sport occurs. A significant platform for the intersection of these two strands—social change advocated through sport and the fight to change sport itself—is the hosting of what scholars have labelled sport mega-events (SMEs).[1]

Recent opposition initially to Games bids and then to the development deemed necessary for hosting events such as the Summer Olympic Games and the FIFA men's World Cup have highlighted the considerable public investment expected in the face of other priorities, the dislocation of marginalized populations for venue construction, and the human rights record of host nations. Some, if not all, of these issues arose during Boston's mooted bid for the 2024 Olympics, South Africa's, Brazil's, and Qatar's hosting of the 2010, 2014, and 2022 men's soccer World Cups, respectively, and will no doubt arise during debates over Saudi Arabia's bid for the 2034 FIFA event.

The Olympic Winter Games are not immune from such pressures. In fact, as the contributors to this book have articulated, the Winter Olympics offer a unique and compelling coterie of case studies through which to consider protest and resistance in sport. These Games comprise sports and events that are almost entirely Western and Northern, with the necessity for snow-covered venues limiting the geographic possibilities for hosting. Despite sport development programs funded by the International Olympic Committee (IOC)—from Samoa and Tonga in the Pacific to the US Virgin Islands and Dominica in the Caribbean (recall the bare-chested Pita Taufatofua carrying the Tongan flag into the PyeongChang 2018 opening ceremonies)—that are intended to broaden participation in winter sports and, cynically, expand the roster of nations marching into Games' opening ceremonies, the Winter Olympics remain a niche event where interest is greatest in predominantly white, privileged nations.

It is within these settings that resistance to and protest at the Winter Olympics has emerged. While Milan-Cortina d'Ampezzo's selection as the host for 2026 may be seen as signaling a return to "traditional" winter Olympic locales, the same trends have continued for the 2030 bidding cycle, with the provincial government in British Columbia opting not to support an Indigenous-led bid for a return to Vancouver/Whistler in Canada (which hosted in 2010) and the Sapporo bid becoming embroiled in a bribery scandal.[2] This is a reminder that the concerns that have informed the long history of Winter Olympic resistance remain current.

That these issues emerged in force in the mid-1960s while the IOC was confronting challenges on a number of fronts (e.g., the multiple impacts on sport of the Cold War and Third World decolonization) made the IOC wary of courting more controversy by selecting Banff as the host of the 1972 Games. The success of efforts to oppose the Banff bid and, six years later, the Denver Games being returned to the IOC by plebiscite can be attributed to the growing prominence of opposition to development (or, more accurately, additional development) of the "natural" world. However, as both Russell Field and Adam Berg detail, in chapters 1 and 2, respectively, these campaigns also achieved their ends in part because of the predominantly white, middle-class citizen-activists, scientists, and professionals who were at the forefront of anti-Olympic initiatives in Northern democracies—and their commensurate ability to influence the public narrative.

While the impact of activists' resistance efforts cannot be overlooked, the perception of them as respectable actors may have enhanced their efforts. A similar deference was not accorded to Indigenous opposition when the Olympic movement finally opted to award the Winter Games to Calgary as Christine O'Bonsawin details in chapter 3. Two decades after the Banff protests, when the Winter Olympics were first hosted by Canada, the 1988 Calgary Games were similarly inflected by resistance, but protests grounded in the dispossession of Indigenous peoples from their traditional lands and territories, whether through European systems of treaty negotiation or outright appropriation, and the associated mining of natural resources with minimal consent or consultation, were considerably less resonant with Olympic officials.

As the Winter Games expanded to new locales—with the first Asian Winter Olympics taking place in Japan (Sapporo 1972, Nagano 1998), Korea (PyeongChang 2018), and China (Beijing 2022)—the demographics of activists drawn to social movements similarly evolved. The local booster coalitions that fueled Winter Olympic growth often worked, at times with the complicity of the IOC, to marginalize opposition. Despite this, local voices concerned by the effect on the environment of the Winter Olympics were having an increasingly influential impact on the institution. As a result, one reason for continued optimism among anti-Olympic activists— or at least those who advocate for a fuller consideration of the economic, environmental, and sociopolitical impact of the Olympic enterprise—is the recent evidence that their messages are gaining mainstream acceptance.

Anti-Olympic arguments resonated with a generation schooled on the lessons that emerged from worldwide protests beginning, perhaps, with the anti-WTO (World Trade Organization) protests in Seattle in 1999 and culminating in the Occupy movement.[3] As Jules Boykoff demonstrates in chapter 4 in the context of the Vancouver 2010 Olympics, resistance to the Winter Games has coalesced around a number of intersecting issues that are increasingly prominent in public discourse, if not always public policy. These include opposing the destruction of the natural environment and wildlife habitats in favor of development, where an arc traced from Nagano 1998 to PyeongChang 2018 passes through Eagleridge Bluffs. In Vancouver, this opposition reflected Indigenous stewardship of the land and informed Indigenous resistance to first the bid and then the Games themselves. With the lower mainland of British Columbia encompassing land never ceded through treaty by Indigenous Peoples, Indigenous leaders and protesters insisted upon "no games on stolen native land." Allied protest movements, in the Games' most urban settings, protested against the size of public expenditures (from multiple levels of government) in the face of more pressing issues, the profiteering that resulted from the development of Vancouver's Downtown Eastside—essentially pricing residents out of their own communities—as well as the prioritizing of the Olympic promotional and security apparatus over the protection of civil rights.

Boykoff argues that the activism that coalesced in Vancouver in the leadup to and during the 2010 Olympics—a moment of movements—contributed to a growing international network of anti-Olympic resistance. However, Sven Daniel Wolfe offers a significant reminder that issues that have transnational relevance are still at root local issues. While Sochi 2014 became the inflection point for a number of global causes, in particular the fight for LGBTQ rights in opposition to Russian state laws, in chapter 5 Wolfe highlights the ways in which for local residents, opposition to the Games in and around Sochi focused on the economic impacts and logistical disruptions on people's lives. The issues of concern to anti-Olympic protestors have the greatest resonance when connected to the day-to-day existence of those affected by Olympic-related dislocations.

Nevertheless, these issues have continued to be relevant, (re)emerging in debates over the 2018 PyeongChang Games as well as the abandoned bids for Oslo 2022 and Calgary 2026. Paradoxically, however, these voices of dissent gained acceptance during a period when the IOC embraced the commercial potential of global sponsors and its power over bid and host cities grew significantly. While anti-Olympic protest has coalesced in the past 15–20 years, these movements have had their greatest success in motivating local opposition and seeing proposed bids rescinded. Because all of the recent iterations of Olympic Winter Games that have faced resistance movements—from Vancouver to PyeongChang—have proceeded, destroying ecosystems and natural habitats in favor of infrastructure and development, safe in the knowledge that once the Opening Ceremonies were underway the public media discourse would shift from newsrooms focused on discord to sports departments interested in feel-good stories and medal-winning performances.

It is in this context that Winter Olympic resistance finds purpose (tactically) and resonance (ideologically). As Liv Yoon explores in chapter 6, in the context of PyeongChang 2018 and the struggle to protect Mount Gariwang, anti-Olympic activists must search for meaning when Games proceed without their concerns being addressed. This meaning can be found in the communities built across the convergence of activist interests and in the bridges built and conversations had with local residents. In this way, resistance can continue after the Games have left town, focusing less on SMEs and more on the broader structural inequities that they reveal. Opposing the costs and impacts of the Winter Olympic Games could, in this way, find resonance with the analysis of the rescinded Oslo 2022 bid offered by Jan Ove Tangen and Bieke Gils in chapter 7. In their formulation, the Oslo bid lost public support as a gulf between Norwegian national moral values and the operational values of the Olympic movement revealed themselves in IOC expectations of bid cities.

This contest between the values of Olympic promoters and bid opponents continues to play itself out as Hokkaido's largest city bid for the 2030 Winter Games. Sapporo's Olympic history is intimately associated with environmental activism: it was the city selected for the 1972 Games when issues were raised with the Banff bid and was itself the site of concerns expressed by local conservationists over the deforestation undertaken to develop ski facilities at Mount Eniwa. Chapter 8 brings the narrative arc of this collection full circle as Keiko Ikeda and Tyrel Eskelson detail the context of the current Sapporo bid and argue for reimagining Pierre de Coubertin's initial Olympic ideals within the framework provided by the UNESCO's Sustainable Development Goals (SDGs). Infusing 21st-century development priorities *might* (even as these are invested with neoliberal ideologies) wrest Olympic rhetoric from the civic boosterism and sporting nationalism that currently fuel Olympic bid advocates.

Nevertheless, the Winter Olympics remain conceptually different from Coubertin's original project. While some of the resistance to and protest through (and directed at) the Winter Games recognizes the event's status among the prominent global SMEs, other grievances stem from the event's unique origins. While the values informing the Winter Games may have diverged from Olympic ideals—without lapsing into reifying the Olympics' purported purpose—much of the protest examined in this collection is embedded in the nature and history of the Winter Olympic project: the negotiation between Nordic and Alpine traditions; the initial inclusion of outdoor-only events that aided the promotion efforts of exclusive resort towns; and the exclusion of some recreational traditions (e.g., mountaineering) that may have taken a very different attitude toward the commercial development of the natural world. Since at least the mid-1960s, the uneasy resolution of these tensions has led quadrennially to winters of discontent.

Notes

1. Maurice Roche, *Mega-Events and Social Change: Spectacle, Legacy and Public Culture* (Manchester, UK: Manchester University Press, 2017).

2. Chris Corday, "IOC Struggling to Find Home for 2030 Winter Olympics—and a Tokyo Games Scandal Is Not Helping," CBC News, December 25, 2022, https://www.cbc.ca/news/world/winter-games-sapporo-japan-tokyo-ioc-1.6692150.

3. Some place the beginning of this period earlier, with Chiapas, Mexico, in 1994. See, e.g., Paul Kingsnorth, *One No, Many Yeses: A Journey to the Heart of the Global Resistance Movement* (London: Free Press, 2003). Also, the significance and resonance, particularly in Canada, of Indigenous assertions of rights through Idle No More should not be overlooked.

Contributors

ADAM BERG is an assistant professor of Kinesiology at the University of North Carolina Greensboro. He teaches about and researches the intersection of sport, culture, and politics in the United States. He is the author of *The Olympics that Never Happened: Denver '76 and the Politics of Growth* (2023).

JULES BOYKOFF is the author of six books on the Olympic Games, including *What Are the Olympics For?* (2024), *NOlympians: Inside the Fight Against Capitalist Mega-Sports in Los Angeles, Tokyo, and Beyond* (2020), and *Power Games: A Political History of the Olympics* (2016). His work has appeared in academic journals like the *International Review for the Sociology of Sport*, *Sociology of Sport Journal*, and the *International Journal of the History of Sport*, and outlets like the *New York Times*, *The Nation*, and *Asahi Shimbun*. He teaches political science at Pacific University in the United States.

Dr. TYREL ESKELSON is a historian who has been working in the Faculty of Education at Hokkaido University since 2017 as a specially appointed assistant/associate professor and adjunct lecturer. He received his MA from Norwich University, Vermont, and his PhD from Hokkaido University. He is the author of various publications such as "Continuity or Change: After the Tokyo Olympic Games 1964: Exploring the Tokyo Games 2020 through Various Critical Reviews" (2019) and *The Island of Mora Mora: A Journey into Madagascar* (2023).

RUSSELL FIELD is an associate professor in the Faculty of Kinesiology and Recreation Management at the University of Manitoba. His research explores the colonial nature of sport with an emphasis on resistance and social justice. He is the author of *A Night at the Gardens: Class, Gender, and Respectability in 1930s Toronto* (2023), co-author of *The History and Politics of Sport-for-Development: Activists, Ideologues and Reformers* (2019), and co-editor of *Decolonizing Sport* (2023). He also has a research interest in visual representations of sport and is the founder of the Canadian Sport Film Festival.

BIEKE GILS is an assistant professor at the University of South-Eastern Norway (USN) with competence in the history and sociology of gender and the body, and with a PhD from the University of British Columbia, Canada. Her research to date has focused on female leading figures in a variety of contexts, including North American entertainment industries around 1900, physical education in Canada in the 1960s–70s, as well as elite coaching in Norway. Bieke is currently working on a three-year research project investigating diversity and inclusion work in the Norwegian elite sport and art sector. She is committed to addressing social inequities on the intersections of gender and racial dimensions, to promote inclusion, diversity, and social sustainability.

Professor KEIKO IKEDA works in the faculty of Education at Hokkaido University. Professor Ikeda researches and publishes in a wide area including topics stemming from the history of sport (particularly British and Japanese), sport journalism, and feminism in sport. Professor Ikeda has been a visiting fellow at both the Centre for the Study of Social History at University of Warwick and in the International Centre for Sport History at De Montfort University. A significant proportion of her research and publications focus upon comparative studies of the British and Japanese Empires during the pre-Victorian and post-Victorian periods. Since 2009, Professor Ikeda has been a member of ISHPES Council, and since 2017 is a vice president.

CHRISTINE O'BONSAWIN (Abenaki, Odanak Nation) is an associate professor of History and Indigenous Studies at the University of Victoria, located on Lkwungen, Wyomilth (Esquimalt) and WSÁNEĆ homelands. Her scholarship in sport history and Indigenous studies takes up questions regarding the appropriation and subjugation of Indigenous peoples, identities, and cultures in Olympic history and the future programming of the Games. Christine's recent scholarship has mainly focused on the legal and political rights of Indigenous peoples in settler colonial Canada, particularly in hosting the Olympic Games and other mega-sporting events on treaty lands as well as those Indigenous territories that remain treaty-less (unceded).

JAN OVE TANGEN is professor emeritus at the University of Southeast Norway. He has a doctorate in sociology from the University of Oslo. He has researched various aspects of sport as a social system—particularly on sports policy topics such as inclusion and exclusion in sports, sports facilities as a political instrument, mega-events in sports, doping among athletes, and now, in recent years, sports and sustainability. This has resulted in a number of scientific articles as well as more popular science chronicles.

SVEN DANIEL WOLFE is Swiss National Science Foundation Ambizione Fellow in the Spatial Development and Urban Policy group at the ETH Zurich, and a vice president of the Swiss Association of Geography. He works on the socio-spatial impacts of mega-events, urban sustainable development, and everyday geopolitics.

LIV YOON is an assistant professor in the School of Kinesiology at The University of British Columbia. Her research is at the intersection of climate change, social inequities, and health, with a focus on community engagement and participatory methods. Her PhD training in socio-cultural kinesiology informs her to think about bodies in sociopolitical contexts, provoking thought about how some bodies are considered more "dispensable," and in turn, rendered more vulnerable to climate-related risks and pollution. Her research considers taking climate change as an opportunity to challenge the status quo and promote structural changes that alleviate social inequities that both led to, and are exacerbated by, the climate crisis.

Index

The University of Illinois Press
is a founding member of the
Association of University Presses.

———————————————————

University of Illinois Press
1325 South Oak Street
Champaign, IL 61820-6903
www.press.uillinois.edu